BEYOND APPEASEMENT

BEYOND APPEASEMENT

INTERPRETING INTERWAR PEACE

MOVEMENTS IN WORLD POLITICS

CECELIA LYNCH

Cornell University Press | ITHACA AND LONDON

First published 1999 by Cornell University Press

Printed in the United States of America

Cornell University Press strives to use environmentally responsible suppliers and materials to the fullest extent possible in the publishing of its books. Such materials include vegetable-based, low-VOC inks, and acid-free papers that are recycled, totally chlorine-free, or partly composed of nonwood fibers. Books that bear the logo of the FSC (Forest Stewardship Council) use paper taken from forests that have been inspected and certified as meeting the highest standards for environmental and social responsibility. For further information, visit our website at www.cornellpress.cornell.edu.

Library of Congress Cataloging-in-Publication Data

Lynch, Cecelia.
Beyond appeasement: interpreting interwar peace
movements in world politics / Cecelia Lynch.
p.   cm.
Includes bibliographical references and index.
ISBN 0-8014-3548-x (alk. paper)
1. Peace movements—United States—History.
2. Peace movements—Great Britain—History.
3. United Nations.   I. Title.
JZ5584.U6 L96 1998
327.1'72'0973—dc21   98-49634

Cloth printing   10   9   8   7   6   5   4   3   2   1

For Tom

Contents

Acknowledgments

I became interested in the complexities, angst, and irresolutions of the interwar period during the antinuclear weapons debates of the 1980s, in which I was involved. My interest then was to understand the antecedents of peace movements, especially whether they had any long-term effects or became mere historical artifacts. The interwar period clearly provided the hardest case for both activists and security specialists. As I began to probe it more carefully I became fascinated by the contemporary hold of perceptions of realism and idealism and their relation to social agency in the minds of journalists, pundits, and academics alike. Though cracks had appeared in the academic discussion of realism, there seemed to be little understanding of how these insights might relate to the concrete debates of the interwar period. This book is the result of my delving into these issues.

In researching this book I became an archive mole, spending many hours (and days, weeks, and months) piecing together the interactions and claims of both peace movement activists and groups and government officials. I gratefully acknowledge the assistance of numerous libraries, archives, and librarians, including those at the Public Record Office at Kew, the British Library, the British Library of Political and Economic Science, the Imperial War Museum, the Library of the Society of Friends, and the Peace Pledge Union, all in London; the U.S. National Archives and the Library of Congress in Washington, D.C.; the Swarthmore College Peace Collection in Swarthmore, Pennsylvania; the Widener Library at Harvard; the Harry S. Truman Library in Independence, Missouri; and the League of Nations Archives in Geneva. The Harvard Law School Library graciously granted permission to cite from the Manley O. Hudson papers.

Parts of "E. H. Carr, International Relations Theory, and the Societal Origins of International Politics" have been reprinted here from *Millennium: Journal of International Studies* 23:3 (1994), reproduced with permission of the publisher.

At various stages of this project I was fortunate to receive financial support from the John D. and Catherine T. MacArthur Foundation and the Institute for the Study of World Politics; I also received much appreciated research support from the Fulcher Fund, a University Research grant, and assistance from the Center for International and Comparative Studies (CICS), all at Northwestern University. Excellent research assistants, including Patricia Goff, Heajeong Lee, Jill Nystrom, and Mike Bosia, brought to light new sources, carried large sections of the library to my office, and provided extremely able computer, fact-checking, and bibliographic assistance.

Intellectually the book has benefited from the comments, criticisms, advice, and suggestions of many friends and colleagues. Fritz Kratochwil provided strong encouragement and excellent advice from the project's inception. Roger Haydon of Cornell University Press expressed interest in the project when it was only partially written. He has helped the book to completion in innumerable ways, and I, along with so many other scholars, know well how lucky I am to have worked with him. My good friend and veteran activist Frank Panopoulos gave me his entire, considerable book and newsletter collection on militarism and peace activism. Jean Cohen, Jane Evans, Peter Grose, Bill Hetherington, Phyllis Lassner, Carol Miller, Bill Munro, Benjamin Page, Tom Rochon, John Ruggie, James Shenton, Jack Snyder, Hendrik Spruyt, Thomas Sugrue, Ann Tickner, Georgia Warnke, Harold Whiteman, Jr., Meredith Woo-Cumings, and Nigel Young provided extremely useful comments, suggestions, and information at various stages of the project. Although in some cases they may not remember and in others they will not recognize their input, I am grateful to all of them. Those who definitely cannot forget their contributions even if they wanted to are Michael Loriaux, Audie Klotz, and Thomas Warnke, each of whom read and commented on multiple drafts of the book and who made it much better than it would have been otherwise. Their friendship, collegiality, and propensity for good suggestions know no bounds. I am equally grateful to Franci Pina, Alva Shaw, Marcia Baxter, Belinda Bester, and all the staff of Home Day Care and the Child Care Center of Evanston, as well as to Peggy Lapke, all amazing individuals whose knowledge, friendship, professionalism, love, and care made this book possible and my children happy.

The production of this book has spanned the birth of my children Brigid and Aidan and very recently the death of my father, Robert E. Lynch. My debts to each of them are very great. My father's humor, generosity, and grace were legendary among those who knew him. I will always be grateful for his insistence on not accepting easy answers and for both his and my mother's love and encouragement. I am especially indebted to my father and children, however, for their active demonstration, in the words of Ecclesiastes, that there is nothing better in life than to be glad and enjoy the fruits of one's labor. I owe a special debt to the various generations of my family, including my parents, many of their siblings, and my five sisters, for their unstinting belief in my abilities, whether or not they agreed with my arguments.

I dedicate this book to Tom, who willingly moved to Brussels, London, and Chicago and never wavered in his conviction of the book's worth. He managed to provide editorial skill, cynicism, prodding, support, reality checks, and a wonderful sense of humor all in the right measures. He will certainly enjoy the fact that the book is done.

C. L.

Chicago

BEYOND APPEASEMENT

Mythological Narratives
and Critical Interpretation

Great Britain and the United States in the interwar period witnessed the most polemical and complex peace movement activity in history. Conventional interpretations of this activity have framed debates in history, international relations, and international security studies. These interpretations, however, are misleading. They have limited our historical understanding of the role, influence, and meaning of interwar peace movements. They have also constrained theories about the role of social movements in world politics.

In contrast to conventional interpretations, I argue that interwar peace movements in Britain and the United States contested traditional security norms and legitimized significant norms that underlay global international organization and, ultimately, the construction of the United Nations. The importance of this activity has been masked, however, by the prevailing narratives of the interwar period, which blame peace movements for appeasement in Britain and isolationism in the United States and ignore social agency in the founding of the United Nations. The power of these dominant narratives, in turn, has reinforced theoretical tendencies that label social agency as "idealist" as opposed to "realist," implying that it is dangerous, simplistically liberal, or unworthy of serious consideration.

Scholarship and conventional wisdom provide contradictory answers to the question about the role and meaning of interwar peace movements, a stance that leads to a double paradox. First, popular and academic discourse blames peace movements for interwar failures, yet scholars argue that the primary causes of specific policies, including arms limitation and appeasement, were rooted in the biases of individual leaders, economic or security requirements, or structural constraints—factors that do not involve social agency. Second, dominant narratives of the construction of the United Nations ignore the role of social movements, yet the very existence of norms underpinning global international organization— universal participation, equality of status, the promotion of peace, economic and social welfare, individual and group rights—makes little sense when divorced from the agency of social movements. The absence of social movements from these narratives is all the more puzzling since a considerable body of research accords nongovernmental organizations a significant role in promoting these norms in contemporary international organization.[1]

Incomplete narratives of the influence of social movements are responsible for these paradoxes. The first paradox is based on a narrative that assigns peace movements significant influence—but only for negative normative and policy effects. The second overlooks the role of social agency in building global international institutions and leads us to disregard the similarities between social movements in the past and in the present. Resolving the inconsistencies in both paradoxes requires historical research that is more balanced and narratives that are more complete.

I thus maintain a critical stance toward entrenched narratives in order to reconstruct interpretations that address the complexity of social movement agency. I argue that the most productive way to understand social movement agency in world politics is to clarify its *normative meaning*, that is, its role in legitimizing and delegitimizing norms of behavior in political practice. I analyze policy, therefore, but not as an end goal. Instead, tracing the role of peace movements in policy debates provides a means to situate both the movements and the debates within a broader normative and

---

[1] Paul Wapner, "Politics beyond the State: Environmental Activism and World Civic Politics," *World Politics* 47 (April 1995): 311–40; Audie Klotz, "Norms Reconstituting Interests: Global Racial Equality and U.S. Sanctions against South Africa," *International Organization* 49 (Summer 1995): 451–78; Kathryn Sikkink, "Human Rights, Principled Issue-Networks, and Sovereignty in Latin America," *International Organization* 47 (Summer 1993): 411–42; Roger A. Coate, Chadwick F. Alger, and Ronnie D. Lipschutz, "The United Nations and Civil Society: Creative Partnerships for Sustainable Development," *Alternatives* 21 (January– March 1996): 93–122; Franke Wilmer, *The Indigenous Voice in World Politics* (Newbury Park, Calif.: Sage, 1993); Thomas G. Weiss and Leon Gordenker, eds., *NGOs, The United Nations, & Global Governance* (Boulder, Colo.: Lynne Rienner, 1996); Ronnie D. Lipschutz and Ken Conca, eds., *The State and Social Power in Global Environmental Politics* (New York: Columbia University Press, 1993); David P. Forsythe, *Humanitarian Politics: The International Committee of the Red Cross* (Baltimore: Johns Hopkins University Press, 1977).

social context. My analysis then explores the relationship among narratives, norms, and social agency.

PEACE MOVEMENTS AND NORMATIVE INFLUENCE

Criticisms of peace movements remain powerful. At the extreme, pundits and scholars accuse interwar peace movements of causing appeasement, isolationism—and hence promoting world war. This thesis is epitomized by Walter Lippmann, who stated unambiguously that "the preachment and practice of pacifists in Britain and America were a cause of the [second] World War. They were a cause of the failure to keep pace with the growth of German and Japanese armaments. They led to the policy of so-called appeasement." Interpretations based on this thesis permeate both popular thinking and scholarship, and leaders in Britain and in the United States from the 1950s to the present post–Cold War era have called upon this interpretation to disparage peace movement dissent and legitimize interventionist policies. The appeasement bogey, for example, has been raised by Anthony Eden against critics of militarism and interventionism in Suez, by Ronald Reagan against European peace movement activists in the 1980s during the Freeze Campaign, and by George Bush against opponents of the Persian Gulf War.[2]

A second critique charges "utopians'" with an unwise and ultimately futile attempt to institutionalize in the international realm moral principles designed for the domestic arena. Exemplified by E. H. Carr's seminal work, *The Twenty Years' Crisis, 1919–1929,* this claim is ultimately as powerful and damning as that of Lippmann. At one point himself an advocate of appeasement (although he skillfully lifts this argument from the revised 1946 edition of his book), Carr does not castigate peace movements for "causing" the policy, and only indirectly scolds them for preventing rearmament. His criticism is leveled at hegemonic ideology, embodied in self-serving faith in the League of Nations, international law, general disarmament, and compulsory arbitration. These peace movement proj-

---

[2] Walter Lippmann, *U.S. Foreign Policy: Shield of the Republic* (Boston: Little, Brown, 1943), p. 53; Victor Rothwell, *Anthony Eden: A Political Biography, 1931–1957* (Manchester: Manchester University Press, 1992), pp. 212–13; Robert J. Beck, "Munich's Lessons Reconsidered," *International Security* 14 (Fall 1989): 161; John Mueller, *Retreat from Doomsday* (New York: Basic Books, 1988), pp. 204–5; George Bush, *Public Papers of the Presidents of the United States,* 1990, Book II (Washington, D.C.: U.S. Government Printing Office, 1991), p. 1108.

ects Carr considered at best naive and at worst morally corrupt vestiges of nineteenth-century liberalism.[3]

A third critique of interwar social forces focuses on the damage that "public diplomacy" could cause to diplomatic efficiency. For example, Gordon Craig and Alexander George address the "excessive preoccupation with the mood of the electorate" during the interwar period. They single out "diplomacy by conference," a method that peace movements actively supported to make the treaty-building process more transparent to the public in the hopes of thwarting Bismarckian-style secrecy. For diplomatic historians, these methods "had the effect of changing the conduct and forms of diplomacy in ways that were not always conducive to efficiency."[4]

All three critiques are variants of classical realism, which sees the interwar period as the prototype for how foreign policy ought not to be conducted. The field of international relations has ever since cast the complexities and paradoxes of the period into binary categories—realism versus utopianism or idealism; scientific man versus power politics; moral man versus immoral society—that typecast social agency and from which enduring lessons are to be drawn.[5]

Yet, when scholars move from castigating peace movements to explaining the outbreak of war, these mythological representations evaporate. Scholarship on the origins of specific interwar policies does not cite peace movement influence as the primary causal factor for any given economic or strategic decision of the period, concluding instead that individual decision making or structural factors were determinative. Early scholarship focused on Neville Chamberlain's inexperience or collusion with the fascists or Franklin Roosevelt's ambivalence about pushing the United States into a leadership role as causes of appeasement and isolationism. After the 1960s structural analyses targeting either economic or strategic constraints for interwar policies became dominant, coalescing into the "post-revisionist" corporatist school in history and the neorealist balance-of-power school in international relations. Each of these schools drew on themes in classical realism, but each also moved away from studying social

[3] E. H. Carr, *The Twenty Years' Crisis, 1919–1939*, 2d ed. (1946; New York: Harper & Row, 1946), pp. 15–18, 62, 140, 178, 202–3. See also Michael Joseph Smith, *Realist Thought from Weber to Kissinger* (Baton Rouge: Louisiana State University Press, 1986), pp. 83–87.

[4] Gordon Craig and Alexander George, *Force and Statecraft: Diplomatic Problems of Our Time*, 2d ed. (New York: Oxford University Press, 1990), p. 60.

[5] Carr, *Twenty Years' Crisis;* John Herz, *Political Realism and Political Idealism* (Chicago: University of Chicago Press, 1951); Hans Morgenthau, *Scientific Man versus Power Politics* (Chicago: University of Chicago Press, 1965); Reinhold Niebuhr, *Moral Man and Immoral Society: A Study in Ethics and Politics* (New York: Scribner, 1960).

movements. Neorealist analysis, in particular, ignored questions of social agency, intentionality, and normative meaning; consequently, the interwar period became a "gap" in balance-of-power politics. Scholarship emanating from the fiftieth anniversary of World War II, however, has revived debates on interwar tragedies and fiascos.[6] Although contemporary debates do not focus on the role of peace movements or echo the vehemence of Lippmann's censures, vague references to the role of "pacifism," the "peace movement," or war-averse "domestic publics" as contributing factors to ill-fated policies remain common and illustrate the endurance of the earlier narratives.

The discrepancy between the negative reputation of interwar peace movements and the inconclusive evidence that they exerted direct policy influence is due to the difficulty of tracing peace movement activity to strategic or military decisions and to theoretical trends. Final policy proposals must pass through domestic elites and legislative institutions to be enacted, and documentary evidence of policy decisions comes from government archives and official papers that reflect socialization into the traditional diplomatic discourse of realpolitik. It is easy, therefore, to ignore social movements in favor of structural analysis, to focus on "domestic factors" that encompass only elites, or to adopt the attitude of government officials who dislike unofficial interference. Thus analysts of the "high politics" of peace and security either dismiss social forces, especially those that draw much of their strength from popular mobilization, or consider them to be a priori nefarious. They thus miss or gloss over, at considerable cost, the social and political ferment that contributes so strongly to debate. It is necessary, therefore, to reexamine both the classical realist critique and the neorealist denial of social agency.

[6] For an overview, see William R. Rock, *Chamberlain and Roosevelt: British Foreign Policy and the United States, 1937–1940* (Columbus: Ohio State University Press, 1988), esp. chap. 1; for a different view of Roosevelt, see Barbara Rearden Farnham, *Roosevelt and the Munich Crisis: A Study of Political Decision-Making* (Princeton: Princeton University Press, 1997). On corporatism, see Michael J. Hogan, "Corporatism," in Hogan and Thomas G. Paterson, eds., *Explaining the History of American Foreign Relations* (Cambridge: Cambridge University Press, 1994), and Thomas J. McCormick, "Drift or Mastery? A Corporatist Synthesis for American Diplomatic History," *Reviews in American History* 10 (December 1982): 318–30. On neorealism, see Kenneth Waltz, *Theory of International Politics* (Reading, Mass.: Addison-Wesley, 1979), and Robert O. Keohane, ed., *Neorealism and Its Critics* (New York: Columbia University Press, 1986). On more recent scholarship, see Richard Cockett, *Twilight of Truth: Chamberlain, Appeasement, and the Manipulation of the Press* (London: Weidenfeld & Nicolson, 1989); Donald Cameron Watt, *How War Came: The Immediate Origins of the Second World War, 1938–1939* (New York: Pantheon, 1989). See also Beck, "Munich's Lessons Reconsidered"; J. L. Richardson, "New Perspectives on Appeasement: Some Implications for International Relations," *World Politics* 40 (April 1988): 289–316; and Anthony Adamthwaite, "War Origins Again," *Journal of Modern History* 56 (March 1984): 100–15.

At the same time, the charges leveled against peace movements are not merely that they "caused" bad policy, or in the worst case, war. Dominant narratives criticize interwar peace movements as much for daring to inject themselves into foreign policy debates, for the types of policies they attempted to enact, and for the underlying guides to action they promoted as for actual policy outcomes. These narratives charge peace movements with normative influence, where norms are seen as both pragmatic "guides to behavior" defined in terms of rights and obligations and as ethical principles.[7]

The critique of diplomatic inefficiency illustrated by Craig and George mildly criticizes social forces and does not accuse them of primary responsibility for failed decisions. It does, however, emphasize that inefficient policy results from demands for inclusion and transparency. It implies that demands to redefine who participates in security decisions disturb pragmatic norms of efficient diplomatic conduct, leading to confusion, misperception, and mistakes.

Lippmann's realpolitik critique castigates peace movements and mass publics much more severely for their inexperience and interference in security decisions, laying a solid foundation for postwar perceptions of the interwar period and judgments about social activism in foreign affairs. Students of public opinion have discredited Lippmann's thesis on mass publics, that is, that they are too volatile, irrational, unintelligent, and ineducable to play a constructive role in foreign policy decision making. But the damning censure of interwar peace movements' "preachment and practice" in preventing rearmament and promoting appeasement continues to resonate.[8] Much of the power of this critique lies in its inherent criticism of movements not merely for "causing" a particular type of policy, but also for shifting the limits of acceptable behavior to norms that delegitimize preparations for the use of force. In this view, such norms prevent a state from developing the necessary means to realize its interests.

The final classical realist variant is the critique of liberalism embodied in Carr, whose interpretation of the interwar period is based on criticism

[7] Stephen Krasner, "Structural Causes and Regime Consequences: Regimes as Intervening Variables," in *International Regimes* (Ithaca: Cornell University Press, 1983), p. 2; Friedrich V. Kratochwil, *Rules, Norms, and Decisions: On the Conditions of Practical and Legal Reasoning in International Relations and Domestic Affairs* (New York: Cambridge University Press, 1989); Terry Nardin and David Mapel, "Convergence and Divergence in International Ethics," in Nardin and Mapel, eds., *Traditions of International Ethics* (Cambridge: Cambridge University Press, 1992), pp. 297–317.

[8] Benjamin Page and Robert Y. Shapiro, *The Rational Public* (Chicago: University of Chicago Press, 1992). See n. 2; also F. S. Northedge, "The Adjustment of British Policy," in Northedge, ed., *The Foreign Policies of the Powers* (London: Faber & Faber, 1968), p. 171.

of liberal hegemony. He implicates peace groups in his trenchant critique of the "harmony of interests," the notion that what is good for the individual is good for the collectivity, even when the "individuals" who define the collective good happen to be those who are most powerful and prosperous. For Carr this false belief in harmony has two interrelated aspects: faith in the liberal doctrine of laissez-faire, and the belief that global peace could be attained through law, international institutions, and the force of reason, although he modified the latter part of the critique in his later work. He deftly blends his critique of liberal norms of morality with realpolitik counsel on the necessity of taking "power" into account in foreign policy decision making; thus both critical theorists and classical realists draw "lessons" from his work.[9]

Here again, much of the power of the critique lies in its normative dimensions. Carr, more clearly than others, zeroes in on the normative content of peace movement projects, and he disparages the specific norms of equality of status and universal participation on which peace group projects for global international organization were based. By creating the realist/utopian dichotomy, he opened debate about the relationship between ideology and power. Carr's peace groups are simplistically liberal, morally naive social agents who promote unworkable norms in world politics. "It may be not that men stupidly or wickedly failed to apply right principles, but that the principles themselves were false or inapplicable."[10] For him peace groups ignore power realities at the same time as they act as unwitting agents of hegemonic interests.

These criticisms each presuppose some judgmental posture regarding "proper" norms of conduct by states, diplomats, and social agents, although they do not use that language. In so doing, they situate peace movement agency within narratives of the interwar experience that are constructed from particular interpretations of security requirements, power, and ideology. More often than not, these narratives are not analytically distinct; rather, ongoing criticisms of peace movement agency tend to combine one or more of them.

Yet each narrative also falls short, raising interpretive problems. The

---

[9] Carr, *Twenty Years' Crisis*, especially pp. 41–62, *The Moral Foundations of World Order* (Denver, Colo.: Social Science Foundation, University of Denver, 1948), and *Conditions of Peace* (London: Macmillan, 1942). Michael Joseph Smith, in *Realist Thought*, discusses the classical realist position on Carr; for critical theorists' appropriation of Carr see Robert Cox, "Social Forces, States and World Orders: Beyond International Relations Theory," *Millenium: Journal of International Studies* 10 (1981): 127–31; Cox, with Timothy J. Sinclair, *Approaches to World Order* (Cambridge: Cambridge University Press, 1996), p. 51; and Paul Howe, "The Utopian Realism of E. H. Carr," *Review of International Studies* 20 (July 1994): 277–97.

[10] Carr, *Twenty Years' Crisis*, p. 40.

realpolitik judgment of peace movements' influence ties norms to appeasement, yet lacks concrete empirical support. The degree to which peace movements are blamed for these norms and policies indicates unacknowledged assumptions and preferences, resulting in analytical confusion. The diplomatic history critique rues overreliance on public participation during the interwar period, yet the demand for participation by nongovernmental organizations has become so institutionalized over time as to make such criticisms today seem like carping. At the very least, we should ask whether the problem might lie with the incapacity or unwillingness of diplomats to recast decision-making procedures to take into account very real public fears and social pressures, especially powerful in the aftermath of World War I. Finally, Carr's critique of liberalism treats social agents as monolithic in their ideological orientation. His work thus opens—and attempts to close—a debate about progressivism, radicalism, and socialism that intellectual historians and social theorists have found much more complex and treated with greater sophistication.[11] Taken together, these interpretations lead to a partial, misleading, and unsophisticated treatment of social agency, resulting in the overly simplistic dichotomization of political action into realist and idealist categories.

These interpretive lapses also fail to help us to understand why, if faith in the League of Nations and its goals of arbitration, disarmament, and economic and social welfare failed so miserably, states would bother to create a new global international organization in the form of the United Nations. Prevailing theories of the founding of the United Nations, like hypotheses about the origins of the universe, fall into either evolutionist or creationist camps. The evolutionist narrative assumes that global international organization, once it was articulated in the Enlightenment schemes of the Abbé de Saint-Pierre and Kant, developed according to an inexorable logic from seventeenth- through nineteenth-century international legal codes to twentieth-century institutions. The creationist school, in contrast, sees the United Nations as part and parcel of the post–World

[11] Frederick Charles Bartol, "Liberal Minds, State-Making Dreams: Politics and the Origins of Progressive Thought in Britain and the United States," Ph.D. dissertation, Yale University, 1995; James T. Kloppenberg, *Uncertain Victory: Social Democracy and Progressivism in European and American Thought, 1870–1920* (New York: Oxford University Press, 1986); David Long, *Towards a New Liberal Internationalism: The International Theory of J. A. Hobson* (Cambridge: Cambridge University Press, 1996); David Long and Peter Wilson, eds., *Thinkers of the Twenty Years' Crisis* (New York: Oxford University Press, 1995); Daniel Rodgers, "In Search of Progressivism," *Reviews in American History* 10 (1982): 113–32; and Morton Keller, "Anglo-American Politics, 1900–1930, in Anglo-American Perspective: A Case Study in Comparative History," *Comparative Studies in Society and History* 22 (1982): 457–77.

War II "realist" restructuring of international politics into a reconstituted and pragmatic balance of great power interests.[12]

Yet there is nothing inherently inevitable about the evolution from legal theories to institutions, especially in times of cataclysmic wars. It is also unclear why states would want to "complicate their lives" by agreeing to construct and participate in costly forms of cooperation in a "multipurpose, universal membership" international organization.[13] Both the evolutionist and creationist narratives, I argue, lack an understanding of the social agents who articulated, promoted, and worked to legitimize global international organization. Twentieth-century innovations in the League and the United Nations are comprehensible only if we examine how social movements promoted and legitimized norms that constrained states' rights to wage war and that elucidated social and economic rights and responsibilities.

My alternative narrative captures social movements' constitutive, or enabling, role in building the United Nations. At issue is not promoting world government or furthering a spurious belief in global international organization to find a solution to the world's ills. Rather, we need to recognize that social groups fostered and exploited norms of behavior in world politics that differed in both form and substance from those that governed traditional diplomatic practice. The result, the legitimization of the League, the construction of the United Nations, and ongoing debates over the role of social movements in international life, represents a significant "move," in David Kennedy's words, in the course of international relations. However short the League and the United Nations fell of the lofty goals stated in the Covenant and Charter, respectively, each organization has represented in its era the primary recourse for social groups who have found the state unable or unwilling to provide security and peace, to address social inequities, and to respond to humanitarian crises. Global international organization embodies significant normative tensions and represents a "site of struggle between conservative and transformative forces."[14] Both the construction of an alternative to the state and the underlying norm that stipulates that the international community, rather

---

[12] F. H. Hinsley, *Power and the Pursuit of Peace* (London: Cambridge University Press, 1963); see also Chapter 5.

[13] John Gerard Ruggie, "Multilateralism: The Anatomy of an Institution," *International Organization* 46 (Summer 1992): 583–84. I address Ruggie's explanation, U.S. geographic exceptionalism, in Chapter 7.

[14] David Kennedy, "The Move to Institutions," *Cardozo Law Review* 8 (April 1987): 841–988; Robert W. Cox, "Multilateralism and World Order," *Review of International Studies* 18 (1992): 161–80.

than great powers, is responsible for maintaining peace emanate from the activities and goals of social movements.

An Interpretive Approach to Understanding Interwar Peace Movements

An interpretive analysis of interwar peace movements addresses these shortcomings. Interpretivism is an approach whose roots are found in hermeneutics, history, philosophy, and jurisprudence, and that has branched out from early twentieth-century debates over the degree to which *Verstehen* (understanding) departs from explanation, to take a firm hold in the social sciences. Interpretivists stress the ways in which intentions and actions emanate from intersubjective understandings, are communicated by actors through discourse and narrative, and reproduce or change the meaning of established practices, rules, and norms. In contextualizing intersubjective understandings, discourse and narrative, and practices, rules, and norms, the interpretive task is "to make a confused meaning clearer."[15] In other words, interpretivists attempt to provide a more complete understanding of the context and meaning of a particular text or set of actions than do alternative interpretations.[16] A "better" interpretation gives coherence to the whole; however, it is not free to draw just any meaning from its subject. Rather, when confronted with specific empirical material, in the form of texts, actions, and/or practices, it must be refined and revised according to the material's content.[17]

Epistemologically, the focus of interpretivism on understanding and meaning differs from the emphasis of logical positivism on explanation through generalizable patterns or covering laws. Ontologically, given its concern with the meaning of intentional agency, interpretivism differs

---

[15] Richard J. Bernstein, *The Restructuring of Political and Social Theory* (New York: Harcourt, Brace, Jovanovich, 1976); Fred R. Dallmayr and Thomas A. McCarthy, *Understanding and Social Inquiry* (Notre Dame, Ind.: University of Notre Dame Press, 1977); Charles Taylor, *Philosophy and the Human Sciences,* Philosophical Papers 2 (Cambridge: Cambridge University Press, 1988) p. 25; Craig Calhoun, *Critical Social Theory* (Oxford: Blackwell, 1995).

[16] Paul Ricœur, *Hermeneutics and the Human Sciences,* edited and translated by John B. Thompson (1981; Cambridge: Cambridge University Press, 1993); Ricœur, *Time and Narrative,* vol. 3, translated by Kathleen Blamey and David Pellauer (Chicago: University of Chicago Press, 1988); Dallmayr & McCarthy, *Understanding and Social Inquiry,* p. 289; Taylor, *Philosophy and the Human Sciences,* 2, p. 25.

[17] Georgia Warnke, *Gadamer, Hermeneutics, Tradition, and Reason* (Stanford: Stanford University Press, 1987); Ronald Dworkin, "Law as Interpretation," *Critical Inquiry* 9 (September 1982): 179–200.

from both structural analysis and choice-theoretic modes of explanation, that ignore or overlook this understanding of social agency in favor of economic, strategic, or individualistic determinism.[18] Although variants of interpretation, like positivism, abound, its adherents join in rejecting monocausal, ahistorical analysis that focuses on "brute facts" or objectively observable behavior. Thus most interpretivists admit some variation of the "hermeneutical circle," that is, that no single interpretation can provide *the* final, complete, or ultimate understanding of events.[19] In other words, some interpretations are clearly better than others, good interpretations make sense in relating action to meaning, and strong empirical evidence is a necessary component of the interpretive task. Yet the adherence to contextuality, whether seen in terms of historical "layering" of translations of meaning for Gadamer or the incommensurability of different discourses for Taylor, means that analysts must also see their own narrations and understandings as situated in a matrix of historically conditioned concerns.[20] Interpretivists do not shy away from articulating well-developed, coherent understandings that improve on past explanations. Indeed, interpretivist research can aid in both "explaining" the role of particular agents in political outcomes and in "understanding" the meaning of such actions in their normative and historical contexts. But, mindful of the pitfalls of the hermeneutical circle, interpretivists stop short of declaring their findings universally applicable or finite.

Thus, intepretivists recognize that the way in which narratives, or "stories," about political events, are constructed is a critical theoretical enterprise, in that stories emphasize particular aspects of evidence for particular purposes. The critique of established narratives, therefore, is a significant component of their work. They are also concerned with the relationship between intentionality and behavior, how behavior is guided by pragmatic and ethical norms and conscious attempts to reproduce or change them. The intentions and beliefs of human agents are not merely subjective; they are, according to Bernstein, "*constitutive* of the actions,

---

[18] The later writings of Wittgenstein provide early examples of this epistemological stance, clarified in the 1950s by Peter Winch. Wilhelm Dilthey represents an early, "psychologizing," version of interpretive ontology, although contemporary versions have moved away from concerns with the cognitive experience of the individual in favor of concern with intersubjective understandings of "social" agents. Dallmayr and McCarthy, *Understanding and Social Inquiry*, pp. 3–10, 137–40; Peter Winch, *The Idea of a Social Science and Its Relation to Philosophy*, 2d ed. (London: Routledge, 1990).

[19] Winch and Taylor see no resolution, whereas Gadamer attempts to provide one. Winch, *Idea of a Social Science;* Taylor, *Philosophy and the Human Sciences*, 2; Warnke, *Gadamer.*

[20] Dallmayr and McCarthy, *Understanding and Social Inquiry;* Taylor, *Philosophy and the Human Sciences*, 2.

practices, and institutions that make up social and political life." This means that interpretivists are concerned with the meaning and possibilities of social agency.[21]

Aspects of interpretive methodology have taken hold in international relations. Diplomatic history is centrally concerned with the problem of interpreting archival evidence and the theoretical issues raised by differing interpretive approaches.[22] Critical theory and postmodernism are concerned with both exposing the material and ideological power relationships underlying dominant discourses and narratives and exploring the relationship between identity and power.[23] As discussed later in this chapter, constructivism focuses on the critical role of rules and norms in providing intersubjective understandings that guide behavior.[24] And many feminist studies of international politics, despite their variants, contextualize dominant narratives and expose the contradictions in constructions of foundational concepts such as power and security.[25] In seeing interna-

[21] Ricoeur, *Hermeneutics and the Human Sciences,* pp. 274–96; Donald E. Polkinghorne, *Narrative Knowing and the Human Sciences* (Albany: State University of New York, 1988), pp. 37–70; Richard J. Bernstein, on Isaiah Berlin's critique of empirical theory, in Bernstein, *Restructuring,* p. 61; Taylor, *Philosophy and the Human Sciences,* 2, p. 27; and Ricœur, *Hermeneutics,* pp. 197–221.

[22] See Michael J. Hogan and Thomas G. Paterson, eds., *Explaining the History of American Foreign Relations* (Cambridge: Cambridge University Press, repr. 1994); and Colin Elman and Miriam Fendius Elman, "Diplomatic History and International Relations Theory: Respecting Difference and Crossing Boundaries"; Jack S. Levy, "Too Important to Leave to the Other: History and Political Science in the Study of International Relations"; Stephen H. Haber, David M. Kennedy, and Stephen D. Krasner, "Brothers under the Skin: Diplomatic History and International Relations"; and Alexander L. George, "Knowledge for Statecraft: The Challenge for Political Science and History"—all in *International Security: Symposium: History and Theory* 22 (Summer 1997).

[23] Cox, *Approaches to World Order;* R. B. J. Walker, *Inside/Outside: International Relations as Political Theory* (Cambridge: Cambridge University Press, 1993); David Campbell, *Writing Security, United States Foreign Policy and the Politics of Identity* (Minneapolis: University of Minnesota Press, 1992); James DerDerian, *On Diplomacy* (Oxford: Blackwell, 1987); Yosef Lapid and Friedrich Kratochwil, eds., *The Return of Culture and Identity in IR Theory* (Boulder, Colo.: Lynne Rienner, 1996).

[24] Nicholas Greenwood Onuf, *World of Our Making, Rules and Ruled in Social Theory and International Relations* (Columbia: University of South Carolina Press, 1989); Kratochwil, *Rules, Norms, and Decisions;* and Rey Koslowski and Friedrich Kratochwil, "Understanding Change in International Politics: The Soviet Empire's Demise and the International System," *International Organization* 48 (Spring 1994): 215–48; Alexander Wendt, "Anarchy Is What States Make of It," *International Organization* 46 (Spring 1992): 391–425; Audie Klotz, *Norms in International Relations: The Struggle against Apartheid* (Ithaca: Cornell University Press, 1995); Martha Finnemore, *National Interests in International Society* (Ithaca: Cornell University Press, 1996); John Gerard Ruggie, *Constructing the World Polity: Essays on International Institutionalization* (London: Routledge, 1998).

[25] V. Spike Peterson, ed., *Gendered States: Feminist (Re)visions of International Relations Theory* (Boulder, Colo.: Lynne Rienner, 1992); J. Ann Tickner, *Gender in International Relations* (New York: Columbia University Press, 1992).

tional relations as gendered, feminist interpretations of international relations emphasize the necessity of highlighting, reinterpreting, and even critiquing the understandings, actions, and role in world politics of "hidden" or ignored social agents.[26]

My preference for the interpretive approach is guided first and foremost by the empirical case at hand and the paradoxes it presents, and second, by the conviction that taking social agency seriously requires an interpretive stance toward intentionality. I therefore ground the problem of narrative construction in a critical case of social movement agency to develop a more sophisticated view of social movements as actors in international politics.

As argued, extant explanations of the role of interwar peace movements in international relations are embedded in variants of a "dominant narrative" of the interwar experience. Some variants attempt to explain the onset of World War II; others stop at the policies of appeasement and isolationism or neutrality; yet others view the interwar period as a "gap" in the normal conduct of foreign affairs. But each weaves the role of social forces, most often from the point of view of diplomatic sources, into a "plot" that contains normative lessons, or guides, for the conduct of foreign policy. These lessons emanate from the way in which concepts such as power, realism, idealism, diplomatic efficiency, security requirements, and the harmony of interests, hold intersubjectively understood meaning in foreign policy and security discourse. The resulting explanations of events point to concepts validated within this discourse to provide support for a given interpretation of events.[27] The dominant narratives "work," even when they lack sufficient empirical evidence, to the degree that their conceptual foundations call upon or validate norms that are deemed intersubjectively legitimate.

Narrative explanations of events thus have normative implications that we must discover and expose. In the case of interwar peace movements, social movement agency has most frequently been understood through the

[26] Not every feminist work focuses on all of these aspects, of course. Ibid. See also Christine Sylvester, *Feminist Theory and International Relations in a Postmodern Era* (Cambridge: Cambridge University Press, 1994); Jean Bethke Elshtain, *Women and War* (New York: Basic Books, 1987); Cynthia Enloe, *Bananas, Beaches, and Bases: Making Feminist Sense of International Politics* (Berkeley: University of California Press, 1990), and *Does Khaki Become You? The Militarization of Women's Lives* (London: Pandora Press, 1988); and, for an overview, Craig N. Murphy, "Gender in International Relations," *International Organization* 50 (Summer 1996): 513–38.

[27] This points to the notion of "conceptual narrative" articulated by Margaret R. Somers and Gloria D. Gibson, "Reclaiming the Epistemological 'Other': Narrative and the Social Constitution of Identity," in Craig Calhoun, ed., *Social Theory and the Politics of Identity* (Oxford: Blackwell, 1994), pp. 37–99.

prism of realpolitik and traditional diplomatic practice. I use an interpretive approach to exit from the traditional security discourse and provide a more coherent understanding of social movement agency than the dominant narratives allow. A more coherent interpretation requires a critical stance toward established ways of thinking. It also requires examining both peace group archives and the diplomatic records of governments and international organizations.

An interpretivist focus on the constitutive nature of rules, norms, and meaning also opens the way to understanding social movements' long-term role in constituting the United Nations. In international relations the study of norms provides a contrast to materialist and individualist theorizing to provide an understanding of the social fabric of international life. Norms are not merely regulative or constraining of behavior, but also enabling, or constitutive of particular practices and institutions. According to Kratochwil, norms are thus "the means which allow people to pursue goals, share meanings, communicate with each other, criticize assertions, and justify action." The study of norms in international relations falls under the rubrique of "constructivism," which relies on interpretive insights to understand why actors make particular claims or choose certain behaviors over others. These reasons may appeal to generalized principles (ethical or pragmatic), rules of behavior, or shared understandings of self-interest, but they are in effect "guides" to behavior that are understood by those to whom the appeal is made. Research has shown that the institutionalization of particular norms, such as those on racial equality, human rights, or humanitarian intervention, can result in significant changes in state interests and in international practice.[28]

Yet constructivists in international relations vary in their adherence to or break away from foundationalism, positivism, and relativism and in whether they believe constructivism belongs inside or outside the modernist tradition.[29] I locate the constructivist enterprise—the questions driving it and its essential assumptions regarding the social construction of

[28] Onuf, *World of Our Making;* Kratochwil, *Rules, Norms, and Decisions;* Wendt, "Anarchy"; Klotz, *Norms in International Relations;* Finnemore, *National Interests;* and Peter J. Katzenstein, ed., *The Culture of National Security: Norms and Identity in World Politics* (New York: Columbia University Press, 1996).

[29] Compare Katzenstein, ed., *Culture of National Security,* to Jutta Weldes, Mark Laffey, Hugh Gusterson, and Raymond Duvall, eds., *Cultures of Insecurity: States, Communities, and the Production of Danger* (Minneapolis: University of Minnesota Press, 1999); see also Onuf, *World of Our Making;* Emanuel Adler, "Seizing the Middle Ground: Constructivism in World Politics," *European Journal of International Affairs* 3 (Fall 1997): 319–63; Alexander Wendt, "Collective Identity Formation and the International State," *American Political Science Review* 88 (1994), 384–96; Ruggie, *Constructing the World Polity;* and Jutta Weldes, "Constructing National Interests," *European Journal of International Relations* 2 (1996): 275–318.

reality—firmly within the interpretivist camp. My use of interpretation rules out either a positivist or a relativist analysis of interwar social movements. Rather, it supports an approach to political and social phenomena that relates each to the other and is, according to Bernstein, "empirical, interpretative, and critical."[30] Thus, following interpretivists such as Ricoeur, I am more concerned with transcending the modernist versus poststructuralist debate than with taking a rigid position in regards to it. In other words, I am more concerned with analyzing how normative understandings give meaning to intentions, behavior, and events than with resolving the debate over whether foundational principles or methods can be "true" or universally applicable.[31] I thus draw on the long tradition of interpretivist social science to highlight the relationship between narratives, norms, and social agency in world politics.

Emphasizing this relationship requires taking social agency seriously. Both Gidden's notion of structuration in sociology and the constructivist interpretation of the "agent–structure" debate in international relations theory have opened the door to social agency by insisting that structures and institutions are not immutable, but instead are socially constructed sets of practices that are reproduced by agents who act knowledgeably and reflexively in the political sphere. Actors can act meaningfully only in a social context, based on mutual understandings and interpretations of events.[32] Yet they may behave in intentional ways, through claims, demands, and actions that *either* reproduce *or* challenge established rules and practices.

Nevertheless, despite the fact that both structurationism in sociology and constructivism in international relations show an awareness of the question of how to interpret social agency, each has thus far relegated the issue to the background. In contrast, I bring social agency to the forefront by informing the analysis of norms with the interpretivist's insight that intentional behavior holds meaning. Neither norms nor narrative interpretations arise in a vacuum, but constantly must be articulated, promoted, and legitimized—that is, reproduced or changed—by social agents. In-

[30] Bernstein, *Restructuring*, p. xiv.

[31] Polkinghorne, *Narrative Knowing*, pp. 66–67; see also Calhoun's defense of a "middle path" between defenders of difference and universalism, in *Critical Social Theory*, pp. xi–xii.

[32] Anthony Giddens, *Central Problems in Social Theory* (Berkeley: University of California Press, 1979, repr. 1990); *The Constitution of Society* (Berkeley: University of California Press, 1986); and *The Consequences of Modernity* (Cambridge, UK: Polity Press, 1990); in international relations theory, see Alexander Wendt, "The Agent-Structure Problem in International Relations Theory," *International Organization* 41, 3 (Summer 1987), 335–70; David Dessler, "What's at Stake in the Agent-Structure Debate?" *International Organization* 43, 3 (Summer 1989): 441–73.

terpretive variants of social movement theory have made a similar linkage in arguing that movements represent a challenge to established practices that in the words of Cohen "involves social contestation around the re-interpretation of norms." This is not to say that change is inevitable or easy, as is implied by some neorealist critiques,[33] or that there is a linear relationship between agents' goals and actions. Rather, it is to insist that it is social agents who make claims to justify particular rules, norms, and actions. They act within an already constituted web of meaning, and their claims may entail justifying or transcending established practices and meanings. Informed more explicitly by interpretive insights, therefore, we can address the question left dangling by much structurationist and constructivist theory, namely, to what degree agents can transcend or change given sets of practices, rather than merely reproduce them.

In the interwar case, peace movements exerted influence on normative understandings by successfully setting the agenda for public debate and adding "new" agenda items such as compulsory arbitration or general disarmament. Movement efforts also delegitimized existing solutions to problems of war and peace founded on states' prerogatives and legitimized new principles and procedures linking security to collective responsibility, "equality," and "justice." Finally, longer-term normative influence occurred to the extent that movements were responsible for continuing to legitimize international organization in ways that affected the form and content of the United Nations.

Thus a key historical and policy debate concerns the way in which meaning has been conferred upon social forces of the interwar period and how we reinterpret their role. Reinterpreting the impact of social movements on norms is particularly critical in the interwar case, first because the charges made against peace movements are so serious, second because they are primarily normative in character, and third because the dominant narratives miss the constitutive role of social movement agency in legitimizing norms underlying global international organization. My interpretation rejects classical realism's labeling of interwar peace movements as either uncritically liberal or dangerously utopian; it also refutes structural perspectives that ignore social agency altogether. My purposes are to unmask the contradictions of dominant narratives at the heart of the realist/idealist dichotomy, to recognize the significance of social movement agency, and to understand the complexity of peace movement activity in a way that is consistent with its normative project.

---

[33] Jean L. Cohen, "Strategy or Identity: New Theoretical Paradigms and Contemporary Social Movements," *Social Research* 52, 4 (Winter 1985): 694; John Mearsheimer, "The False Promise of International Institutions," *International Security* 19 (1995): 5–49.

It is not my purpose, however, to exempt peace movements (or any other agent) from all responsibility for interwar fiascos. Tactical choices can lead to normative problems. For example, although I find it incorrect to blame the British peace movement for appeasement and misleading to equate neutrality with isolationism in the United States, I criticize certain U.S. peace groups for aligning themselves tactically with elements of the far right in the late 1930s and for adopting slogans such as "Keep America out of War." These choices muddied the normative goals of the movement and helped to legitimize the identification of "internationalism" with militarism and U.S. national interests after World War II. Developing a more sophisticated view of social movements, therefore, means seeing them as constant, intentional actors on the world scene and recognizing the complexity of their interactions with other types of agents, existing sets of practices, and norms.

In critiquing dominant narratives of the influence of peace movements, I present several interrelated alternative narratives of interwar peace movements' role in delegitimizing traditional security norms in Great Britain and the United States and in legitimizing norms underlying the formation of the United Nations. Chapter 1 begins this process by contextualizing interwar peace movement agency and developing an interpretive approach to the study of social movements. The second chapter explores the nineteenth- and early-twentieth-century ebb and flow of peace movements in Britain and the United States, analyzing their varied ideological composition and the way in which their normative project interacted with socioeconomic and political practices and concerns. Chapters 3 and 4 evaluate the British peace movement during the interwar period from the early 1920s through the controversies over Abyssinia, Munich, and war in the late 1930s. They highlight the fact that Britain could not achieve all of its conflicting goals, raising questions on what positions were "realistic," and they present an alternative narrative of British peace movement influence that breaks down its utopian moniker. Chapters 5 and 6 examine the U.S. peace movement in the same time period and provide an alternative interpretation of activity from the Washington Naval Conference of 1921–1922 through the neutrality debates of 1935–1941. The U.S. movement attempted to keep the debate over the content of internationalism from veering toward a uniquely military approach. Although it ultimately lost this battle, its understanding of the relationship between equality, justice, and peace would influence the future development of global international organization. Chapter 7 explores the ways in which the constitutive norms of equality of status, humanitarianism, and universal participation promoted by peace movements influenced the construction and legitimization of the United Nations. The conclusion explores three primary implications: first, seeing social movement participation as a constant in world politics, particularly in the legitimization and delegitimization of norms; second, understanding the problem of narrative construction and the need for critical reinterpretation of dominant narratives; and third, freeing theoretical inquiry from the remaining discursive power of the realist/idealist dichotomy. These conclusions open the way to a more thorough, yet critical, understanding of the continuing significance of social movements in world politics.

An Interpretivist Approach to Social Movements and the Interwar Peace Movements

Social movements are constant and significant, if overlooked, actors in international politics. They contest, legitimize, and delegitimize norms of behavior. They do this for society, the state, and global international organization. Interwar peace movements engaged in this contestation in extremely important ways, particularly by delegitimizing preparations for war and legitimizing norms that underlay global international organization and hence the construction of the United Nations.

In this chapter I use insights from social movement theory and interpretive social theory to outline an interpretivist approach to analyzing interwar peace movements in Britain and the United States. I argue, against perspectives that equate peace groups with insouciant liberalism, that these peace movements were not ideologically monolithic. Rather, they emanated from the diverse intellectual, social, and political currents of radical progressivism, romanticism, feminism, liberalism, and socialism. Yet, despite their internal diversity, they represented a loosely coherent normative project for world politics. To develop this argument and lay the foundation for reinterpreting peace movement actions in subsequent chapters, I situate the interwar British and U.S. peace movements vis-à-vis other social forces (domestic and transnational) and the state.

I conceptualize interwar peace movements as social movements for two reasons. First, the term has a long history that denotes the coming together of social forces in intentional ways. Social movements set out to influence both the normative and the material direction of politics and society. Second, interwar peace groups themselves used the term *peace movement* to describe the links between themselves and other associations. The British No More War Movement (NMWM), for example, sponsored annual "No More War" demonstrations in the 1920s; each year much discussion ensued about which aspects of the peace movement would agree to participate under its socialist banner. The U.S. National Peace Conference (NPC) considered itself the umbrella organization of the U.S. peace movement and consistently used the term in its external propaganda and internal debates.[1] In each country, interwar peace groups thus thought of themselves as "movements" linked together in action for a common cause, advocating for change in society, the state, and the international polity.

Today, however, multiple literatures debate the definition of the term *social movement*. All are useful in highlighting the concept of quasi-organized, intentional social agency, but they ask very different questions about it. My concern is to put interwar peace movements in context by relating them to the social and political norms and practices of their time, to understand their claims and demands (i.e., the reasons for their intentional actions), and to interpret their normative impact on global politics. Thus I highlight social movement literatures that are useful to this project.

An Interpretive Approach to the Study of Social Movements in World Politics

I define a social movement as a loose association of actors that works for its goals (out of necessity or choice) at least in part outside of traditional political channels. Social movements emanate from civil society and may be nationally bounded, transnational, or even global (at least theoretically, since evidence that global civil society exists is sparse at best). They are relatively autonomous from traditional political institutions, although individual social movement members often have direct experience in, for example, government bureaucracies, political parties, or labor unions.[2] Social movement goals are both normative, that is, pragmatic and ethical guides to behavior, and material. They target both governments (national

---

[1] Frederick Libby, *The American Peace Movement* pamphlet (National Council for Prevention of War, 1932). NPC minutes, Swarthmore College Peace Collection (SCPC); *No More War,* Peace Pledge Union (PPU), London; LNU Minutes, British Library of Political and Economic Science (BLPES), London.

[2] Claus Offe, "New Social Movements: Challenging the Boundaries of Institutional Politics," *Social Research* 52 (Winter 1985): 817–68; and Jean L. Cohen, "Strategy or Identity: New Theoretical Paradigms and Contemporary Social Movements," *Social Research* 52 (Winter 1985): 663–716.

and international) and society. Social movement claims and demands may defend existing norms and practices, promote institutionalization to ensure the reproduction of contested norms and practices, or work to construct new norms and practices that may then be institutionalized. Thus the concept of a social movement denotes the notion of both defensive challenges against perceived threats (e.g., technological advances such as industrialization or militarization, or imposed regimes, such as fascism) and offensive challenges against established practices (e.g., traditional diplomatic practice or self-help security logics). Most often, however, a defensive challenge has offensive aspects, and vice versa. For example, in attempting to halt militarization, social movements generally articulate new norms of behavior rather than simply reverting to those of the past.

A social movement's internal constitution must be relational, and both its internal construction and its actions must have some element of intentionality. This intentionality possesses an identifiable normative coherence. Some social movement literatures distinguish, for example, between "spontaneous" and "deliberate" social movements. In my construct, spontaneous action counts as a social movement as long as it contains the three characteristics of relationality, intentionality, and normative coherence. Even spontaneous movement groupings tend to be in contact with each other, that is, they exhibit a relational awareness, most often through the process of discovering mutual grievances or goals and acting to redress or defend them. In this sense also, even seemingly spontaneous action, such as German noncooperation during the Franco-Belgian invasion of the Ruhr in 1923, is intentional.[3] But for noncooperation to be more than an isolated case of protest, those participating in it must also hold intersubjectively understood beliefs that prompt their action and allow it to be articulated as a normative agenda. Once social action exhibits these characteristics, we may interpret its meaning as a social movement rather than merely as a manifestation of a different type of agency.

Saying that social movements emanate from civil society is a complex statement. The meaning and utility of the term *civil society* is contested and debated across the disciplines of social theory, sociology, and international relations. Jean Cohen and Andrew Arato, drawing on Hegel, Marx, Gramsci, and especially Habermas, have provided one of the few contemporary definitions of civil society, renewing a useful dialogue on the meaning of the concept. Their definition is an attempt to understand

---

[3] Wolfgang Sternstein, "La Bataille de la Ruhr: problèmes économiques de la défense civile," in *Résistance dans une Allemagne en crise* (Brussels: MIR-IRG, 1983), pp. 7–47.

Eastern European dissidents' challenges to the state during the 1980s. In their construction of the term,

> It is necessary and meaningful to distinguish civil society from both a po-
> litical society of parties, political organizations, and political publics . . .
> and an economic society composed of organizations of production and
> distribution. . . . Political and economic society generally arise from civil
> society, share some of its forms of organization and communication, and
> are institutionalized through rights (political rights and property rights
> especially) continuous with the fabric of rights that secure modern civil
> society.[4]

This definition is a useful point of depature. But rather than viewing political and economic society as "arising from" civil society (or the inverse),
I see them as "co-constituted," in a constructivist sense, into a system of
norms, rights, and practices. Nevertheless, Cohen and Arato's definition is
useful in the British and U.S. interwar contexts because it highlights the
role of civil society apart from political and economic logics and "fabrics"
of rights. In making this distinction, it meets the interpretivist emphasis on
agency: civil society is not merely a predetermined "outcome" of either political (in this case, power politics) motive forces, or of economic (i.e.,
market) logic. Although both political and market logics obviously condition civil society, the agents who act in the arena of civil society—social
movements—can also influence these logics, the norms on which they are
based, and the practices that ensue from them. Moreover, Cohen and
Arato's definition also distinguishes civil society from the free market. It
thus makes it possible to take issue with E. H. Carr's critique of interwar
peace groups as unwitting agents of hegemonic economic interests and
with the contemporary discourse on liberalism that tries to posit that civil
society can best coexist with capitalist markets (especially in Third World
and Eastern European contexts).

The analytical distinction between social movements, civil society, market society, and political society is helpful for understanding the limits and
possibilities of interwar peace movements, as well as many Western social
movements (the "new social movements" of the 1970s and 1980s) and
much transnational social movement activity. But, as R. B. J. Walker aptly
warns, we must be wary of the definitional slide through which domestic
(Western) societal attributes, theoretical assumptions, or aspirations are

---

[4] Jean L. Cohen and Andrew Arato, *Civil Society and Political Theory* (Cambridge: MIT
Press, 1992), pp. ix–x.

either idealized or universalized.[5] The distinction between civil and economic (or political) society may be quite thin,[6] or it may not apply in all state or historical contexts. For example, the promoters of capitalism exhibit relational awareness, intentionality (especially in the post–Cold War era of globalization), and normative coherence. As Warren Magnusson argues, capitalism is thus a prime example of a social movement. It has "its ideology, its exponents, its true believers. It rouses millions of people in its support, generates hundreds of political parties, and inspires the most incredible personal sacrifices."[7] In this construct, the capitalist social movement crosses both economic and civil society, targeting, defining, and controlling the system of rights and rules practiced in economic society while constantly performing the function of ideological cheerleader in civil society. Yet, for definitional purposes, what is important is the crossover into civil society and the debate engendered by this permeation. An interpretive approach to social movements thus differs from perspectives that either collapse civil and economic society or those that posit a rigid distinction. Social movements both emanate from and attempt to influence the normative development of civil society; civil society both conditions and enables social movements' normative contestation of political and economic practices. But the distinction between civil, political, and economic society is neither rigid nor necessarily permanent.

Although notions of contestation and challenge form the foundation for these definitional understandings,[8] critical theories of social movements emanating from the "new social movement" literature, along with more recent attempts to articulate the workings of social agency and civil society on a global basis, inform conceptions of their embeddedness in civil society.[9] But other social movement literatures are less productive for

[5] R. B. J. Walker, "Social Movements/World Politics," *Millennium, Journal of International Studies* 23 (Winter 1994), esp. 680–83.

[6] For example, Justin Rosenberg, *The Empire of Civil Society* (London: Verso, 1994), and Paul Wapner, "Politics beyond the State: Environmental Activism and World Civic Politics," *World Politics* 47 (April 1995): 311–40, identify civil with economic society.

[7] Warren Magnusson, "Social Movements and the Global City," *Millennium, Journal of International Studies,* 23 (Winter 1994): 637.

[8] For different conceptions of these notions, see Sidney Tarrow, *Power in Movement* (Cambridge: Cambridge University Press, 1994); and *Struggle, Politics, and Reform: Collective Action, Social Movements, and Cycles of Protest* (Ithaca: Cornell University Western Societies Paper no. 21, 1989); Charles Tilly, *From Mobilization to Revolution* (Reading, Mass.: Addison-Wesley, 1978); Charles Tilly, Louise Tilly, and Richard Tilly, *The Rebellious Century, 1830–1930* (Cambridge: Harvard University Press, 1975); and Giovanni Arrighi, Terrence K. Hopkins, and Immanuel Wallerstein, *Antisystemic Movements* (London: Verso, 1989).

[9] See the contributions in two special journal issues: "Social Movements," *Social Research* 52 (Winter 1985); and "Social Movements and World Politics," *Millennium, Journal of International Studies* 23 (Winter 1994).

this enterprise. Some are firmly situated in the field of sociology or comparative politics and do not travel well to international relations for reasons that have as much to do with IR's obstinacy in ignoring social agency as with comparativists' focus on intranational politics. Others are not helpful because they simply do not address the same questions.

Many researchers seek to explain the rise of social movements in terms of why individuals choose to join them or what structural or resource conditions "cause" them to form. These questions are less interesting for my purposes. I am concerned with the "rise" of interwar peace movements in a broad sense, that is, with how interwar British and U.S. peace movements differed from pre–twentieth-century ones (explored in Chapter 2) and with the impact of World War I on peace group concerns. Interwar peace movements were part of a trend of peace activity that had been ebbing and flowing in Britain and in the United States since the post-Napoleonic era. Their enormous growth and mass manifestations during the 1920s and 1930s, however, must be related more specifically to the tremendous destruction and shock to civilian populations engendered by World War I. Because of the conjuncture of political, social, and economic forces that proved conducive to movements' development among particular strata of society during the nineteenth century, along with the structural crises produced by World War I (both explored in Chapter 2), I do not frame the movements' existence as overcoming a "collective action problem."[10] Nor is it very productive to look for a growth in resources unrelated to these forces to explain the rise of interwar peace movements.[11] I take the peace movements' origins as unproblematic once they are contextualized historically. This historical contextualization, however, does not see interwar peace movements purely as an emanation of changes in the means of production (such as capitalist expansion) either. The debate over imperialism, for example, pitted socialist and humanitarian groups against liberal internationalist ones, but World War I brought these warring sides together on the issue of peace.[12]

[10] Thus I do not survey the considerable literature on collective action begun by Mancur Olson's *The Logic of Collective Action* (Cambridge: Harvard University Press, 1965). For a critique of its bases, see Donald Green and Ian Shapiro, *Pathologies of Rational Choice* (New Haven, Conn.: Yale University Press, 1994).

[11] For discussion and critique, see Aldon D. Morris and Carol McClurg Mueller, eds., *Frontiers in Social Movement Theory* (New Haven: Yale University Press, 1992).

[12] David S. Patterson, *Toward a Warless World: The Travail of the American Peace Movement, 1887–1914* (Bloomington: Indiana University Press, 1976); C. Roland Marchand, *The American Peace Movement and Social Reform, 1889–1918* (Princeton: Princeton University Press, 1973); Warren F. Kuehl, *Seeking World Order: The United States and International Organization to 1920* (Nashville: Vanderbilt University Press, 1969); James Hinton, *Labour and Socialism: A History of the British Labour Movement, 1867–1914* (Amherst: University of Massachusetts

In characterizing interwar peace movements as ideologically complex, but normatively coherent, it is important not to reduce their scope to that of "identity" or "lifestyle" politics, or to inflate it by equating it with "public opinion." Like most movements that target global politics, peace movements had multiple identities. Their coherence was based more on normative goals and broad-based motive forces (World War I; the legacy of imperialism; global inequalities) than on group identity, although aspects of identity often played a role in the formation of particular groups (i.e., women's, religious, pacifist, or labor movements). Moreover, some peace groups and individual activists were motivated at least in part by a concern for what has become known as "lifestyle politics." The notion of lifestyle politics can be two-pronged: on one hand, it suggests a mode of acting in the public sphere that attempts to fuse issues of internal group democratization and the elimination of inequalities within the group to broader political goals. On the other, it may include an antimodernism that attempts to "return" to a more holistic view of social, economic, and political life. It is interesting that the "lifestyle issues" considered to be relatively common and understandable responses to the pressures of postindustrial society by contemporary social movement theorists are denigrated as abnormal peculiarities when transposed to interwar politics. For example, Martin Ceadel asserts that interwar British pacifism "was indeed characterized by many of the left-wing idiosyncracies which, in Orwell's famous list, ranged from fruit-juice drinking to feminism."[13] But here again, even though some activists in pacifist, women's, religious, or socialist groups were primarily motivated by the concern to integrate their activism into a more progressive lifestyle, this concern was negligible for others. It thus cannot be said to characterize the peace movements as a whole.

Neither is it productive to equate movements with public opinion, in the sense public opinion holds for us today. In practical terms, an approach that equates social movements with public opinion is impossible for the interwar case because no official polls existed until 1935 in the United States and until 1937 in Britain. Leaving aside this obstacle, the equation of social agency with public opinion remains problematic for analytical reasons. This is because the concept of social movements highlights analytically that portion of the public that does more than hold passive opinions that can be measured by polls—a segment that is also willing to act to further its beliefs. In an interpretivist approach to social movements, therefore, the measures of public opinion that do exist may

---

Press, 1983); Marvin Swartz, *The Union of Democratic Control in British Politics during the First World War* (Oxford: Oxford University Press, 1971).

[13] Martin Ceadel, *Pacifism in Britain* (New York: Oxford University Press, 1980), p. 84.

be helpful to contextualize or to lend support to a particular narrative, but they do not lend themselves to a sustained analysis.

In seeking to understand peace movements' impact on norms, an interpretivist approach to social movements is secondarily concerned with their influence on policy. Despite a growing interest in the relationship between social movements and "culture," social movements' direct impact on policy remains the major indicator of their "success" and a primary focus of movement supporters, detractors, and social movement theorists representing significant epistemological differences.[14] Policy influence is, of course, important, especially for a comparative study that evaluates the effectiveness of domestic social movements or analyzes the consequences of international "issue-networks."[15] But an exclusive focus on policy travels less well to other aspects of international politics. It is precisely the type of impact that is extremely difficult to determine in monocausal ways for security issues and, as argued in the preceding chapter, results in misleading narratives. This is also why interest-group theories are not of much use in analyzing interwar peace movements. Because it ignores the legitimization and delegitimization of norms, an exclusive focus on policy also overlooks movements' influence on society. My interpretivist approach to social movements does not, however, ignore movements' role in policy debates. In fact, I trace debates on policy empirically to understand the movements' normative claims and demands, changes in governments' interests, and the degree to which discourses used by the movements and governments differed, evolved, and converged.

In the interwar case, the difficulties inherent in demonstrating direct policy impact, especially against the background of serious normative charges against peace movements, paradoxically has resulted in attempts to downplay movement influence. Particularly in the short term, the focus on the policy of political appeasement enables movement sympathizers to label interwar peace movements unsuccessful. James Hinton, for example, argues against the thesis that peace movements "caused" appeasement. He asserts, "Many diverse factors have been shown to have influenced the decision makers, amongst which pacifism was of minor importance. . . . Popular movements made little impact on [the] Establishment."[16] Most

[14] See Frances Fox Piven and Richard A. Cloward, *Poor People's Movements* (New York: Pantheon, 1977); J. Craig Jenkins and Bert Klandermans, eds., *The Politics of Social Protest, Comparative Perspectives on States and Social Movements* (Minneapolis: University of Minnesota Press, 1995).

[15] Kathryn Sikkink, "Human Rights, Principled Issue-Networks, and Sovereignty in Latin America," *International Organization* 47 (Summer 1993): 411–42.

[16] James Hinton, *Protests and Visions: Peace Politics in Twentieth-Century Britain* (London: Hutchinson Radius, 1989), p. 92; Bill Hetherington, "Stopping War," *The Pacifist* 27 (Janu-

historical analyses of the interwar movements, therefore, treat peace groups as tragic actors rather than causal factors, buffeted and ultimately defeated by the devastating drama played out on the international scene. Beginning with Manchuria and continuing with Abyssinia, the Spanish Civil War, and finally Munich, peace movement historians emphasize the fact that the tragedies of the 1930s caused anguish and irreparable divisions within the movements, so much so that by 1940 they had for all practical purposes disintegrated. Although valid in many respects, this interpretation negates any possibility that social movements had power. In fact, peace movements were sometimes able to alter the normative and discursive terrain on which policies (and "interests") were debated and formulated (for example, from bilateral initiatives to multilateral ones).

Moreover, an exclusive focus on policy "success" in the interwar case is reactive in that it implicitly or explicitly frames the analysis of peace movements to answer the criticisms and charges of dominant narratives. Thus much work on interwar peace groups has adopted a "divide and absolve" strategy. For example, some scholars in Britain, particularly those sympathetic to Labor, distance themselves from the strict pacifist wing of the movement, arguing that socialists were the first to admit and comprehend the evils of Hitler's regime and the growing international fascist threat. In one of the earliest examples of this type of analysis, the British University Group on Defence Policy contended, "If we except the extreme wing of the Pacifists . . . at every point the body of opinion represented by the peace movements stood for resistance to the aggressions of Hitler, Mussolini and Japan."[17] Others defend the liberal internationalist wing of the peace movement. Peter van den Dungen differentiates between the pro-collective security stance taken by the largest British peace group, the League of Nations Union (LNU), and other peace groups, implicitly acknowledging that the burden of responsibility for interwar fiascos still rests on peace movements.[18]

Historical scholarship has not resolved, therefore, questions regarding the influence of interwar peace movements. Consequently, as argued in

---

ary 1989): 11; and Peter Brock, *Twentieth-Century Pacifism* (New York: Van Nostrand Reinhold, 1970), chap. IV.

[17] British University Group on Defence Policy, *The Role of the Peace Movements in the 1930s,* Pamphlet No. 1 (London: 1959), p. 6. See also Martin Shaw, "War, Peace, and British Marxism, 1895–1945," in Richard Taylor and Nigel Young, eds., *Campaigns for Peace: British Peace Movements in the Twentieth Century* (Manchester, Eng.: Manchester University Press, 1987), p. 63.

[18] Peter van den Dungen, "Critics and Criticisms of the British Peace Movement," in Taylor and Young, eds., *Campaigns for Peace,* p. 266.

the Introduction, charges against peace movements remain confused. Nevertheless, students of interwar peace movements have long attempted to come to grips with the fact that movements often wield significant influence in the political arena, even when the specific policies they advocate are not enacted. Charles DeBenedetti, for example, argues that the interwar U.S. peace movement failed to rouse the majority of Americans out of their indifference to its activity, but that it nevertheless "succeeded" in two ways. First, it created an "organizational substructure," establishing many new movement organizations that "demonstrated their effectiveness by their very durability over the rest of the century." Second, it kept "the peace issue far forward in the public consciousness" by defining and articulating intelligent critiques of U.S. policies. "If the peace movement failed to alter national policy, it succeeded in doing the next best thing that can be expected of a movement for change and reform: it questioned prevailing dogma and advanced fresh alternatives. It cut and cleared other paths."[19]

The problem for social movement theory, as Thomas Rochon points out, is that "no unified jargon has yet emerged to summarize these perspective shifts."[20] Indeed, students of peace movements have been frustrated by the weakness of theoretical frameworks in illuminating the impact of social movements' political "effects." Yet "delegitimizing prevailing dogma" on state security policies and "cutting and clearing other paths" point to a deeper influence on the level of ethical and pragmatic norms. An interpretive approach focuses on the relationship among social context, policy debates, and norms to understand the significance of social movements.

Conversely, the problem for international relations theory is its frequent misunderstanding of work on social agency. Researchers either collapse social agency with the state or elites, or worry that students of social movements regard them all "as ipso facto benign or progressive."[21] Yet the field of international relations increasingly has to grapple with various questions of agency, such as nationalism and "ethnic" conflict that lead to war, and environmental consciousness, feminism, and "peace" that may (or may not) lead to some form of "progress." Moreover, constructivists have engaged in a self-critique for not probing sufficiently "the ori-

[19] Charles DeBenedetti, *Origins of the Modern American Peace Movement, 1915–1929* (Millwood, N.Y.: KTO Press, 1978), p. 245.

[20] Thomas R. Rochon, "Political Movements and State Authority in Liberal Democracies," *World Politics* 42 (January 1990): 302.

[21] Robert W. Cox, "An Alternative Approach to Multilateralism for the Twenty-First Century," *Global Governance* 3 (Jan.–April 1997): 107.

gins of norms."[22] International relations theory would do well to embrace the growing interest in social movement agency and seek to apply its developing insights to both nationalist and "internationalist" movements and issues.

The interpretivist approach to social movements I advocate addresses the weaknesses of international relations theory by viewing intentional action by social agents as meaningful. This approach also relates social movements to civil society, highlighting the importance of social movement agency vis-à-vis both "society" (viewed in national or transnational terms) and the state. In contrast to conventional theories of international relations, it takes social movements' actions seriously rather than reducing them to mere manifestations of economic or political structures. Thus, if civil society collapses into economic (or political) society, my approach sees such a collapse as produced at least in part by the actions of intentional social movements. Moreover, this interpretive approach highlights the role of social movements in *social contestation* and argues that this role is at least equally as important for developments in world politics as the ability of movements to influence policy directly.

An interpretive approach to the study of social movements in world politics also addresses weaknesses in social movement theory. By insisting on historical contextualization, such an approach provides an understanding of movements' origins that does not prejudge individual motivation. More significantly, by focusing on movements' influence on *norms*, it provides a way to understand their significance without having to rely exclusively on often unprovable "policy" success. An interpretive approach thus integrates social movements into international politics. It argues that both "perspective shifts" and the "origins of norms" can be better comprehended by focusing on normative contestation and the social agents who seek to legitimize or delegitimize accepted rules and practices.

Contextualizing U.S. and British Interwar Peace Movements

To lay the groundwork for critiquing dominant narratives and reinterpreting interwar peace movements, it is necessary to disentangle the component parts of interwar peace movements and to contextualize their claims and demands vis-à-vis those of other social forces of their time. Seeing

---

[22] Paul Kowert and Jeffrey Legro, "Norms, Identity, and Their Limits: A Theoretical Reprise," in Peter J. Katzenstein, ed., *The Culture of National Security, Norms, and Identity in World Politics* (New York: Columbia University Press, 1996), p. 469.

peace movements in context helps to illuminate their complexity and makes their normative project understandable against that of traditional diplomatic practice.

Peace movements incorporated analytically complex social and political components, motives, and goals. Their ideology can be characterized as liberal in the sense of encompassing pluralistic debate over issues of militarism, international law, the content of peace, the causes of war, economic exploitation and inequalities, capitalism, and the causes of human suffering. But this type of liberalism is quite broad. For peace movements, trends in pacifism, feminism, socialism, radicalism, and internationalism informed debate over all these issues, making an exclusively liberal label problematic.[23] Although emphases varied, all peace groups, whether considering themselves internationalist, pacifist, socialist, or "centrist," encouraged the linkage of these issues to their promotion of "peace."

The basic structure of interwar U.S. and British peace movements was similar, but the relative power and impact of movement factions differed in each country. Each peace movement contained liberal internationalists who favored both sanctions and a liberal economic order, although they also campaigned for controls on the arms trade and the inclusion of both Germany and the Soviet Union in the League. "Centrists," including primarily sectarian organizations and women's groups, developed a humanitarian critique of international economic and political injustices. Although initially pacifist, many centrists eventually regarded sanctions, both economic and political, as a necessary means of containing and condemning aggression. Religious pacifists sympathized with, and socialist pacifists adhered to, a Marxist explanation of the causes of war and injustice. Both rejected sanctions, economic or political, as window-dressing that failed to address the underlying causes of war. Nonpacifist socialist and radical political individuals and organizations also maintained relationships with peace groups. Their opposition to imperialism, developed during the pre–World War I heyday of syndicalist organizing, lent support to the movements' economic critique of war. Student organizations, farm groups emanating from radical agricultural traditions, and labor groups formed much of the organizational rank and file of peace group memberships.

---

[23] See James T. Kloppenberg, *Uncertain Victory: Social Democracy and Progressivism in European and American Thought, 1870–1920* (New York: Oxford University Press, 1986); Frederick Charles Bartol, "Liberal Minds, State-Making Dreams: Politics and the Origin of Progressive Thought in Britain and the United States," Ph.D. dissertation, Yale University, 1995; and Daniel T. Rodgers, "In Search of Progressivism," *Reviews in American History* 10 (December 1982): 113–12.

Thus peace groups did not represent a monolithic force advocating a single policy—indeed they often could not agree on specific policy paths. Groups such as the British National Peace Council, an umbrella organization that attempted to unite the various sections of the movement, acknowledged this lack of agreement, frankly admitting, "the penalty of this comprehensiveness is that there are occasions where the N.P.C. cannot commit itself . . . the lowest common denominator of agreement may reduce its policy at times to a platitudinous level."[24] Peace groups engaged in passionate debates, internally, among themselves, against their conservative movement opponents, and with governments. Internal debates concerned the definition and desirability of pacifism versus an "enforced peace"; the means of attaining economic equality internationally; the importance of cultural pluralism; and promoting the existing League versus pouring time and money into a reformed organization that would be less reflective of states and their interests and more representative of "peoples."[25]

The primary goal of liberal internationalists was to promote and popularize the League of Nations. The British League of Nations Union (LNU), for example, was created to "secure the whole-hearted acceptance by the British people of the League of Nations as . . . the final arbiter in international differences, and the supreme instrument for removing injustices which may threaten the peace of the world" and to "advocate the full development of the League," including the "immediate creation of the Permanent Court of International Justice" and the "progressive limitation of armaments . . . in all countries."[26] The LNU, by far the largest membership group in either country, peaked at almost half a million annual dues-paying members in the early 1930s.

The LNU ties to political elites were the strongest of any peace group in Britain or the United States to date, especially as governmental participation, on a nominal level at least, was built into the LNU's structure. The prime minister of the day was always asked to serve as honorary president (paradoxically only the Labour Prime Minister Ramsay MacDonald declined the honor in 1924, to the consternation of many in the group). Other Cabinet ministers were registered as vice-presidents, duties that included little more than being listed on LNU stationery and making an occasional speech in favor of the League of Nations. The LNU led the Brit-

---

[24] *The N.P.C.: 1908–1958* (London: NPC, 1959), pp. 14–15.
[25] See George W. Egerton, *Great Britain and the Creation of the League of Nations* (Chapel Hill: University of North Carolina Press, 1978), pp. 7–23; Thomas J. Knock, *To End All Wars* (Princeton: Princeton University Press, 1992).
[26] LNU General Council Minutes, January 21, 1919.

ish movement, largely through its considerable sources of funding and organizing techniques. It successfully organized church, women's and students' peace committees, and was more than willing to incorporate pacifists into its ranks.[27] But many rank-and-file LNU members took both a more pacifist stance and a critical line toward the government than did the leadership. This resulted in many instances of grass-roots pressure for open opposition to government economic and political policies.

The League of Nations Non-Partisan Association (LNNPA), which simplified its name to the League of Nations Association (LNA) in 1927, represented Establishment internationalists in the United States. In contrast to its British counterpart, the U.S. group remained small (it peaked at approximately 19,000 members in 1930) and, despite attempts at mass education campaigns, elitist in attitudes and membership.[28] It failed to gain a mass membership both because it failed in its primary goal—U.S. membership in the League of Nations—and because of its restrictive understanding of its purposes and work. Liberal internationalism in the United States thus remained divided between "legalists" (specialists in international law who devoted most of their efforts to developing a functioning world court) and those, including pacifists, for whom internationalism formed part of a larger project. The LNA focused on the former and did not attempt until the mid-1930s to influence the direction of the peace movement at large. Yet the LNA was closely tied to endowed peace research organizations, including the Carnegie Endowment and the World Peace Foundation, and was able to draw on their vast financial resources for its pro-League campaigns. Moreover, successive administrations often called on its members (Manley O. Hudson, Norman Davis) to lend expertise to official U.S. diplomatic delegations.

The center-pacifist axis of the peace movements was, however, stronger in the United States than in Britain. Led by the National Council for Prevention of War (NCPW), an umbrella group originally organized to act as coordinator and clearinghouse for the U.S. peace movement's campaign for the Washington Naval Conference, this component was the most effective in the United States in publicizing its message across a wide spectrum of U.S. society, as well as in forming links with Congress and other peace groups. The U.S. section of the Women's International League for Peace and Freedom (WILPF) was one of the more pacifist and probably

[27] Donald Birn, *The League of Nations Union, 1918–1945* (Oxford: Oxford University Press, 1981), p. 135.

[28] Lawrence Wittner, *Rebels against War: The American Peace Movement, 1933–1983* (Philadelphia: Temple University Press, 1984); Charles DeBenedetti, *Origins of the Modern American Peace Movement, 1915–1978* (Millwood, N.Y.: KTO Press, 1978).

the most influential U.S. women's group. It cooperated with ten additional women's groups (some, like the League of Women Voters and the American Association of University Women, not exclusively peace groups) to form the National Committee for the Cause and Cure of War.

The membership of WILPF never included more than 15,000 women during the interwar period, but it remained influential throughout the period. Leaders such as Jane Addams and Emily Greene Balch had international reputations from their humanitarian work during the war, and the group's early decision to concentrate its headquarters in Washington in an attempt to sway votes in the U.S. Senate increased its potential for influence in official circles.[29] Both the NCPW and WILPF became widely credited during the period for their lobbying skills, which they developed virtually from scratch. Frederick Libby of the NCPW and Dorothy Detzer of the WILPF, despite their reputations as committed pacifists, proved deft at crafting coalitions of congresspersons, administration officials, and peace activists in debates over disarmament, U.S. membership in the World Court, and the arms trade.

The British National Peace Council (NPC), the NCPW's cross-Atlantic umbrella group counterpart, never attained the level of notice gained by the U.S. group, although it improved its position considerably relative to other British peace groups after 1937 when it inaugurated a "peaceful change" campaign. The NPC included most of the major British peace groups as organizational members, but because the LNU refused formal affiliation, pacifist groups tended to dominate.

The British section of WILPF, known simply as the Women's International League (WIL), tended toward pacifism and socialism. But by 1935 it advocated oil sanctions against Italy as punishment for its aggression in Abyssinia, and it afterward supported collective security. The WIL was probably the most influential British women's group, although women in other peace societies organized dynamic women's committees. The British women's groups formed an umbrella council in 1928 that was especially active in pressing for substantive results at the 1930 London Naval Conference.

Church peace organizations rounded out the center-pacifist groups in both countries. Jewish and Catholic peace committees cooperated on the major campaigns, but it was primarily the Protestant Christian umbrella groups such as the World Alliance for International Peace through the Churches (well organized in the United States and Britain), the U.S. Federal Council of Churches (FCC), and the U.S. Church Peace Union,

---

[29] *Pax International* 1:1, November 1925.

that wielded power in the peace movements. In the United States, the churches' ability to mobilize their constituents remained significant throughout the interwar period. In Britain most of the major Protestant denominations, including the Church of England, organized peace councils or boards on both the local and national levels. These councils often joined with local LNU, No More War, or NPC chapters to campaign for arbitration and disarmament.

Religious pacifists, who had become increasingly politicized by the war, became both sources of membership for the larger organizations and a faction in their own right. Quakers (in the United States, the American Friends Service Committee) and the Fellowship of Reconciliation (FOR) formed the base of religious pacifism. Radical/socialist pacifists formed the War Resisters League (WRL) in the United States. In Britain the No More War Movement (NMWM) became the British chapter of the War Resisters International. The Union of Democratic Control (UDC), created by radical dissenters in Britain at the beginning of World War I, remained influential during the war but declined thereafter. These groups remained small, but they often included well-known intellectuals and wielded significant influence in the larger umbrella groups, steering them away from supporting the military implications of collective security. In the mid-1930s, the Peace Pledge Union (PPU) became the predominant British pacifist organization.

Peace group memberships were not mutually exclusive: overlapping memberships facilitated grass-roots influence on larger, more hierarchically organized groups. Most groups also maintained a rigorous policy of nonpartisanship. Groups in Britain tended to have a majority of either Labour or Liberal Party members, but attempted to recruit nonparty and conservative members as well. In the United States the peace movement spanned party ranks. The LNA and internationalist legal groups included many Republicans, and many members of centrist and pacifist groups were Democratic or Socialist party members.

The overlap between peace groups assisted intramovement cooperation on disarmament and arbitration campaigns, although it could not prevent the eventual realignment and split within the movements in the 1930s. After an initial growth spurt for all peace groups, membership in the pacifist groups, whose identity was grounded as much in lifestyle politics as in a political program, held steady or declined. Conversely, membership in internationalist, centrist, and center-pacifist groups peaked during the arbitration and disarmament campaigns of the late 1920s and early 1930s. At first, centrist and liberal internationalist groups continued to gather steam even after it became obvious that some of their major campaigns, especially the campaign for substantive general disarmament, would fail. In the United States, a new umbrella organization, the National Peace Conference (NPC) was created to coordinate group efforts, competing with the center-pacifist NCPW for influence. In Britain, the Peace Ballot, a successful center-internationalist effort to demonstrate widespread support for the League of Nations, followed after the failure of the Geneva disarmament conference.

Successive foreign policy crises, the renewed debate over the worth of collective security through sanctions, and heightened fears of bombing brought about by the experiences of Spain and China, rejuvenated pacifism in the mid- to late 1930s in both countries. In 1935 the smaller pacifist groups organized with the NCPW and WILPF an Emergency Peace Campaign (EPC) in the United States, followed by cooperation with the Keep America out of War Committee (KAOWC), led by Norman Thomas. In Britain, the PPU, organized in 1935–1936, immediately attracted 100,000 pledges not to participate in war. Pacifists in Britain combined their critique of sanctions with a critique of international economic inequalities, whereas in the United States, pacifists blamed the move to sanctions on European balance-of-power politics.

Peace movements, therefore, represented organizationally and ideologically complex entities. Yet, despite their different claims regarding sanctions, collective security, and promoting economic liberalism versus an economic critique of war, peace groups agreed on the fundamental norms of placing restraints on state capacities to wage war, enabling new forms of international conflict resolution, and universalizing participatory mechanisms on issues of security, humanitarianism, and economic welfare. Thus they can be distinguished analytically from other social forces in the interwar period.

For example, peace movements overlapped partially, but not completely, with the Left in both countries. Because of the link made by peace groups between notions of economic fairness, social welfare, and peace, most elements of the Left had explicit ties to the peace movements, through labor unions, progressive farm organizations, or groups with an explicitly socialist orientation. Thus peace movements were perceived in both countries as explicitly leftist in orientation, illustrated by State Department memos labeling peace activists as "pink," if not outright "red."[30] Moreover, peace groups rarely hesitated to advocate positions put forth at the League by the Soviet Union if they believed these positions would advance their

[30] E.g., "List of Civic Leaders to Plead China's Cause in Parley," Sept. 5, 1925, 811.00B/473, RG59, U.S. State Department, National Archives.

goals. Even establishment groups such as the LNU promoted the 1927 proposal for complete disarmament made by Soviet delegate Litvinov. Yet any synonymous identification of peace movements with the Left is erroneous. Not only were many in the Left suspicious of pacifism or the military implications of collective security, but also centrist and liberal peace groups in both countries explicitly distanced themselves from organized communist parties. Moreover, the peace movements in both countries bemoaned the difficulty of attracting working-class members. One U.S. organizer from the National Council for Prevention of War, one of the more successful groups in this regard, complained that "the peace movement needs in it more men that chew tobacco."[31]

The differences within the Left over the definition of peace and the causes of militarism surfaced most explicitly during the Spanish Civil War. The war became an epiphany for many, especially the former pacifists who began to advocate violence to fight oppression. It caused a painful split within the Left and within the peace movements at large, but it also sharpened the arguments and claims of both advocates and opponents of military assistance to Republican Spain. As part of this rearticulation, some peace activists adopted an overtly antifascist orientation that led to increasing opposition to Hitler and Mussolini (and would have repercussions over Abyssinia and Munich). This was also a path of rejuvenation taken by besieged communists. But the Spanish Civil War also caused a rearticulation of anti-imperialist demands among socialists and even many pacifists, who developed a new critique of fascist imperialism. Many began to oppose fascism as a danger to peace without making it their central target. Still others in the peace movements, however (and this included both "liberals" and "socialists"), muted their concerns about fascism in the hopes of productive negotiations with Germany to reverse the slide toward war.[32] This meant that there was partial, but not complete, overlap between the growing antifascist movement and the peace movements.

Peace movements were more clearly distinguishable from the right-wing, anti-Bolshevist movements. In Britain the Conservative Party represented institutionalized opposition to the claims and demands of most peace movements. Quasi-institutionalized opposition in the press was also significant. The Beaverbrook Press and the pro-Conservative papers, such as the *Morning Post*, staunchly supported British imperialism, a stance that automatically distanced them from League internationalism and socialist

---

[31] NCPW Minutes, April 19, 1933, SCPC.
[32] Hinton, *Protests and Visions;* van den Dungen, "Critics and Criticisms."

egalitarianism. But the British peace movement also had to contend with both the influential rhetoric of Sir Oswald Moseley's Union of Fascists and the elite right-wing centered in the "Cliveden set."[33]

In the United States a countermovement on the right grounded in powerful unofficial social groups actively promoted claims in favor of a Big Navy and U.S. isolation from the World Court. This countermovement included nationalist patriotic societies such as the American Legion and the Daughters of the American Revolution (DAR); far-right demagogues epitomized by Father Charles E. Coughlin; and the Hearst press and a few other newspapers, including the *Chicago Tribune*.[34] Millions tuned in to Father Coughlin's weekly radio program, and Hearst press readers represented twelve percent to fourteen percent of total U.S. newspaper readership in the mid-1930s.[35] Nationalist groups also collaborated to discredit peace groups, organizing anti-peace movement and anti-League speakers at public meetings, and channeling information to the Executive Branch that implicated peace group members in suspect activities.[36]

Finally, peace movements, despite the overlap between liberal internationalist groups and government elites, represented a normative project distinct from that of advocates of traditional diplomatic practice. Some peace groups, such as the LNU in Britain and the LNA and WILPF in the United States, maintained considerable contact with governments, both officially through lobbying or overlapping memberships or unofficially through meetings and friendships. Through these official and unofficial contacts many peace groups demonstrated a willingness to compromise on policy positions with their governments. But even the LNU, whose leadership on paper always included government elites, promoted a discourse that remained critical of traditional diplomacy and that articulated a normative project that differed from that of promoting state interests as conceived by governments.

The relationships of peace movements with the "state," therefore, were ambivalent. They treated the state in a variety of seemingly incompatible

---

[33] On these relationships, see Alan Foster, "The Beaverbrook Press and Appeasement: The Second Phase," *European History Quarterly* (1991): 5–38; Ceadel, *Pacifism in Britain, 1914–1945;* and John Ramsden, *The Age of Balfour and Baldwin* (London: Longman, 1978).

[34] Rodney Carlisle, "The Foreign Policy Views of an Isolationist Press Lord: W. R. Hearst and the International Crisis, 1936–41," *Journal of Contemporary History* 9 (July 1974): 217–27; James Shenton, "The Coughlin Movement and the New Deal," *Political Science Quarterly* 73 (1958): 352–73; "Fascism and Father Coughlin," *Wisconsin Magazine of History* 44 (1960): 6–11; and Warren F. Kuehl, "Midwestern Newspapers and Isolationist Sentiment," *Diplomatic History* 3 (Summer 1979): 283–385.

[35] Shenton, "The Coughlin Movement," 352; Carlisle, "Foreign Policy," 217.

[36] NCPW papers; e.g., May 8, Sept. 19, 1924; RG59, "Surveillance of Radicals."

ways: as a negotiating partner, as an actor in international negotiations and organizations, and as something to be superceded in ensuring the security of "peoples" or "societies." Although apparently contradictory, the movements' understanding of the multiple roles of the state enabled them to "target" the state to attempt both to influence policy (although there was little direct success in this regard) and to dilute the state's influence on decisions of war and peace through pursuing forms of global organization.

Peace movements in both countries, therefore, represented complex entities. Movement components emanated from reactions to practices of imperialism, lifestyle and identity beliefs, the rise of a feminist critique of politics (national and international), religious opposition to militarist "ethics," labor (in both countries but especially in Britain) and farm (especially in the United States) activism, and the liberal internationalist move to contain conflict through law. It is difficult to find a homogeneous label for interwar peace groups aside from the label of "peace movement" they chose for themselves. World War I united previously diverse trends in peace activism and gave them a more urgent purpose. Yet, even with the impetus of war, peace movements did not remain static. Different ideological currents present in the movements intersected with political practice and events to rise to prominence at different historical points: the promotion of League internationalism in early to mid-1920s; the resurgence of a socialist critique in the mid to late 1920s and early 1930s; and the conflict between a growing left-pacifism and a smaller, but extremely influential, collective security push in the late 1930s. Yet these fluctuations still exhibited normative coherence in promoting extranational solutions to conflict, restraints on states' capacity to wage war, and a humanitarian and egalitarian ethic.

Chapter 2 situates these currents more firmly and reinforces the complexity and continuous "construction" of peace movements by examining their historical roots in the nineteenth and early twentieth centuries.

The Evolution of U.S. and
British Peace Movements since 1815

P eace movements in the nineteenth and the twentieth centuries promoted a vision of international life based on inculcating particular standards of state behavior into international practice. Pacifists and religious activists conceptualized these standards in the ethical terms of respect for human life, whereas socialists conceptualized them in terms of the promotion of economic justice and equity in international relations. Internationalists, many of whom were professionally trained lawyers who promoted the "rule of law" in international as well as national affairs, conceptualized them in terms of legality and order. All of these societal elements—religious, pacifist, socialist, and internationalist—traditionally comprised peace movements in both Britain and the United States, moving both within and beyond the dominant liberal ideology. Yet, despite their differing motive forces and objectives, all advocated common programs and minimum international norms to achieve international peace.

Some elements in peace movements' programs remained constant through the nineteenth and early twentieth centuries, although they evolved and recast themselves in reaction to social and political circumstances. To appreciate the relationship between peace movements and the evolution of international relations, therefore, it is crucial to understand both the continuities and changes in how social movements articulated norms.

This chapter assesses the role of peace movements in articulating and promoting international norms during five periods in the nineteenth and early twentieth centuries, beginning with movement foundations in the post-Napoleonic era and ending with the institutionalization of some (but not all) movement programs in the form of the League of Nations. E. H. Carr covered much of the same historical ground in *The Twenty Years' Crisis,* but my contention is that, in treating this historical ground in a sweeping manner, he glosses over social, economic, and political changes that have had important implications for peace movements' composition and activities and that pose significant challenges to his critique.[1] I thus take Carr as emblematic of the way in which realist international relations theory, despite its variations, views members of groups that supported these causes—as agents who act inappropriately in the international arena by attempting to institutionalize legal and ethical principles designed (and only suitable) for the domestic realm. If one looks carefully at the character and goals of peace activism vis-à-vis norms, one sees not only that Carr, Morgenthau, and other classical realists have vastly oversimplified complex historical phenomena in creating the realist/idealist dichotomy, but also that Carr's critique of the harmony of interests and his linkage of that notion to peace activism in fact applies primarily to the height of Cobdenism in the middle of the nineteenth century, somewhat less to turn-of-the-century progressivism, and little to other periods covered in his broad historical sweep. If the critique of social forces is inaccurate or incomplete, then we must also question the resulting implicit and explicit criticisms of the role of interwar peace movements in world politics.

Carr misses three insights in his analysis of social forces, law and ethics, and the harmony of interests. Once recognized, these insights better enable us to understand the role of interwar peace movements, both in delegitimizing traditional norms of statecraft and in legitimizing norms underlying the United Nations. These insights are, first, that idealism is neither an unchanging nor a monolithic strand of belief and activism in international affairs. Both the historical overview and the more in-depth understanding of interwar peace movements illustrate this point. Second, the notion of a "harmony of interests" is based on both economic and political foundations and practices that Carr conflates in a manner that confuses the stance of movements toward one another from the early nineteenth century into the 1920s and 1930s. These must be disentangled if we are to see more clearly how movements changed international relations. Third, the persistence of societal attempts to create legal/ethical standards of behavior, the fact that standards have been created, and the fact that such standards evolve with changing international circum-

---

[1] E. H. Carr, *The Twenty Years' Crisis, 1919–1939: An Introduction to the Study of International Relations,* 2d ed. (New York: Harper & Row, 1964).

stances indicate that at a minimum they are phenomena worthy of serious analysis.

Looking at the history of the development of peace movements in the societies on which Carr focused—Great Britain and the United States—during the nineteenth and early twentieth centuries, one sees that he has skillfully pointed out what theorists of social movements who analyze the relationship between movements and *policy* neglect: that social forces may have real political effects through articulating and promoting standards of behavior, be they legal or ethical norms. Yet a closer look first at the history of nineteenth- and early twentieth-century movements and, second, at the interwar movements themselves, indicates that classical realism's broad-brush treatment mischaracterized this strand of social activism in significant ways that hinder, rather than help, our understanding of the impact of such movements on international politics.

THE HISTORY OF ANGLO-AMERICAN PEACE MOVEMENTS IN THE NINETEENTH AND EARLY TWENTIETH CENTURIES

Five periods mark peace movement activism in the nineteenth and early twentieth century in Britain and the United States: (1) the foundational period in the post-Napoleonic and war of 1812 era; (2) the period of radical/institutionalist debates in the 1830s and 1840s; (3) the era of midcentury conflicts (during and after the Crimean and Civil wars) that resulted in the temporary decimation of peace movements; (4) late-nineteenth and early-twentieth-century progressivism; and (5) the post-progressive era of the partial institutionalization of movement goals in the form of the League of Nations. Despite this periodization, which is done for heuristic clarity, these phases of peace movement activity were only partially discrete. Peace movements grew, reformed, transformed themselves, and declined in response to varying national and international developments. Sociological developments in each period affected them as did their consequent interaction with other types of domestic issues and movements. Wars and international economic rivalries often transformed their goals and composition, and nascent attempts at institutionalized international cooperation encouraged their growth.

Movements broadened in their sociological composition throughout the nineteenth century, gradually expanding from their base in Protestant nonconformism to include secular, radical, and internationalist elements. National and international security concerns also affected the movements in both countries, influencing their growth, decline, ability, and desire to promote specific kinds of normative standards and institutional mechanisms for the maintenance of peace. If we situate peace movements' development in the midst of the domestic and international influences of their times, it is evident that they should not be typecast solely as static representatives of particular interests or "pie-in-the-sky" utopians incapable of evolution or reflexivity regarding political and economic practices. Many movement elements did not ignore power considerations in international politics. Although they attempted to formulate norms and mechanisms that might in their view enable states to transcend power politics, their evolving programs and goals were an explicit response to their understanding of the nature and effects of states' use of power. This understanding remained nascent in the first foundational period of movement activity, when newly formed peace groups focused on the renunciation of aggressive war.[2] In the middle of the century, movements articulated more forcefully norms of arbitration and adjudication of disputes, while promoting the idea that peace and prosperity through free trade went hand in hand. During the latter part of the century, movements continued to push arbitration, now promoted through the mechanism of a world court characterized by universal membership. For late-nineteenth-century internationalists this was to be complemented by the codification of international law, which would impose concomitant rights and obligations on all states and thereby reinforce the boundaries of acceptable state behavior.[3] The early twentieth century, and particularly the interwar period, was marked by the continuation of attempts to increase the effectiveness of the World Court and international arbitration machinery, to expand the meaning of universalism and equality of status through a league of nations, and to create new types of control of state war-making powers, particularly through disarmament conventions and treaties. During World War I peace movements saw a league of nations as the primary means of

[2] See A. C. F. Beales, *The History of Peace* (New York: Dial Press, 1931); Merle Curti, *Peace or War: The American Struggle, 1636–1936* (New York: Norton, 1936); Peter Brock, *Pacifism in Europe to 1914* (Princeton: Princeton University Press, 1968), and *Freedom from War: Nonsectarian Pacifism, 1814–1914* (Toronto: University of Toronto Press, 1991); Sandi E. Cooper, *Patriotic Pacifism: Waging War on War in Europe* (New York: Oxford University Press, 1991); and Charles F. Howlett and Glenn Zeitzer, *The American Peace Movement: History and Historiography* (Washington, D.C.: American Historical Association, 1985).

[3] David S. Patterson, *Toward a Warless World: The Travail of the American Peace Movement, 1887–1914* (Bloomington: Indiana University Press, 1976); Warren F. Kuehl, *Seeking World Order: The United States and International Organization to 1920* (Nashville: Vanderbilt University Press, 1969); C. Roland Marchand, *The American Peace Movement and Social Reform, 1889–1918* (Princeton: Princeton University Press, 1973); and Keith Robbins, *The Abolition of War: The "Peace Movement" in Britain, 1914–1919* (Cardiff: The University of Wales Press, 1976).

restraining great powers from promoting their interests at the expense of smaller states and of "peoples": international organization, by extension, became key to preventing war.[4] The following section delineates these continuities and changes.

PEACE MOVEMENT FOUNDATIONS

In the United States, three peace societies were founded separately in New York, Massachusetts, and Ohio between August and December 1815. All three fused into the American Peace Society under the leadership of William Ladd in 1827. In Britain, William Allen founded the London Peace Society (technically, the Society for the Promotion of Permanent and Universal Peace) in June, 1816. Although ostensibly nonsectarian in orientation and membership, both promulgated overtly Christian ethics (the London Peace Society rejected collaboration with nonbelievers, and the American Peace Society also made Christian beliefs a prerequisite for membership until 1901, although the requirement was rarely enforced) and were led by clergy. Their historical importance lies in the fact that they represented the first solid attempt by pacifist (Quaker) or pacifist-leaning churches to organize a political expression of their antiwar beliefs. As Peter Brock points out, this endeavor to engage in the political expression of antiwar beliefs, rather than the former practice of rejecting the political realm altogether, marked a new phase for nonconformists and other Protestant churches in the nineteenth century.[5]

Thus, the original peace societies sprang up almost simultaneously in the United States and in Britain as a direct reaction to the War of 1812 and to the Napoleonic wars. These first peace societies grew out of what was, before 1815, scattered disaffection in Britain with war policies toward revolutionary and then Napoleonic France, and disapproval in the United States of persistent fearmongering against Britain. They coalesced in response to these conflicts to propagate their opposition. They also were

---

[4] Peter Brock, *Twentieth-Century Pacifism* (New York: Van Nostrand Reinhold, 1970); Donald Birn, *The League of Nations Union, 1918–1945* (Oxford: Oxford University Press, 1981); James Hinton, *Protests and Visions: Peace Politics in Twentieth-Century Britain* (London: Hutchinson Press, 1989); Charles Chatfield, *For Peace and Justice: Pacifism in America, 1914–1941* (Knoxville: University of Tennessee Press, 1971); Charles DeBenedetti, *The Peace Reform in American History* (Bloomington: Indiana University Press, 1980), and *Origins of the Modern American Peace Movement, 1915–1978* (Millwood, N.Y.: KTO Press, 1978).

[5] Beales, *History of Peace*, p. 45; Brock, *Pacifism in Europe*, pp. 345, 383, 355–56.

"surprised and delighted" to learn of each others' existence, and after a time began to initiate mutual contacts.[6]

The efforts of the British and American peace societies between 1814 and 1816 represented, then, the first organized noninstitutional expression of antiwar sentiment. There appears to be no evidence to suggest these societies were influenced, or gained much encouragement from, the simultaneous official attempts to control hegemonic war exercised by leaders of the Great Powers in the form of the Concert of Europe. Cooper, for example, argues that the end of the Napoleonic wars spawned three *unrelated* groups to seek ways of controlling future wars in Europe: "the international political and diplomatic elites, individual writers and intellectuals, . . . and, finally, citizen activists."[7] Peace society activism, modest, mainstream, and middle-class, did not yet seek to lobby or influence officialdom directly, but rather concentrated on education and the propagation of antiwar ideas in first Christian, and later wider, public circles. This in and of itself still embodied a new type of politicization of security issues and state policies of war and peace, since social forces had not previously organized and sustained attempts to influence citizen acquiescence in such policies.

The primary questions first debated by early nineteenth-century movements included whether opposition to all war was required by Christian ethics. The debate over opposition to particular versus all wars brought into the open a fundamental division that would plague all Anglo-American peace movements thereafter. Pacifist opposition to war took the form of ethical opposition to all killing, while many who opposed war on a more selective basis, later to be called "pacificists" and some to become "internationalists," promoted a Whiggish belief in international progress and reform.[8]

The London group expended a considerable amount of energy and resources to spread its ideas on the Continent, while the U.S. society concentrated on proselytizing and disseminating tracts to religious congregations. During this period and until the middle of the century, they did not attempt to pressure governments, promote large participatory institutions for resolving conflict on the international level, or champion free trade as

[6] Cooper, "The British Contribution," in Sandi E. Cooper, ed., *Internationalism in Nineteenth-Century Europe: The Crisis of Ideas and Purpose* (New York: Garland, 1976), p. 21; Beales, *History of Peace*, p. 45; and Cooper, *Patriotic Pacifism*, p. 15.

[7] Continental Europe had no similar societies until 1830, when Jean-Jacques de Sellon founded a peace society in Geneva. This society, however, was short-lived, disintegrating with de Sellon's death in 1839. Cooper, *Patriotic Pacifism*, pp. 16–19, 14.

[8] On these distinctions, see Martin Ceadel, *Pacifism in Britain, 1914–1945* (New York: Oxford University Press, 1980), pp. 1–8.

part and parcel of a peace program. However, despite the fact that movements tended not to target political institutions, they did begin discussing and debating methods of reversing and transcending war as "custom." Noah Worcester, the founder of the Massachusetts peace society, and William Ladd, a younger adherent, wrote continually on the need to abolish "the custom of war."[9] Both pacifists and other antiwar society members agreed even at this stage on the need to renounce wars of "aggression"; their joint call of opposition to the "customary" character of war represented a nascent aspiration and the beginnings of action to influence international norms.

During this initial period movement leaders had little connection to elites, and movement goals were neither representative of nor strongly opposed to state interests. Although the peace movements in both countries had begun to discuss and debate projects of international law and organization, their ideas were vague, and they had developed no economic program or critique either. Consequently, it is difficult to categorize the movements of this era as either conscious or unconscious abettors of a harmony based on particularistic political or economic notions.

THE 1830s AND 1840s: RADICAL JUSTICE VERSUS FREE TRADE HARMONY

This period was categorized first by radical challenges to the "respectable" religious domination of peace societies in both countries. These challenges, had they succeeded, would have drawn peace groups further away from either political or economic notions of harmony. But working-class and radical movement elements were coopted by the free-trade liberalism of the 1840s. It is this period, therefore, that provides the best evidence for Carr's critique. The 1840s were also marked by a series of international peace congresses that provided a forum to articulate and debate a wide range of normative projects (including the idea of a "congress of nations"), some of which would endure beyond the era of belief in the unity of free trade and peace.

Membership in peace societies declined in the 1820s after the initial postwar spurt of organization. But new forms of radicalism in the 1830s and 1840s arising primarily out of the Garrisonian wing of the abolitionist movement in the United States and labor organizing in Britain began to permeate peace movements in both countries. Just as the original American and London Peace societies were aware of each other's work

---

[9] Brock, *Pacifism in Europe*, pp. 379, 384; *Freedom from War*, pp. 37–44.

and took steps to communicate, William Lloyd Garrison's New England Non-Resistance Society, founded in 1838, sent emissaries to Britain to recruit working-class Chartists to the methods of Non-Resistance. Their success was limited, although some well-known Chartists, including Thomas Cooper and Henry Vincent, also became peace advocates. Likewise, labor activism for peace began to spread to the United States: in 1846 Elihu Burritt founded the League of Human Brotherhood, an international organization that attempted to attract a working-class membership. The League enjoyed considerable organizing success on both sides of the Atlantic. However, the natural conservatism of the older peace societies' leadership and the difference in methods between their temperate proselytizing and the radical rejection of government by the Garrisonians, on the one hand, and the overt political organizing of the British workers' movement, on the other, limited cooperation between the older societies and the new movements in both countries.[10]

Moreover, the changing economics of agriculture in Britain increasingly forced working-class radicals to compete with free traders for legitimacy on peace issues. The Quaker John Bright became the first persuasive proponent of the "liberal" movement soon taken up by Richard Cobden. This creed rested on three assumptions: (1) that peace and prosperity were indissolubly linked; (2) that all levels of the citizenry could attain them; and (3) that both could be attained only by eliminating barriers to transnational (and especially commercial) exchange. After the repeal of the corn laws in 1846, which had previously protected domestic agricultural producers against foreign exports, it was clear that Cobdenism had won in Britain. The Anti-Corn Law League had become "the most powerful national pressure group England had known"; Cobden, its leader, "thought the interlocking of the world economy, as international specialization developed, would prevent war—despite the politicians doing their worst."[11] The explicit linkage of free trade and peace provided the peace activism of the 1840s with a new focus, a new lease on life, and a secular tone. This linkage, however, also entailed the cooptation of British working-class radicalism by the middle-class concern with prosperity through tariff reduction, which in turn affected the course of peace ac-

[10] Brock, *Freedom from War*, pp. 30–31, 104–13; and *Pacifism in Europe*, pp. 396–97, 398; Howlett and Zeitzer, *American Peace Movement;* Ronald G. Walters, *American Reformers, 1815–1860* (New York: Hill & Wang, 1978), pp. 115–17; Brock, *Pacifism in Europe*, p. 347.

[11] Arnold Wolfers and Laurence W. Martin reprint many of Cobden's speeches in their edited book, *The Anglo-American Tradition in Foreign Affairs* (New Haven: Yale University Press, 1956), pp. 196–205; Peter Mathias, *The First Industrial Nation: An Economic History of Britain, 1700–1904* (London: Methuen, 1976), pp. 301, 293.

tivity by mooting demands for peace based on economic equality in favor of the promise of peace based on a belief in future prosperity.[12] After 1840 the peace and free-trade movements in Britain became explicitly linked, and Cobden himself began to speak of both issues as one and the same cause, providing grist for the mill of Carr's critique of the "harmony of interests."

The coalition of midcentury peace forces on both sides of the Atlantic, however, also began to organize "international" peace congresses during the 1840s, inspired by the success of the 1840 World Anti-Slavery Congress held in London. These congresses were designed to spread the faith more widely and, in particular, to encourage continental Europeans to engage more actively in the discussion of how to attain a pacific world. Their significance lies in the fact that they debated and articulated over a six-year period plans for international institutions that embodied norms of arbitration, adjudication, and, to a lesser extent, universal participation.

At the first International Peace Congress, held in London in 1843, delegates primarily from England and the United States agreed on resolutions advocating arbitration clauses to settle international disputes and a "high court of nations" to keep the peace in Europe.[13] The Brussels Congress of 1848 and the Paris Congress of 1849 continued to emphasize the need for international arbitration mechanisms and the creation of some type of international court. Other proposals, however, such as the argument for a "congress of nations" (a project continually pushed by Burritt, who was originally inspired by William Ladd's writings of the 1820s), could not overcome the opposition of Europeans, especially the French, who opposed a congress in which representatives from states that suppressed revolutionary movements would sit as equals with those from "republican" states. Likewise, delegates easily agreed on the need for disarmament and reductions of weapons expenditures at the 1843 Congress, but by 1848 and 1849 "disarmament" held different meanings for Anglo-Americans, revolutionary sympathizers, and advocates of the European status quo. Although the majority of British and U.S. delegates refused to sanction attempts to change oppressive domestic regimes through (violent) revolution, they registered "ringing denunciations" of British and French foreign

[12] See Gregory Claeys, "Mazzini, Kossuth, and British Radicalism, 1848–1854," *Journal of British Studies* 28 (July 1989): 225–61; Brock, *Pacifism in Europe*, p. 396; Asa Briggs, *The Making of Modern England, 1783–1867* (New York: Harper & Row, 1965), p. 321; and E. P. Thompson, *The Making of the English Working Class* (New York: Vintage Books, 1966), pp. 807–30.

[13] Cooper, *Patriotic Pacifism*, pp. 22–23; Beales, *History of Peace*, p. 67.

policy in Tahiti, China and Afghanistan for engaging in bloody repressions of non-European peoples.

The peace congresses did not receive much, if any, official notice, and their proceedings and plans were ridiculed by those segments of the press who did pay attention.[14] Still, they represented the first public discussions of and agreement by various movement factions (religious pacifists, members of Burritt's League, and centrist peace society members) on incipient institutionalized expressions of the international legal norm of conflict resolution through arbitration. In addition, the discussion (without agreement) of disarmament obligations attendant on all states and the condemnation of the control and repression of territories and peoples outside of Europe represented a further step toward the recognition of the responsibility of all states in ensuring peace (an aspect of the norm of universalism) and the rights of peoples to determine their own fate in international society (an aspect of the norm of equality of status).

Yet the belief that peace and harmony could be attained through prosperity brought about by liberal economic policies gained the upper hand with these newly called "internationalists," who convinced many pacifists in both countries of their logic. The second international peace congress, which Cobden himself attended, was shaped more clearly by a liberal political-economic agenda. Free-trade rhetoric increasingly suffused the British movement, particularly after 1846, and Cobden strengthened the explicit link between notions of liberal harmony and peace activism by publicly crediting the nonconformist peace testimony with influencing the broader repudiation of war that he popularized.[15]

Peace groups tended to support the international status quo against revolutionary movements, linking liberalism and peace during this period and justifying Carr's critique of the liberal harmony of interests. Cobden and other liberals in the movement, for example, "had little sympathy . . . with the contemporary movements for national liberation on the continent" because they feared that the breakup of states into smaller political units would worsen nationalism and hamper free trade.[16] However, neither strict pacifism nor Cobden's brand of free-trade liberalism survived the midcentury wars fought by Britain and the United States. Newer sociological-intellectual currents in the latter part of the century supplemented both pacifism and Cobdenism and contributed to discussion and debate of international legal/institutional mechanisms to ensure peace.

[14] Beales, *History of Peace*, p. 68.
[15] Cooper, *Patriotic Pacifism*, p. 23; Brock, *Pacifism in Europe*, p. 406.
[16] Brock, *Pacifism in Europe*, p. 389.

These new currents demonstrated that agreement on norms of arbitration and the observance of legally sanctioned rules of state conduct did not automatically go hand in hand with free-trade notions of harmony.

THE CRIMEAN AND CIVIL WARS

The midcentury wars shattered the fragile unity between the original religious peace groups, the small radical components, and the then-dominant free-trade leadership. For Britons, the Crimean War, which broke out in 1854 and involved Britain in a major European war for the first time in forty years, roused patriotic fervor, and some peace activists' attempts to stop the war once it had begun discredited the movement. Moreover, the 1857 elections became to a large extent a referendum on Palmerston, including his activist foreign policy in both the Crimea and China. With nationalism and imperialism on the rise, both Cobden and the Quaker liberal John Bright, the leaders of the then more or less fused free-trade and peace movements, lost their seats in Parliament.[17] Cobden and Bright were some of Palmerston's most vocal critics, and their loss resulted in "the almost complete annihilation of the Manchester School" and its liberal economic ethic in Parliament.

In the United States the war with Mexico seemed to improve the peace movement's status during the 1840s, but the Civil War fifteen years later, like the Crimean War for the British, seriously curtailed peace activism and decimated the membership of peace societies. The American Peace Society, fearful of losing its raison d'être, refused to take a position for or against slavery, while the war made many who had previously believed violence to be an unmitigated evil conclude that force provided the best means of eliminating slavery and the danger of breaking apart the Union. Moreover, in addition to the negative effects that involvement in war produced for the individual movements in each country, the Civil War caused a breech of the heretofore amicable communications between the British and American peace societies: the British could not approve of the majority of U.S. peace workers' endorsement of the war.[18] Consequently, peace activity remained meager for at least two decades.

This period cleansed the peace movements of their early faith in the power of Christian values and public opinion to achieve national and

---

[17] Beales, *History of Peace,* p. 132; Briggs, *Making of Modern England,* pp. 420–22.

[18] Brock, *Pacifism in Europe,* p. 390; Howlett and Zeitzer, *American Peace Movement;* Patterson, *Toward a Warless World,* p. 2.

international peace. It forced many, especially in the United States, to re-think the boundaries of what they previously considered to be absolute pacifism, a dilemma that would arise anew during the 1930s. The experi-ence of devastating wars also compelled movement activists who began to reorganize peace efforts in the latter part of the century to replace their faith in the power of public opinion and free trade with more insistent demands for legal and institutional supports for peace.

THE PROGRESSIVE ERA

New domestic reform movements again infused peace activity in the 1890s and broadened the issue base as well as the social base of the peace move-ment. The last decade of the 1800s and the first two decades of the 1900s are often referred to as the "progressive" era, one characterized by a "search for order," when "the gospel of expertise and efficiency merged with economic regulation, social control, and humanitarian reform to be-come a conspicuous part of the public life of both countries." Some his-torians view progressivism as a distinctly U.S. phenomenon and see in liberalism its British counterpart as both were opposed to toryism and so-cialism, others point to its amorphous transatlantic and ideological na-ture.[19] This second reading accords with progressivism's relationship to peace activism: many progressive reformers joined forces with older, bour-geois peace groups to work for arbitration, and increasingly added dis-armament and the development of international organization to their peace programs.[20] The most significant new push during the late nine-teenth century, however, was the move by international legal specialists in favor of the codification of international law. During this period move-ments began to have a more direct impact on the state policies regarding accepting and institutionalizing two legal norms: conflict resolution through arbitration, demonstrated by the creation of the World Court;

[19] Robert Wiebe, *The Search for Order, 1877–1920* (New York: Hill & Wang, 1967); Morton Keller, "Anglo-American Politics, 1900–1930, in Anglo-American Perspective: A Case Study in Comparative History," *Comparative Studies in Society and History* 22 (July 1980): 463. See also Daniel T. Rodgers, "In Search of Progressivism," *Reviews in American History* 10 (December 1982): 127, n. 1.

[20] Howlett and Zeitzer, *American Peace Movement*, pp. 17–18; Nigel Young, "Tradition and Innovation in the British Peace Movement: Towards an Analytical Framework," in Taylor and Young, eds., *Campaigns for Peace: British Peace Movements in the Twentieth Century* (Manchester: Manchester University Press, 1987), pp. 8, 12, 14; Cooper, *Internationalism in Nineteenth-Century Europe*, pp. 14–16; Marchand, *American Peace Movement and Social Reform*.

and universal participation in and responsibility for decisions about peace and security, demonstrated by debates over plans for a league of nations.

In the last decades of the century peace activism first appeared to take up where it had left off in the 1850s. The decline of the quasi-pacifist and radical wings of the two movements (begun in the 1840s with their co-optation into free-trade liberalism), combined with the fact that both Britain and the United States were major players on the world stage, gave a greater voice to the growing number of Establishment internationalists who emerged as leaders of the movement, especially in the United States.[21] This revival of peace activism also appears at first glance to confirm the hold that liberal economic norms, including free trade, held over peace activism. Yet the fact that both Britain and the United States were also caught up in a new competition that affected security relations—the imperialist rivalries of the late nineteenth and early twentieth centuries, attested to by Britain's participation in the scramble for Africa and the Boer War and by the Spanish-American War waged by the United States—again split peace activists. Peace groups coexisted uneasily with nationalist claims, although a number of internationalists in both countries resolved the dilemma by justifying their own country's imperialism in the name of a "civilizing mission" of spreading liberalism and democracy to "backward" peoples. Advocating internationalist solutions to conflict provided a way for many in the United States, for example, to plan to increase the American presence in world affairs, engineering the growth of U.S. power and influence in what they believed to be a benevolent manner. Consequently, renewed imperialist policies during the late nineteenth and early twentieth century split progressives and caused the Left in both countries to cultivate an increasingly antiwar stance, which it would maintain during the lead-up to World War I as the Anglo-German naval race heated up and hostilities on the European continent became more pronounced.[22]

Progressivism and its impact on politics, including foreign affairs, is open to a wide variety of assessments and interpretations.[23] In one interpretation, the focus on reform by virtually all types of U.S. activists—Eastern liberals, Republican legalists, other assorted internationalists, and those

[21] Cooper, *Patriotic Pacifism,* pp. 13–14.

[22] See Robert E. Osgood, *Ideals and Interests in America's Foreign Relations* (Chicago: University of Chicago Press, 1953), pp. 86–87; Patterson, *Toward a Warless War,* pp. 126, 131; Marvin Swartz, *The Union of Democratic Control in British Politics during the First World War* (Oxford: Clarendon, 1971); Martin Shaw, "War, Peace and British Marxism, 1895–1945," in Taylor and Young, eds.; Osgood, *Ideals and Interests.*

[23] Rodgers ultimately argues against any single interpretation in "In Search of Progressivism," pp. 113–32; see also Keller, "Anglo-American Politics," pp. 458–77; and Wiebe, *The Search for Order,* chap. 9, "The Emergence of Foreign Policy."

who tied domestic reform issues to international peace—demonstrated a strong belief in internationalizing domestic economic practices in a way that still very often fit with the notion of a harmony of interests. Patterson, for example, points out that for elite leaders of the movements in this era, the equation of peace with free trade was at its apex.[24] The trends toward professionalization of many occupations (e.g., teaching, medicine, law, social work) did little at first to negate the growing elite Establishment influence on the movements—indeed, well-connected spokespersons were most often seen as a boon to the cause. In Britain, Establishment activists who felt that the traditional peace societies were "too closely identified with Nonconformist pressure groups" joined the American-led International Law Association to further projects for international arbitration among elite classes of lawyers and public officials.[25] Nevertheless, many progressive reformers made new connections between peace and economic and social needs, both at home and abroad, connections that engendered a distinct unease with liberal notions of harmony. Indeed, a number of progressives came to peace activity *because of* their work for reform of domestic economic and political practices and extended their concerns about the exclusionary aspects of turn-of-the-century liberal society (e.g., the concern with the unemployed and marginalized by the settlement house movement imported into the United States from Britain by Jane Addams or the suffragists' efforts to end the exclusion of women from political participation in both countries) into their peace activities on the international level (e.g., less support for laissez-faire economic policies by the Women's International League for Peace and Freedom; work for the "democratization" of security decisions to reflect the will of "peoples" rather than "states").[26]

Moreover, a left-wing critique of war was also growing in influence during the Progressive era. Although socialists were not consistently concerned with foreign policy issues during the latter half of the nineteenth century, the birth of the Labour Party in Britain and the activism of the Independent Labour Party (ILP) engendered a more developed critique of war. Meanwhile U.S. union organizers and radical pacifists did the same

[24] Although followers of this interpretation do not necessarily use the term. See, for example, Marchand, *The American Peace Movement;* Patterson, *Toward a Warless World,* pp. 12–13, 126–29; and Warren F. Kuehl, *Seeking World Order: The United States and International Organization to 1920* (Nashville: Vanderbilt University Press, 1969); and, for a more introspective view, Osgood, *Ideals and Interests.*

[25] Robbins, *Abolition of War,* p. 8.

[26] Charles De Benedetti, *Origins of the Modern American Peace Movement, 1915–1929* (Millwood, N.Y.: KTO Press, 1978); Chatfield, *For Peace and Justice;* and Peter Brock, *Twentieth-Century Pacifism* (New York: Van Nostrand Reinhold, 1970).

across the Atlantic. Despite their different views on economic practices and the causes of war, Establishment liberals, progressive reformers, and the socialist Left all worked to legitimize norms that constrained states' right to wage war and to promote institutionalized mechanisms for engendering interstate cooperation. In Britain, for example, not only did the elitist International Law Association advocate arbitration, but also the International Arbitration League, first known as the Workmen's Peace Association, which had "extensive trade union contacts."[27]

Through the nineteenth and early twentieth centuries, then, peace groups gained adherents in fits and starts, broadening their sociological base as other domestic social movements grew and found common ground in promoting peace through arbitration. In the 1840s and 1850s the dominant theme in peace group activism encouraged the notion of a harmony of interest between the promotion of individual prosperity and international peace, and the concomitant promotion of both "civic rights" among states and rights to private property, with trade on the international level occuring among property owners according to a free-market regulation of supply and demand. The linkage between free trade and peace also encouraged a status quo conception of international order, with movement leaders arguing against intervention in support of revolutionary movements on the Continent. The decimation of the midcentury movements, however, made the notion of "harmony" a moot point for effective peace activism; the turn-of-the-century infusion of progressive reformers and the marriage of peace with social concerns made the reconstitution of the idea of a harmony of interests problematic.

Thus, as a result of both the changing sociological composition of groups interested in "peace" and the new competition between states for colonies and prestige, the mix of norms and institutions that peace activists attempted to internationalize evolved away from the notion of a harmony of interests. As new actors struggling for additional rights on the domestic level became interested in the peace issue (abolitionists, labor unions, settlement house workers, suffragists), peace groups increasingly reflected a concern with "humanizing" international relations and with ensuring the participation of all peoples and political entities in decisions affecting their welfare. Rather than equating the promotion of "harmony" with the promotion of universal participation in international institutions,

---

[27] Hinton, *Protests and Visions,* p. 32; also Hinton, *Labour and Socialism: A History of the British Labour Movement, 1867–1914* (Amherst: University of Massachusetts Press, 1983); Asa Briggs and John Saville, eds., *Essays in Labour History, 1918–1939* (London: Croom Helm, 1977); Swartz, *Union of Democratic Control;* and Shaw, "War, Peace, and British Marxism"; Robbins, *Abolition of War,* p. 8.

peace activity should be seen as an evolutionary process that moved from the former in the middle of the century to the latter at the century's end. This evolution was related to both the change in the balance of social groups composing peace movements over time and the domestic and international political crises with which they had to contend. At the turn of the century, the Darwinian struggle among the powers for colonies and influence left a great number of these new peace activists uneasy with, and many openly critical of, founding international harmony on rights to ownership and control of resources, people, and territory. As a result, some began to question the "civilizing effects" of empire building, and most concentrated their "peace" efforts on the promotion of international order through universalist civic rights and the creation of an international judiciary and "legislature" for discussing and resolving disputes. Many saw the two international congresses at the Hague of 1899 and 1907, which resulted in the creation of the World Court, as the first tangible institutional fruits of their efforts; some new critics of old notions of harmony also saw in these mechanisms the means by which imperialism might be delegitimized, "subject peoples" granted rights as participants in international society, and peaceful change made possible. Movement influence on governments in the pre–World War I period probably peaked with the Second Hague Conference of 1907, "a meeting that the powers would not have spontaneously convoked without considerable pressure exerted on them."[28]

Connections and Dislocations between Pre–World War I and Interwar Movements

Until recently, peace movements have not been given much direct credit for influencing states to create international institutions to facilitate arbitration and help to ensure peace. Now, however, historians are revising their analyses of Wilsonianism and the foundation of the League of Nations to grant peace movements a greater and potentially determinative role.[29] Even more significant, perhaps, is the role that peace movements during and after World War I played in ensuring that the normative foun-

[28] Cooper, *Internationalism in Nineteenth-Century Europe*, pp. 17–18; see also Kuehl, *Seeking World Order*.

[29] See, for example, Thomas J. Knock, *To End All Wars: Woodrow Wilson and the Quest for a New World Order* (New York: Oxford University Press, 1992); Martin David Dubin, "Toward the Concept of Collective Security: The Bryce Group's 'Proposals for the Avoidance of War,' 1914–1917," *International Organization* 24 (Spring 1970): 299; Peter Yearwood, "'On the Safe and Right Line': The Lloyd George Government and the Origins of the League of Nations, 1916–1918," *Historical Journal* 32 (1989): 131–55; George W. Egerton, *Great Britain*

dations of their projects would provide new standards of diplomacy and guides for state foreign policy practice—standards that would be debated throughout the twentieth century.

Interwar movements differed from their nineteenth- and early twentieth-century predecessors in their direct experience of worldwide, cataclysmic war, conducted with enormously destructive weapons such as submarines, poison gas, and airplanes that for the first time directly targeted civilians. Consequently, interwar movements no longer expressed qualms about disarmament. Arms reduction, either unilateral or multilateral, became the primary focus of many in the movements on both sides of the Atlantic. By the end of World War I disarmament supplanted the Progressive Era push for codification of international law because peace activists viewed the mere codification of existing practices in international law, particularly the foundational respect for states' sovereign rights and the concomitant disregard for the self-determination of peoples, as helping to perpetuate an unjust status quo. Peace groups saw themselves as challenging the international status quo, including their own governments' policies toward the League, mandatory arbitration, and disarmament. After World War I faith in state security practices and traditional forms of diplomacy plummeted, resulting in a widespread willingness to criticize government policies and put forth detailed alternatives that were based on principles of international law and organization. Peace movements promoted the League, international law, and principles of universal participation and equality of status not to further the particularistic state interests of Britain, France, or even the United States, but rather to restrain them and enable the discussion of how collective interests might be determined that were not based on false notions of harmony.

Peace movements made an impact during the period because many groups could legitimately claim to represent thousands (and in the case of the British League of Nations Union or the U.S. National Council for the Prevention of War, tens or even hundreds of thousands) of adherents, increasing their chances of being heard in the press, Parliament, Congress, and Cabinets in both countries.[30] Their activity constitutes what Carr labeled the "popularization of international politics" in the interwar period.

---

and the Creation of the League of Nations: Strategy, Politics, and International Organization, 1914– 1919 (Chapel Hill: University of North Carolina Press, 1979); and Kuehl, *Seeking World Order.*

[30] Birn, *League of Nations Union;* Martin Ceadel, "The Peace Movement between the Wars: Problems of Definition," in Taylor and Young, eds., *Campaigns for Peace,* pp. 80–81; Wittner, *Rebels against War: The American Peace Movement, 1933–1983* (Philadelphia: Temple University Press, 1984), pp. 13–15; Chatfield, *For Peace and Justice,* pp. 95–101.

But far from being a continuation of mid-nineteenth-century notions of "harmony," or even the continuation of ideas favoring the international-ization of liberal standards on the part of Progressive Era elites, interwar peace movements and their supporters by and large believed that inter-national norms and institutions had to possess the capacity to control, in addition to reform, states' war-prone tendencies. Both the experience of imperialism and that of the pre–World War I alliance system had con-vinced many peace activists that Great Power concordats needed to be re-placed by universal participation in decisions regarding international security, universal responsibility for maintaining peace, and equality of treatment at the international level.

Peace movements emphasized these norms in a number of ways. First, peace activists expected the newly created League of Nations to represent all states and if possible all peoples, and worked for self-determination and in some cases independence of colonies as well as the inclusion of both the Soviet Union and Germany in the League. Second, they differed from pre–World War I activists in their concentrated and relatively unified stance in favor of the principles that all states should disarm and that trade in arms should not be allowed to continue unfettered, even while they continued to disagree on whether disarmament should be unilateral or multilateral and on whether the arms trade should be banned or nation-alized. Arbitrating conflict had been the leitmotif of the nineteenth-century peace movements, and although peace groups in the immediate pre–World War I era agitated against the Anglo-German arms race, dis-armament as a movement goal finally gained an equal footing with arbi-tration in the aftermath of the Great War. The continuing development of weapons of mass destruction during the interwar period, particularly the bomber and various chemical weapons, encouraged the perception that civilization could not survive another war and fueled the fire for disarma-ment. Finally, post–World War I movements put international economic and social issues, such as the effects of reparations, the blockade of for-merly enemy countries, the international "traffic in women and children," and during the Depression, the effects of disarmament on employment, at the forefront of international concerns.

These developments had significant implications for peace groups' ac-tivism and identities. Peter Brock, for example, asserts that "the new pacifism" of the post-1914 era "came to possess a social concern" not pres-ent earlier, in that both pacifists and other sections of the wider post–World War I peace movement became "acutely aware of the need for so-cial change in effecting the elimination of war and violence from the world." Although still vaguely defined, the new willingness to challenge the "institutions of war" (including secret diplomacy among the Great Powers, rearmament, and the arms trade), for both pacifists and internationalists would entail a wider change in consciousness and the beginnings of a deeper critique of state and international practices than that provided by either the idea of a "harmony of interests" that dominated the mid-nineteenth century or the reformist spirit prevalent in the Progressive Era. For Charles DeBenedetti, "the modern American peace movement that arose during 1914–20 was radically different from its prewar counterparts in its methods of understanding and analysis, its transnational humanism, its left-wing political orientation, and its explicit lines of alternative action." As James Hinton succinctly describes this transformation in his study of British movements, "Nineteenth-century peace movements set out to improve the world: twentieth-century ones struggle to save it."[31] Mid-nineteenth-century and late-nineteenth-century "idealism" was a vacillating product of liberal political institutions, of a belief in a British and/or American *mission civilisatrice,* and of faith in the unity of the free-trade ethic and peace. The fundamental difference between the pre- and post-1914 eras was the disintegration of precisely these assumptions about how peace could be attained and maintained.

PEACE MOVEMENT AGENCY AND CHANGE

Contextualizing peace movements historically and focusing on the confrontation of their normative projects with social, economic, and political trends reveals that Carr's construction of the "harmony of interests" is too sweeping to aid our understanding of *how* and *why* movements attempted to internationalize principles embedded in domestic beliefs and practices.

Students of liberal "harmony" generally recognize both its economic and political components. Carr erred in conflating the liberal economic doctrine of harmony with moves toward international problem-solving mechanisms. Peace groups gradually developed a program founded on agreement to internationalize the juridical equality of states and mechanisms for conflict resolution through global international organization. They first provided the foundation for peace groups' primary focus during the 1900s: the institutionalization of arbitration procedures to prevent conflict and proposals for the codification of international law.[32] Through-

---

[31] Brock, *Twentieth-Century Pacifism,* p. 12; Charles DeBenedetti, ed., *Peace Heroes in Twentieth-Century America* (Bloomington: Indiana University Press, 1986), p. 9; Hinton, *Protests and Visions,* p. 1.

out the century peace activism focused on arbitration, promoting bilateral arbitration treaties and clauses in treaties. Over time, nineteenth-century peace activists also demonstrated an increasing interest in the second type of institution by drawing up plans for an international tribunal or congress of some type.

Peace groups have often disagreed on whether an economic critique of war obtained. Recognizing private property rights and the forces of supply and demand as the best regulators of economic decisions have often been matters of contention within peace movements. During the middle of the century, peace and free trade became tightly linked, and many prominent peace workers and groups adhered to a harmony of interests, in this case the belief that free trade and the right to ownership of private property increased both the prosperity of the individual and the prospects for peace in the international polity. However, although belief in this tenet remained strong amongst many upper middle-class activists throughout the century, accord on issues of economic organization and distribution within peace movements *as a whole* often proved problematic. Peace activism had broadened from a small reformist religious base to include abolitionists, suffragists, business interests, and socialists, and its rank-and-file membership was drawn largely from the service professions: teaching, the clergy, medicine, law, and social work. Consequently, though peace activism remained rooted in the middle-class,[33] both overlapping membership with other movements concerned with social and economic practices (labor, abolitionism, feminism) and crises and wars (the U.S. Civil War, the Crimean War, and the second wave of imperialism) tended to disrupt peace movement accord on harmony in the latter half of the century. By the outbreak of World War I, agreement among peace groups was limited to internationalizing norms and methods of political conflict resolution.

Nineteenth-century peace activism can be seen as a struggle between those who would prioritize universalist legal norms and their institutionalization and those who would stress founding peace on rights to private property and free trade. By the end of World War I, peace groups' focus had coalesced around plans to internationalize participatory institutions (and their concomitant rights) in the belief that "peace" required universal participation and equality of status—norms that, it was believed, would

[32] Brock, *Twentieth-Century Pacifism*, p. 7.
[33] This sociological profile fits with that of other peace movements. See Frank Parkin, *Middle-Class Radicalism: The Social Bases of the British Campaign for Nuclear Disarmament* (Manchester: Manchester University Press, 1968).

allow for peaceful change rather than legitimate an unjust status quo. Peace movements believed that these norms, when institutionalized through a league of nations, would also replace conflict management by either unstable alliances or Great Power machinations. By the interwar period, agreement on the use of liberal economic institutions to foster peace had disintegrated, but accord on what might be called the "republican compromise," that is institutionalizing universal norms of both rights to participation and obligations, was quite strong.[34] Thus, in addition to working to recognize the rights of Germany and the Soviet Union to full membership in the League and the principle of equality of status in armaments, interwar peace movements promoted the recognition of parity in the naval arms race between the United States and Britain and obligatory arbitration of conflict on a basis of juridical equality.

Peace movement activism and goals, therefore, have evolved over time. In assessing the influence of some movements on the promotion and legitimization of norms—from arbitration to free trade liberalism to disarmament and universal participation and equality in a congress of nations—Carr begins with the interwar period and, criticizing the failure of legal and moral standards and their institutionalization in League mechanisms to keep peace, works backward to assert that efforts to ensure peace through institutionalizing principles of conduct are misleading, often dangerous, and inevitably shallow covers for furthering the interests of the powerful. However, if we begin with early-nineteenth-century peace movement activity and work forward, we see that dismissing such activism as irrelevant to political necessities misses the fact of its persistence and the facets of its evolving character. When we see the ways in which movements have reacted to and interacted with the norms, events, and practices of their times—the Napoleonic wars, protectionism, imperialist competition, the social dislocations brought about by both laissez-faire and neomercantilism, World War I, arms races—their goals and actions become understandable, sometimes logical, and even perhaps "realistic."

Yet realist international relations theory has created a narrative that uses the rhetorical device of dichotomization to set itself up as the standard of prudent statecraft against the utopianism of "idealists." To overcome this erroneous dichotomization of action in international relations theory, it is necessary to recognize explicitly the importance of the interaction between peace movements as social agents and the forms taken by domestic

---

[34] See Michael Doyle's discussion of the components of republicanism, in "Kant, Liberal Legacies, and Foreign Affairs, Part I," and "Part II," *Philosophy and Public Affairs* 12 (Summer and Fall, 1983).

and international political and economic practices.[35] Moreover, although Carr's theory of liberal hegemony places both movement groups and liberal states in the same category, a normative focus on nineteenth- and early-twentieth-century peace movements demonstrates that these movements increasingly formulated agendas critical of British and U.S. state policies and practices. The reasons for this growing divergence between movement and state agents can be understood only by looking at the interplay of social activism with political and economic practice in a manner that does not characterize social forces in a monolithic fashion. The following chapters assess the interplay of social and political activism for British and U.S. peace movements during the 1920s and 1930s.

[35] An interaction highlighted by Alexander Wendt, "The Agent–Structure Problem in International Relations Theory," *International Organization* 41 (Summer 1987): 335–70; and David Dessler, "What's at Stake in the Agent–Structure Debate," *International Organization* 43 (Summer 1989): 441–73.

Reinterpreting the British
Peace Movement in the 1920s

Beginning with the Versailles Treaty and League of Nations Covenant through Munich and the invasion of Poland, realist interpretations present British interwar diplomacy as something of a farce in which prudent statecraft takes one step forward, only to be forced two steps back by the naïveté of social forces, the League of Nations' impotence, or a combination of the two. Sir Eyre Crowe, permanent under-secretary in the Foreign Office in the first half of the 1920s, put it well in his 1923 complaint, "In many ways the spread of democracy is tending to impede rather than to facilitate the amicable settlement of international differences . . . it is a common experience of statesmen desirous of peace to find that public opinion . . . prevents them from making the sacrifices and compromises which they themselves see the justice and the advantage of offering as the price of an amicable settlement."[1]

This type of official complaint undergirds the "diplomatic inefficiency" critique of interwar peace movements. Combined with other aspects of the realist narrative, the traditional view of the 1920s holds that revulsion to war marked the decade. Promoted by peace activists, the demands resulting from this revulsion resulted in the utopian belief that the League of Nations either would automatically work to prevent war or could be made to do so. Unrealistic faith in collective institutional arrangements—the League, international arbitration, the Kellogg–Briand Pact—set a dangerous precedent that helped to make governments incapable of addressing the crises of the 1930s.

[1] Crowe memorandum, 24–25 June 1923, FO 371/9419/5047/30, PRO.

This and the following chapter present another narrative of the role played by the interwar British peace movement—one that is much more complex but also provides a more thorough understanding of the implications of peace movement activity. In this narrative, neither peace movement forces nor the government maintains a monopoly on realistic or idealistic policy. Structural constraints matter (e.g., Britain's historic position as balancer, the importance of global trade to British hegemony, Britain's commitments to its Empire), but the narrative sees these "structures" as themselves socially constructed. Moreover, their relative weight and importance are subjects of interpretation for Cabinets, the military, and social forces alike. This narrative rejects realism's dichotomization and delineates the process by which the claims of government officials and peace groups at times intersect, but more often vie for, normative legitimacy.

In this narrative peace groups (internationalists, pacifists, socialists, religious groups) often diverged in their specific policy proposals, depending on the degree to which an economic, humanitarian, or legalist critique of war informed their purpose. Yet, despite their differences, the claims and demands of peace groups coalesced in significant ways, providing a considerable amount of normative coherence. Peace groups worked to restrict states' rights to prepare for and wage war, normalize the practice of resorting to multilateral mechanisms to resolve conflicts (political and economic) and address humanitarian problems, and claim broad rights to break down traditional diplomatic practice and secrecy by widening public participation in security debates.

Peace groups first claimed that armaments, especially highly advanced and destructive weapons such as bombers and chemical weapons, were at best counterproductive. If they did not cause war (and many believed they did), they at least made warfare so destructive, painful, and widespread that civilians could no longer be protected in the name of "defense." This claim resulted in the demand for general disarmament (peace groups' primary demand) and for control or elimination of the arms trade, although peace groups disagreed over specific policy proposals.

For the peace movement the Anglo-German naval arms race and secret diplomacy led to World War I; disarmament, therefore, was the only way to prevent a recurrence of the war's carnage. More important, money spent on weapons meant money wasted and unavailable for more pressing social needs; for many, weapons expenditures also demonstrated capitalist manipulation of state interests. World War I had quickly lost popular support, had provoked enormous suffering, and had precipitated widespread economic insecurity; continued arms races would compound the disaster in the short term and risked engendering another war in the long term. For disarmament to occur, states had to accept the principle of equality of status, and the sooner this was accomplished, the easier it would be to prevent competitive rearmament not only in warships, but also in terrifying new weapons such as bombers and chemical gas. Any efforts to stall or obstruct disarmament therefore added to the movement's frustration and fear of another war.

The peace movement focused its disarmament goals on three primary demands. Each had both normative and policy implications. The overarching goal was to realize Article 8 of the League Covenant, in which state signatories recognized "that the maintenance of peace requires the reduction of national armaments to the lowest point consistent with national safety," by means of a General Disarmament Conference under League of Nations auspices. Although in this article of the Covenant, also incorporated into the four peace treaties concluded at Paris, members of the League merely *recognized* the necessity to reduce armaments, the peace movement interpreted this phraseology as a *pledge* to disarm on the part of the signatory powers, and this interpretation gained wide currency.[2] Moreover, the peace movement took its distinction between "aggressive" and "defensive" weapons directly from the Versailles Treaty. According to the military provisions of Versailles, Germany was forbidden to acquire "aggressive" weapons, including tanks, heavy guns, military aircraft, submarines, battleships over 10,000 tons, and "poison gases." Universalizing this standard became in effect the foundation for the peace movement's ongoing disarmament campaigns. More important, it became the basis for claims regarding what the peace movement deemed realistically possible; if Germany could carry out this degree of disarmament, even though forced to do so, then the British government's contrary claims that it could not do likewise were untenable. Finally, to be enacted successfully both claims required universal compliance and some recognition of equality among states.

The efforts of peace groups to normalize multilateral (especially League) conflict-resolution mechanisms rested on dual claims. Groups saw multilateral mechanisms as either a "good" in their own right, a necessary improvement on Great Power politics that provided for a more democratic airing of grievances and therefore more legitimate solutions to conflict than those worked out through force; or as in the case of the No More War Movement (NMWM) or the Union of Democratic Control (UDC), they viewed multilateral mechanisms as the most readily available means to

---

[2] John Wheeler-Bennett, *The Pipe Dream of Peace* (1935; New York: Howard Fertig, 1971), pp. 2–3.

redress the wrongs of imperialism and the Versailles treaties. For some groups and many individuals, both claims obtained. In particular, a developing sense of the injustices of both imperialism and capitalism pervaded even nonsocialist peace groups. For example, the manifesto issued in 1923 by the Women's International League for Peace and Freedom (WILPF) stated: "the Governments of the great States have all in various degrees and at different periods of their history pursued imperialist interests to the detriment of their neighbours, or have imposed their domination on Peoples desiring independence, or have employed force to obtain economic and political advantages." Thus the WILPF, "while not refusing *a priori* to work with Governments whenever this is possible, addresses itself directly to the Peoples victimised by politics and capitalism." Similarly, as Donald Birn points out, although the League of Nations Union (LNU) leadership maintained a relatively pro-imperial posture, "In the Union rank and file there were many signs of a critical attitude towards imperial abuses."[3] For almost all groups, these wrongs were to be redressed through the institutionalized arbitration mechanisms of the League, including strengthening the World Court and making the resort to arbitration compulsory.

This cautiously supportive stance of the League weakens the idealist tag attached to peace groups. To be sure, peace groups used the League differently from Lloyd-George, Ramsay MacDonald, Stanley Baldwin, and Austen Chamberlain. But the peace movement also demonstrated an awareness of the limits of the League that subsequent critics refused to acknowledge. Peace groups' debates indicate that they did not delude themselves into thinking that a league composed of powerful status quo and vulnerable revisionist powers could ensure peace or that its mandate system, run by colonial powers, would encourage self-determination or promote economic equality. Even the League of Nations Union, the only "quasi-pro-imperial" peace group, periodically warned the government not to abuse its position as a mandatory power; the LNU's rank and file also pressured it to adopt a more critical stance toward mandates.[4] Moreover, groups such as the National Peace Council (NPC) and sympathizers such as the Labour Party implicitly admitted, through their continued debates over the ethics and practicality of sanctions, that they did not know how best to contain conflict. But they did, by and large, agree that

[3] Women's International League (British Section) *Monthly News Sheet*, vol. XI, no. 6, October 1923, p. 2, BLPES; Donald Birn, *The League of Nations Union, 1918–1945* (Oxford: Oxford University Press, 1981), p. 55.

[4] Birn, *League of Nations Union*, pp. 24–25, 55.

the League furnished a necessary forum for working out the means to peace that was not provided by traditional diplomacy.

Peace groups disagreed about what to do if arbitration failed, which led back to the thorny issue of economic and military sanctions. But they did agree that all conflicts, potential and actual, should be resolved through "open," institutionalized arbitration procedures and that aggression should be defined and either averted or condemned. International institutions should be vigilant in attempting to resolve conflict; failing this, they should condemn aggression and member states should adjust national policies to punish the aggressor.

For their claims to be successful, power politics (or Great Power politics) had to be replaced by an overarching norm of equality of status. More widespread participation in security decisions, and the accompanying breakdown in traditional forms of diplomatic practice, also depended on a recognition of equal status over Great Power politics and worked on two levels for peace groups. First, participation had to be broadened to include Germany, the Soviet Union, and the "small states," and colonial possessions had to have a say in their own affairs, leading inexorably toward independence. Second, peace groups believed that they—and the public opinion they hoped to influence—should be considered legitimate participants in foreign policy decision making. The realist/idealist debate was not initiated by Carr; the Foreign Office and peace groups engaged in a lively struggle to define what was possible in foreign policy throughout the interwar period. "Idealism" and "utopianism" were labels that women's groups worked especially hard to refute. They strongly asserted their rights to participate in foreign policy debates without being labeled idealist.

DISARMAMENT AND ARBITRATION: WASHINGTON AND THE RUHR

The claims of peace groups regarding war, destructive armaments, imperial possessions, and equality of status underlay their work in favor of achieving disarmament and strengthening institutional mechanisms to resolve conflicts. Rather than seeing the League or the Kellogg Pact as a panacea for war, peace groups treated them as second-best options. They used, and at times helped to initiate and legitimize, "realist" openings such as the Washington Naval Conference and the Locarno treaties to advance their normative agendas. Successive British governments fought peace movement proposals and interpretations of events on many occasions, but on others reformulated British "interests" and/or employed language conducive to meeting peace movement demands. The question of whether appeasement was evitable or inevitable given military and economic developments becomes less significant in this narrative. Instead, the important question is how social forces produced reasons and arguments to articulate, debate, and claim legitimacy for particular norms, and the ways in which governments responded to their claims—by attempting to refute them, by taking them into account in policy formulation, or by reconfiguring state "interests" to include them. Both policy debates and private correspondence illustrate the normative confrontation engendered by peace movement activity. Building on peace groups' critique of Versailles, the hopes created by the Washington Naval Conference, and the problem of the 1923 Franco-Belgian occupation of the Ruhr, this confrontation is well demonstrated by the debates over the Geneva Protocol, Locarno, and the Kellogg–Briand Pact. My narrative focuses on these debates and their implications.

For the peace movement, arbitration and disarmament related to each other in both symbiotic and dialectical ways. Progress on one could not occur without progress on the other; indeed, peace groups used progress in one area as a rationale for their claims that progress in the other was possible and desirable. Yet failure in one area also prompted peace groups to regroup and demand success in the other. Disarmament and arbitration, therefore, represented intertwining objectives that rested on the same normative assumptions, and peace movement campaigns moved from one to the other throughout the interwar period. Once the League began to function, peace groups immediately turned their attention to both problems. As they saw it, the two were interdependent for the purpose of establishing a peace in which inequitable provisions of the status quo could be challenged and the Covenant improved.

The necessity of demobilizing after the war opened the way for peace groups to demand deep and immediate cuts in aggressive weapons and troop levels. But peace groups' arguments in favor of disarmament through the League had to be put on hold because of developing plans in the United States for a multinational naval disarmament conference. Examined in Chapter 5, this effort resulted in the Washington Naval Conference of 1921–1922 and Treaty of 1922. The series of naval arms conferences competed throughout the interwar period with the goal of disarming under the auspices of the League, but it also provides an excellent example of the way in which peace groups used diplomatic initiatives to further their own normative agenda.

For the Lloyd George government in Britain a naval arms limitation conference could control the postwar budget and stabilize Japan's growing power in the Far East. Some in the government agreed with peace movement members that the Anglo-German arms race had contributed to the war.[5] Yet the government was loathe to bargain away potential political advantages (renewing the Anglo-Japanese alliance) by dealing with them during a naval conference called by the United States, and the United States insisted on linking the two issues. As a result the government adopted an equivocal stance on naval disarmament that opened the way for peace movement claims to gain a wider audience.

The British peace movement, for its part, had its own reasons for welcoming the Washington Conference proposals and for criticizing the Lloyd-George government's equivocal stance. The proposal for naval arms limitation circumvented the League, dealt only with naval armaments, and included only selected powers, but the peace movement's strategy, ultimately, was pragmatic. First, a naval agreement could gather some momentum to help to strengthen demands for more general disarmament under the League. The LNU's journal, *Headway,* insisted that "Washington is not a rival, but a complement to Geneva." The Women's International League (WIL) designated the week before the Conference's opening "International Disarmament Week" to draw attention to the proceedings, but called for "universal disarmament" instead of the more limited "reduction of armaments." Consequently, when the Foreign Office tried to dampen public expectations of a successful conference, peace groups increased their support. According to the U.S. Embassy in London, public approval correlated with a change in the government's attitude: "The public . . . is strongly in favor of disarmament as being the obvious way in which to attain peace and economy. Lately, too, the attitude of the Government has changed from being luke-warm to being as enthusiastic as any British government can be expected to be regarding another government's project."[6]

Second, scrapping actual ships could set a normative precedent, demonstrating that disarmament was indeed possible. Thus peace groups guardedly praised the Washington Naval treaties, but did so to open the

---

[5] Malcolm H. Murfett, "Look Back in Anger: The Western Powers and the Washington Conference of 1921–1922," in B. J. C. McKercher, ed., *Arms Limitation and Disarmament: Restraints on War, 1899–1939* (Westport, Conn.: Praeger, 1992), pp. 85–91; Robert Gordon Kaufman, *Arms Control during the Pre-Nuclear Era* (New York: Columbia University Press, 1990), chap. 3; Dick Richardson, *The Evolution of British Disarmament Policy in the 1920s* (New York: St. Martin's Press, 1989), pp. 13–14; Kaufman, *Arms Control,* pp. 32–36; Richardson, *Evolution,* pp. 1–2.

[6] Birn, *League of Nations Union,* p. 38; WIL, British section, Annual Council Meeting, 2 February 1922, in 6th Yearly Report, October 1920–January 1922, BLPES; U.S. National Archives, Record Group 59, 500.A.4002/93, 25 October, 1921.

way to air and land, in addition to naval, disarmament. Robert Cecil asserted that the "triumph" of Washington would prove illusory if not followed by "military" (land) disarmament, and the WIL resolved, "In view of the lessons learned from the Washington Conference" to "work towards universal total disarmament, including the abandonment of chemical warfare."[7]

The Ruhr crisis followed the Washington Conference almost immediately, forcing British peace groups to turn their attention to resolving political and economic issues left outstanding by the Treaty of Versailles. Peace activists viewed the French invasion of the Ruhr Valley in early 1923 as the clearest signal yet that the peace treaties, especially the reparations clauses, insufficient disarmament, the lack of obligatory arbitration, and the exclusion of Germany from the League of Nations, were severely flawed. The LNU, the peace group that was, initially at least, least critical of the government, at first ignored the Franco-Belgian action for fear that criticism would harden the French against compromise in the Ruhr. But the Ruhr invasion created a major internal crisis for the LNU. For several months, Robert Cecil, at that time a member of the Cabinet attempting to pave the way for disarmament and arbitration by convincing the French to sign the Treaty of Mutual Assistance, pressured the LNU leadership not to act on the Ruhr. But the subcommittee assigned to formulate a policy position on the issue resigned en masse in protest at the leadership's inaction. The LNU's general secretary reported that the grass-roots membership and local branches "were urgently enquiring why the League of Nations and the LNU is doing nothing to avert the catastrophe threatened by the French occupation of the Ruhr," eventually prompting the LNU leadership to put forth its own plan and to urge the British government and League Council to resolve the crisis. The WIL, who worked closely with its affiliates abroad, kept perhaps the closest watch on events in the Ruhr and actively supported the German passive resistance (which, although largely spontaneous, was seen as the first European test of Gandhian/Tolstoyan nonviolent techniques). The Ruhr crisis reignited the WIL's Campaign for a New Peace, launched in December 1922 to force revision of the League Covenant, and spurred the WIL's efforts to meet with diplomats from northern Europe, France, Belgium, Germany, Great Britain, and the United States to press for arbitration and an international conference on reparations to redress the harshness of the Ver-

---

[7] Birn, *League of Nations Union*, pp. 38–39; Barry Buzan, "The British Peace Movement, 1919–1939," Ph.D. thesis, London School of Economics, 1973, pp. 185–86; WIL Annual Council Meeting, 2 February 1922, BPLES.

sailles settlement. The Franco-Belgian occupation of the Ruhr and the British government's "attitude of benevolent neutrality"[8] in the face of this violation of the peace treaties momentarily strengthened the claims of peace groups that the treaties were inequitable and untenable and that the peace groups had a better grasp than governments of the bases of international stability. The WIL, for example, took the offensive to claim that regarding the Ruhr, equality of status, and revision of the reparations clauses in the Treaty of Versailles, "what the whole world needs so urgently *must* be regarded as practical politics and not as unpractical utopianism."[9]

The Washington Naval Treaty and the Ruhr crisis inspired peace groups to step up their campaigns to link arbitration and disarmament through the League of Nations. These campaigns first resulted in a draft Geneva Protocol, finally rejected by the Baldwin government in 1925. But the Protocol debates had two significant repercussions. The peace movement's role in publicizing and campaigning for it, coupled with their belief in unnecessary government intransigeance, affected security debates through the early 1930s (and most immediately in the subsequent Locarno Treaties of 1925) and contributed to delegitimizing the government's own arguments regarding the content of the national interest. Moreover, the Protocol's explicit linkage through the League of disarmament and arbitration reinforced norms regarding the proper purview of global international organization and the necessary restraints to be placed on the state.

DELEGITIMIZATION OF ALLIANCES: THE GENEVA PROTOCOL AND LOCARNO

Both the Geneva Protocol and Locarno originated on one hand in the British government's attempt to provide for French security and on the other in the attempts of many peace groups to lay the foundation for disarmament by members of the League of Nations by institutionalizing collective security measures. The first attempt to meet both peace movement and government concerns, the 1923 Draft Treaty of Mutual Assistance initiated by Lord Robert Cecil (former wartime cabinet minister, leader of the League of Nations Union, and nominal Conservative), had fallen flat. The Foreign Office called it utopian because of its provisions for general collective security. Most peace groups criticized its stipulations for "par-

---

[8] LNU-Executive Committee Minutes, 2/27/23, BLPES; Birn, *League of Nations Union*, pp. 44–46; WIL Annual Council Meeting, 23 February 1923.

[9] Women's International League, *Monthly News Sheet*, Vol. XI, No. 6 (October 1923), p. 1.

tial" (i.e., regional) guarantees as warmongering. In their view, any regional guarantees risked negating international checks on state militarism and could easily reestablish the "old" system of alliances.[10]

The Geneva Protocol, in comparison, placed primary stress on compulsory, "all-in" arbitration to achieve security and thus was much more palatable to a wide range of peace groups. It originated in speeches by British Prime Minister J. Ramsay MacDonald and French Prime Minister Eduard Herriot at the 1924 League Assembly. MacDonald argued that "security could not be based on military alliances, and [Britain] hesitated to become involved in any agreements which committed them to vague and indefinite obligations." His rationale thus spoke to both peace sentiment and traditional military concerns. Suggesting that aggression could be forestalled by arbitration, he urged the League to establish a commission to create specific arbitral mechanisms under Article 36 of the Statute of the Permanent Court of Justice. Arthur Henderson and Lord Parmoor, both Labour Party officials active in peace movement circles, then developed a document officially known as the "Protocol for the Pacific Settlement of International Disputes" under the auspices of the League's Fifth Assembly.[11]

The draft protocol not only defined aggression and instituted compulsory arbitration of all disputes, but also provided for sanctions against an aggressor state, including military sanctions, if arbitration failed. It thus represented an attempt to provide for French security by "filling the gaps" in the Covenant, which merely provided for nonbinding economic and financial sanctions, with military sanctions put into effect only after a unanimous vote of the Council. The Protocol's "improvement" on the Covenant consisted of the fact that sanctions would become obligatory immediately after the Council declared an aggressor. The Covenant, according to Protocol supporters in the League, would thereby be "made a living and effective instrument" for preserving international security and defending the victims of aggression. With security then assured via effective arbitration, states could proceed to disarm. But the Protocol would not become binding on governments until after the League successfully con-

[10] FO 371/9418, W1075/30/98, 7 February 1923, comments by G. W. Villiers, PRO; Union of Democratic Control Resolution discussed by LNU Executive Committee, LNU-EC minutes, 20 March 1924; LNU-EC minutes, 22 May 1924; Gertrude Bussey and Margaret Tims, *Women's International League for Peace and Freedom* (London: Allen & Unwin, 1965), pp. 46–47; Birn, *League of Nations Union*, pp. 44–45.

[11] Report on Fifth Assembly Proceedings, FO371/10571/146653, 1 November 1924, PRO; David Carlton, *MacDonald versus Henderson: The Foreign Policy of the Second Labour Government* (London: Macmillan, 1970), pp. 26–27.

cluded its general disarmament conference (originally slated for June 15, 1925, but not convened until February 1932).[12]

The peace movement during the 1920s has often been criticized for its unreflective pacifism. Yet, despite the fact that the Protocol included measures for both economic and military sanctions, most peace groups supported it as a positive step toward disarmament: "on these lines alone will the nations feel sufficiently secure to agree upon and carry out plans of disarmament." The LNU urged its branches to educate public opinion to support the Protocol and urged the British government to take the lead in promoting it.[13] The National Peace Council (NPC) devoted the first three months of 1925 to a campaign in favor of the Protocol. The NPC focused its support on the Protocol's clauses on compulsory arbitration, interpreting them as instances of "international solidarity," whereas the WIL asserted that "the main principle of the Protocol" was "definitely ruling out private war as a means of attempting to settle international disputes and accepting the principle of arbitral settlement." Pacifist groups vigorously debated the sanctions provisions of the Protocol. Some pacifists decided to limit their support to the arbitration provisions while continuing to repudiate military sanctions, others, such as the No More War Movement ultimately rejected support of the Protocol, although it allowed lively debate on the subject and published favorable and opposing views in its newsletter.[14]

Thus for the peace movement, the Protocol once again represented a compromise. It checked states' power to resort to war by defining unlawful "aggression" and instituting procedures for compulsory arbitration, and it laid the foundation for much-desired disarmament. But two successive British governments refused to sign it, despite MacDonald's initial inspiration and the knowledge in the Cabinet and Foreign Office that the principles underlying it were deeply popular. The government's concern was to resolve the French security problem in such as way as to confine "stability" to the European situation. The government wished to prevent any institutionalization of arbitration procedures that either would draw it

[12] Benes comments, FO371/10570, W8208/134/98, 25 September 1924; FO 371/10570, W8078/134/98, 19 September 1924.

[13] WIL, 10th Yearly Report, Jan.–Dec. 1925; LNU, General Council Minutes, 19 December 1924; Birn, *League of Nations Union*, p. 57.

[14] NPC/NPCW Minutes, 23 March 1925, BLPES; WILPF British Section 9th Yearly Report, Jan.–Dec. 1924, p. 34; 10th Yearly Report, Jan.–Dec. 1925; LNU-Executive Committee minutes, 9 October 1924; and NPC Quarterly Meeting minutes, 23 March 1925. For a general discussion of pacifists' attitudes toward sanctions, see Martin Ceadel, *Pacifism in Britain, 1914–1945* (New York: Oxford University Press, 1980); "Quakers and the Protocol," *No More War*, April 1925, *No More War*, January and February 1925, PPU.

into an area of conflict in which it had no economic or security concern or would permit quasi-independent territories such as Egypt to raise complaints against it. Finally, the government did not want to open the door to further disarmament under Article 8. MacDonald, following the lead of senior civil service officers who were skeptical of the League of Nations, refused to act on the Protocol, even though he often expressed support for it while leading the Opposition later in the decade.[15]

Stanley Baldwin's Conservative government, which came to power in October 1924, was resolutely opposed to compulsory jurisdiction of disputes in matters of maritime law. It strongly opposed the Protocol, primarily to avoid placing Britain in the position of having to submit to arbitration for conflicts within its empire. The Conservatives decided early on, therefore, to reject the draft, but the government's discussions show that the problem at hand was not whether, but rather how, to reject it. By mid-December 1924, Lord Curzon, a former foreign secretary, agreed with Austen Chamberlain that it would be all too easy to knock down the Protocol like "a castle of cards" because of its failure to ensure British maritime and imperial interests. However, the government had to move cautiously. This point was emphasized in the Committee on Imperial Defence (CID): "But, whether you look at it from the point of view of the feeling in Europe ... or from the point of view of public opinion at home, clearly we should shock the world and shock our own public very considerably if we simply knocked it down and substituted nothing in its place." The Conservatives decided privately to reject the Protocol in December 1924, but the government needed to find a way to scrap it without appearing to abandon the goals of compulsory arbitration and disarmament for which it stood in the eyes of peace groups and of the public.[16]

Consequently Chamberlain frequently professed publicly that the government needed time to study the issue to make up its mind. He also agreed to receive a deputation from the LNU peace group to press its case for the Protocol. The LNU, believing that "the proposals have been so much misrepresented in the Press, both at home and overseas," was taking every opportunity to outline its understanding of the draft treaty. Chamberlain convinced Baldwin to be present, despite Eyre Crowe's argument that, "So far as I know, ministers have always hitherto declined to receive deputations from this society. They would only misuse the occasion for

[15] Carlton, *MacDonald versus Henderson*, pp. 27–28. Also FO371/10570, Cabinet Meeting Conclusions, 29 September 1924, PRO.

[16] FO371/10572/146745, CID meeting, 16 December 1924, PRO; Jon Jacobson, *Locarno Diplomacy: Germany and the West, 1925–1929* (Princeton: Princeton University Press, 1972), pp. 14–15.

their own propaganda." Chamberlain did, however, impose conditions on the deputation to inhibit any propaganda value it may have wished to obtain: it was to be confidential, no reporters were to be allowed, only six LNU members could be present, and they could give no more than two speeches outlining the LNU position. This would set a precedent for attempts to control peace group participation in security debates throughout the interwar period. The LNU used the occasion to press its case against regional arrangements, reading aloud a letter from Lord Grey that argued that "the system of exclusive alliances and competition in armaments, that existed in Europe before 1914, proved a lamentable failure. The Protocol adopts another and more hopeful principle."[17]

Chamberlain, who personally opposed the Protocol in favor of a limited defensive alliance with the French, was faced with another problem in that the French themselves supported any effort to put "teeth" into the Covenant. Chamberlain realized that "France is pledged to the Protocol. . . . They feel that by ratifying the Protocol they put themselves right with the public opinion of the world and are morally reinforced." In his talks with the French, therefore, he was careful to point out the differences between the MacDonald and Herriot versions of the document and shrewdly asked Briand whether the Protocol would really give France all the security it required. But Chamberlain had to be careful about proposing the Protocol's obvious alternative and his own preference, a limited defensive pact, to the French. Britain and France had attempted, unsuccessfully, to conclude a bilateral defensive pact at Cannes in 1922; the effort was widely criticized and seen as a major failure of Lloyd-George's foreign policy.[18] Chamberlain knew he could not attempt another defensive pact. "I felt it my duty to warn [Briand] that [British] public opinion was less favourable to such a pact at the time of the Cannes Conference than it had been at the time of the Versailles Agreement, and that to-day any such proposal would meet with more opposition than at the time of the Cannes meeting." Chamberlain, "frankly at a loss," also wrote to British Ambassador to France Lord Crewe, warning that any proposal for a regional pact would meet with opposition. In addition to the Liberal and Labour parties, "the League of Nations Union is equally on the alert and equally predisposed against partial and particular arrangements."[19]

[17] FO371/10572, W10126/134/98, 20 December 1924. LNU-Executive Committee minutes, 5 February 1925 (C.13. 13/2/25).

[18] Jacobson, *Locarno Diplomacy*, pp. 14–18; FO371/10572/146745, CID meeting, 16 December 1924, PRO; FO371/10572, W10854/134/98, Dec. 5, 1924; Birn, *League of Nations Union*, p. 39.

[19] FO371/10572, W10867/134/98, 9 December 1924; FO371/11064, W362/9/98, 4 January 1925; Austen Chamberlain papers, FO800, 16 February 1925.

The solution to the "problem" finally arrived in the form of the German proposal for a four-power pact, the genesis of Locarno. Chamberlain later admitted:

> I changed my policy at one point. When I came into office I saw no way of getting Europe out of the rut of stagnating and festering hate and bitterness except by making as a first step a triple alliance with France and Belgium which should be the prelude of a quadruple arrangement . . . I had to admit, however, that public opinion would not understand and would not support this policy. They would see in it only the first step and not the ultimate goal. It was at this moment that the German proposal was first made and gave me a possible alternative.[20]

Thus, after initially resisting the German proposal for a quadro-partite agreement and declining to draw up a draft agreement for discussion by the Cabinet, Chamberlain reluctantly came to the conclusion that Germany needed to be included in any revised security arrangement.[21]

The government thus sensed that the old norm of defensive alliances had lost legitimacy and cast about to find a new normative and policy solution. But it still operated according to restrictive norms of regionalism and of exclusive diplomatic control of security debates. It therefore chafed at the peace movement's insistence on participation and tried to mute its criticisms of regional pacts in favor of compulsory arbitration. Chamberlain, for example, complained to Cecil that the LNU's Birmingham branch was supporting demonstrations "all over the country" opposed to Government policy. He then followed with a sharply worded letter to the LNU leadership:

> Is not the League or its Committees acting beyond its proper duties when it advocates the specific solution of a particular difficulty to which it knows the Government of the day is opposed and to which, I might add, previous Governments have been clearly opposed—here I refer to the petitions which it circulates in favour of compulsory arbitration in cases to which no British government has been willing to apply it. And again, to certain resolutions about the Protocol . . . or again, when . . . the Executive Committee undertakes to tell the British Government how its delegation should be composed.[22]

---

[20] Chamberlain papers, FO800, Chamberlain to Hugh Spender, 19 September 1925, PRO.

[21] Jacobson, *Locarno Diplomacy,* pp. 16–20.

[22] Chamberlain papers, FO800, 19 June 1925, Chamberlain to Cecil; 8 August 1925, Chamberlain to Major Hills.

For peace group members, such complaints rang hollow, particularly at a time when government rationales for security decisions appeared confused and weak. Rank-and-file Labour supporters of the LNU in particular expected the peace movement to promote compulsory arbitration to avoid future splits in international labour. Thus the LNU continued to organize mass meetings and petitions in favor of the Protocol.[23]

Nevertheless, the Baldwin government successfully negotiated the quadro-partite pact, which became the Locarno Treaties of 1925. Locarno guaranteed the Franco–German border in Europe while incurring no further British responsibilities and preserving the Empire's "freedom of movement" among its imperial possessions. The Treaties can thus be interpreted as a successful attempt by the conservative Baldwin government to circumscribe both collective security and arbitration to issues "safe" for the British Empire. But the "spirit of Locarno" so touted by Austen Chamberlain had to take into account peace movement claims regarding fair treatment of Germany, the necessity of addressing the problem of armaments, and dissatisfaction with government claims on imperial commitments. German inclusion in an international treaty of such significance also tended to remove any further rationale for excluding its membership in the League of Nations, an exclusion that peace groups had long criticized. Consequently, one of the pact's key features provided for full German membership in the League, including a place on the League Council. A better interpretation of the Protocol and Locarno debates, therefore, highlights the growing delegitimization of partial security arrangements, as well as the legitimization of broader public participation in security decisions.

Yet, as far as the peace movement was concerned, neither the issue of compulsory arbitration nor the problem of disarmament were settled. For example, although the LNU muted its criticisms of the government after Locarno, it found itself less and less able to control its rank and file. Moreover, along with the National Peace Council and pacifist organizations, the LNU cooperated in an "Arbitration Petition" drive organized by the WIL from March to August of 1925. The WIL campaign, launched as a direct reaction to Baldwin's rejection of the Protocol (the WIL's report said the government's decision against the Protocol "gave the Women's International League its call" to demand progress in institutionalizing arbitration mechanisms), resulted in over 500,000 signatures gathered to enlist British public support for arbitration at the 6th League Assembly the following September. This, as well as subsequent efforts, sustained movement activity in support of the principles underlying the Protocol, remained a

[23] Birn, *League of Nations Union*, pp. 58–61.

thorn in the government's side, and kept the issues of compulsory arbitration and disarmament at the forefront of public discussion long after the Protocol itself was rejected. Several years later, for example (in 1928), Chamberlain was still protesting to Gilbert Murray against the LNU's actions on behalf of the Protocol: "I do not think that it is any part of the business of the Union to advocate the Protocol. The Union, as you say, is formed to induce people to understand and support the League and to assist the League in its development. It seems to me no part of the business of such a body to advocate a particular scheme such as the Protocol."[24]

After Locarno, peace groups turned again to disarmament, basing their approval of the Locarno Treaties on their appraisal of the extent to which the Treaties would facilitate a League disarmament conference. The LNU made its endorsement contingent on its understanding that the Treaties would pave the way for such a conference. For the left-pacifist No More War Movement, "Unless there follow very drastic provisions for disarmament, Locarno will not only have failed miserably, but it will have been responsible for large increases in armaments." Although the WIL welcomed the improvement in European relations resulting from Locarno, it questioned "Britain's guaranteeing the Treaty . . . with no provision for general disarmament. According to the London *Times,* the ultimate result of Locarno was a situation in which the League of Nations decided, and Britain agreed, "that from now on disarmament is a matter for discussion and decision by the League," a decision that "encourages all the pacifists in Europe."[25]

Normative Confrontation: The Coolidge Naval Conference

Because of its demand for international organization to remain the primary means through which disarmament was accomplished, the British movement during the mid-1920s concentrated its efforts on the creation

[24] WIL 10th Yearly Report, Jan.–Dec. 1925; WIL, British Section, 10th Yearly Report, Jan.–Dec. 1925; NPC, Annual Meeting Minutes, 29 June 1925, and General Council Minutes, 11 November 1925; Chamberlain to Murray, January 11, 1928, Austen Chamberlain papers, FO800, PRO.

[25] *No More War,* March 1926, p. 4; WILPF Annual Council Meeting Resolution, 12 and 13 February 1926; LNU General Council Minutes, 6th Annual Meeting, 23 June 1925, General Council Meeting, December 16, 1925, and 7th Annual Meeting, 22–23 June 1926; Birn, *League of Nations Union,* p. 62; From an internal *Times* editorial staff memo obtained by F. A. Sterling (Counselor in the U.S. Embassy in London) and reported to the State Department, 23 October 1925, see National Archives, RG59, 500.A12/79.

of the Permanent Commission to plan for the League Disarmament Conference, originally to take place in 1925. The series of interwar naval disarmament conferences became a critical part of this process during the Geneva Conference of 1927, which was intended to prepare for the League's General Disarmament Conference. At that time, there were Anglo-American differences not only on naval issues, but also on a more comprehensive disarmament package.[26] Peace groups did not initiate major campaigns for naval disarmament before either the Washington or the Geneva Conferences. But when planning for general disarmament stalled, they used the naval conferences to keep their broader disarmament goals at the forefront of public debate.

In the aftermath of the Locarno Treaties, the government apparently decided that moving forward with a Preparatory Commission for the Disarmament Conference could do little harm. But the Preparatory Commission soon became bogged down in endless debate between the British and French over whether to count reserve forces in land armies and how to calculate naval tonnages, and impatience among the peace groups intensified. Peace groups thus used the Coolidge proposals presented to Britain in February 1927, which resulted in the Geneva Naval Conference from June to August, as a catalyst for comprehensive arms reductions. The LNU, for example, requested that the government, "conscious of public support" continue to work through the League's Preparatory Commission for a draft Disarmament Treaty and that any accord reached at the naval conference would be fitted into the framework of such a general treaty.[27]

Foreign Office diplomats in London mistrusted Coolidge's intentions, complaining of the U.S. administration's use of calculated, public moves to improve its image on foreign affairs. Nevertheless, they took the opportunity to show their goodwill and, along with the Japanese, accepted Coolidge's invitation; the French and Italians refused to take part.[28] Austen Chamberlain appointed Lord Robert Cecil, along with the First Lord of the Admiralty, Admiral Bridgeman, as delegates to the Conference; Cecil clearly desired arms limitation and Bridgeman was considered a reasonable negotiator who was capable of compromise.

---

[26] B. J. C. McKercher, "Of Horns and Teeth: The Preparatory Commission and the World Disarmament Conference, 1926–1934," in *Restraints on War: Arms Control and Disarmament in British Foreign Policy* (Westport, Conn.: Praeger, 1992), p. 117.

[27] Richardson, *Evolution*, p. 48; McKercher, "Of Horns and Teeth," p. 254; LNU-General Council Minutes, 8th Annual Meeting, 22–24 June 1927.

[28] See Norman Gibbs, "The Naval Conferences of the Interwar Years: A Study in Anglo–American Relations," *Naval War College Review* 30 (1977): 50–63.

Problems developed almost immediately on both sides, and the Conference proceedings quickly sank into a hostile jousting between Britain and the United States. The British Admiralty in London refused to budge from its original negotiation position, which entailed maintaining naval superiority in cruisers and establishing the six-inch gun (as opposed to the eight-inch gun favored by the United States) as the cruiser's standard-size weapon. The British position was based on the Admiralty's calculations that the six-inch gun and a minimum of forty-five cruisers were needed to defend trade routes adequately. According to its figures, the Americans required only twenty-two cruisers for trade protection and the Japanese six, thus there was no need for parity. Meanwhile a lobbyist paid by U.S. naval building interests fed negative perceptions of the British and fueled U.S. hostility during the conference. The Americans, therefore, played on public perceptions of British chicanery to press for a formal recognition of U.S. naval parity.[29]

The peace movement's elite and its rank and file grew angry at what they perceived to be government intransigeance on the demand for parity. This perception grew when, after essentially agreeing to grant the U.S. parity in cruisers, the British retracted, largely due to the machinations of Winston Churchill, then Chancellor of the Exchequer. Churchill led the fight to redefine the meaning of parity, distinguishing "mathematical parity," which he opposed, from "maritime parity," a vague term he created to justify British naval superiority on the grounds of British imperial commitments. Churchill rounded up Cabinet support for the position that, given Britain's imperial responsibilities, parity would mean de facto inferiority, a position that in the end Cecil and Bridgeman were powerless to counter.[30]

The government's refusal to adhere to equality of status, even with an ally like the United States, was especially galling to peace groups. No More War was incredulous:

Does anyone doubt the hypocrisy of our own Government? As recently as July, in Parliament, the Foreign Secretary declared that "between the United States and this country war is already outlawed, not on paper, but in the heart and soul of every citizen." . . . Such, however, is not the case. The whole British case at Geneva was argued on the assumption that

[29] Norman H. Gibbs, *Grand Strategy.* Vol. I, *Rearmament Policy* (London: HMS Office, 1976), pp. 26–27; Gibbs, "Naval Conferences," p. 124.
[30] Richardson, *Evolution,* pp. 128–29.

America was a potential enemy of this country against whom we might one day be at war.[31]

Cecil argued that many members of the Cabinet at a minimum did not favor disarmament, and therefore "it is unlikely that any direct steps towards limitation, etc., will be taken by the present Government."[32]

Cecil threatened to quit his official position several times during the course of the negotiations when it became evident he would have to backtrack on the issue of parity. In the end he did resign in a move much publicized by peace groups. Even his critics in the peace movement praised his resignation from the government. The No More War Movement admitted a rocky relationship with the LNU and Cecil, but argued he was "an honest man" in resigning. Chamberlain and others, cognizant of Cecil's popularity in peace movement circles, worried that his resignation would be seen as a justification for the U.S. position on parity because of its potential effects on peace opinion.[33] The government at this point did not acknowledge the broader peace movement claim that parity was a necessary step toward equality of status in armaments. Nor did it realize that its position contributed to delegitimizing its own interpretation of British interests.

After the breakdown of the Geneva Naval Conference in the summer of 1927 and the publicity surrounding Cecil's resignation, peace groups stepped up criticisms of the government's responsibility in the Geneva conference's failure and the seemingly endless deliberations of the Preparatory Commission for the General Disarmament Conference, which continued to plod along without result. The government then began to see danger in ignoring pro-disarmament sentiment.

The LNU initiated a fresh disarmament campaign after Cecil's resignation, although it soon toned down its overt criticism of the government. Other peace groups, however, severely reproached the Conservatives for the Geneva Conference's collapse. *No More War*'s September 1927 issue was headlined, "Hypocrisy Unmasked at Geneva," and the resolution passed for use by the 1927 No More War demonstrations (in which the majority of movement groups participated) stated "after eight years the

---

[31] *No More War*, article by Ernest Thurtle, M.P., September 1927, p. 1.

[32] Chamberlain papers, FO800, Cecil to Chamberlain, 16 August 1927, PRO.

[33] *No More War*, October 1927, p. 4; See Richardson, *Evolution*, pp. 140–41. The correspondence between Cecil and Chamberlain on this issue has been quoted often, including in Richardson, pp. 140–44; see also Cecil's autobiography, *All the Way* (1941). The official correspondence is in FO800, Austen Chamberlain papers, 9–25 August 1927, PRO.

pledges as to general disarmament . . . have not been honoured" and urged the government to propose "a far more radical reduction and limitation of armaments than hitherto." The NPC circulated a "General Disarmament" petition, WILPF initiated a similar effort for "a flood of Resolutions and Memorials," and the No More War Movement, with help from the Quakers, initiated a campaign in support of the Russian proposals "for immediate and total disarmament."[34]

The peace movement's severe criticism of the government in the wake of the Geneva Conference soon began to coincide with official attempts to take the high road and reformulate its position on disarmament. Whereas Chamberlain during the Coolidge Conference negotiations had reasserted the efficacy of traditional diplomatic practice, writing to Cecil, "I have never thought that the idea of beginning with a great world conference was the most practical form of approach to the problem,"[35] others in the government began to warn their colleagues of a potential public opinion backlash. Increasingly critical of the Admiralty's positions against disarmament after the Conference, Lord Cushendon, Cecil's successor as minister responsible for disarmament, argued in favor of reopening naval disarmament questions with the United States to enable progress to be made in the Preparatory Commission's discussions:

> If the Admiralty's present position is essential [sic] in the national interest, there is nothing more to be said; but the Government should clearly realise that in that case a breakdown of the whole movement for disarmament by international agreement is inevitable, and that the responsibility for that breakdown will be laid upon us. There is no use disguising the fact that there is a large body of opinion in this country which will severely blame H.M. Government for such a failure.[36]

The Foreign Office then began to reevaluate its stance on naval arms limitation and on the use of the blockade and the importance of negoti-

[34] Birn, *League of Nations Union*, pp. 68–72; *No More War*, September 1927, PPU; National Peace Council, minutes, 29 September 1927, BLPES; NPC Council Meeting, 15 December 1927 and 29 March 1928; *No More War*, September 1927, p. 2, and March 1928, p. 7; *Pax International* 3 (September 1928).

[35] Chamberlain papers, FO800, Chamberlain to Cecil, 14 August 1927; Selby to Lord Grey, 3 September 1927. Chamberlain's defense of British diplomatic "savoir faire" extended to his heated reaction to U.S. press reports that pointed accusingly at "Tory reaction" for the conference's failures: "Briefly, the U.S. seem to resemble England under George III far more than does the democratic England of today. . . . I wonder, by the way, whether it ever occurs to Americans that while many nations fear the U.S., they haven't a single friend in the world. We, on the contrary, with all our 'Imperialism' and 'Toryism' have a good many." FO371/12040, A4794/133/45, 5 and 24 August 1927, PRO.

[36] Chamberlain papers, FO800, Cushendon Memorandum, 1 May 1928.

ating an agreement with the United States. A secret Foreign Office memo reevaluated British interests, arguing:

> The reason why an agreement with the United States of America is important is . . . not only because we do not wish to risk a war with them, nor so much because we desire to preserve a free hand in dealing with private property at sea in the future, as that we want to prevent the United States from themselves having a free hand as soon as their naval power becomes greater than ours. . . . It is much more important that American claims should be limited by agreement than that we should nominally maintain our claims and yet in practice be unable to assert them, whilst the United States by that time would be able to assert any they chose to make.[37]

The government thus constructed a realpolitik rationale for its new position, but only after the end of the conference and in the wake of a barrage of peace movement protest against the government's bad faith. The memo argued for "two subsidiary advantages" of early negotiations: (1) they "would take place in a comparatively calm atmosphere before the American election campaign was fully launched"; and (2) if successful, "Such an agreement would make a strong impression upon the mind of the [British] electorate. It would be further evidence of our determination to promote peace in the world, an important factor now that the female vote is being increased, and it would obviously be the forerunner of reduced naval programmes in the future."

Moreover, the Baldwin government's sensitivity to criticism from peace groups after the Geneva Conference once again caused Austen Chamberlain to complain that the LNU was overstepping its bounds by engaging in antigovernment rhetoric. Chamberlain's grievance centered on a public meeting at which a speaker for the LNU praised Grotius, Woodrow Wilson, and Litvinov, the Russian delegate to the Preparatory Commission, for his proposal for universal disarmament, but "not a word" was said of the government's efforts for disarmament.[38] This time, however, Chamberlain's objection focused not on whether the LNU should presume to put forth a policy in opposition to that of the government, but rather on its public portrayal of the government as antidisarmament, an image Baldwin and his ministers were trying to shed.

The Coolidge Naval Conference, therefore, represented the most direct normative confrontation yet between the peace movement and the gov-

---

[37] FO371/12041/(148710)/A6820/G, 21 November 1927, PRO.
[38] Chamberlain papers, FO800, Chamberlain to Gilbert Murray, 28 January 1928, PRO.

ernment. The government could no longer persuade the peace movement (or much of the public) that its rationales for refusing to give
ground on security prerogatives were either coherent or sound. The peace
movement then used the upper hand it gained in this confrontation to
press for an explicit reconstruction of security norms in the form of the
Kellogg–Briand Pact and the Optional Clause.

Normative Reconstruction: The Pact of Paris

While the government continued to scramble to address the fallout from
the failed Geneva naval conference, another "peace" initiative struck from
across the Atlantic. The Kellogg–Briand proposals, culminating in the signing of the Pact of Paris in July 1928, originated in French attempts during
the summer of 1927 to negotiate a bilateral arbitration agreement with
the United States, on the one hand, and the efforts of Salmon O. Levinson,
a Chicago lawyer, to outlaw war, on the other. These negotiations became
the basis for a multilateral pact proposal in April 1928. Signatories to the
final pact agreed to renounce the use of war for aggressive purposes and
to resolve international differences by "pacific means."

Realist international relations theory considers the Pact of Paris to represent the apex of interwar idealistic folly. But here again, from the British viewpoint, the dichotomy is not useful. Peace groups were well aware
of the pact's limitations, but used the negotiations to get disarmament negotiations back on track and as a step toward British submission to compulsory arbitration under the Optional Clause of the Permanent Court of
International Justice. The British government partially reinterpreted British interests to accord with signing the Pact.

Levinson began to communicate his ideas to British peace groups in the
mid-1920s. Although some groups, including the WIL, kept tabs on the
idea from 1923, they continued to focus on arbitration and disarmament
through the League in their demands to the government and public campaigns. Yet, when the official Franco-American discussions got under way,
British groups considered their support for a pact to outlaw war almost as
a given. This was due in part to their wish to support U.S. peace initiatives,
both official and unofficial. Always eager to draw the United States into
world organization as much as possible, the British movement was especially anxious to improve relations in the tense aftermath of the Coolidge
Naval Conference, whose failure they blamed on government intransi-
gence. The Coolidge Conference's failure had been followed by increasing strains and even talk of war between the United States and Britain.

Some press reports spoke of the "inevitability" of war; Esme Howard, British Ambassador to the United States, and Herbert Hoover, then Secretary of Commerce, tried to relieve tensions by discussing measures to prevent open conflict. Thus for British supporters "The nature of the proposal was of secondary importance. . . . It was not Levinson's theory of Outlawry that motivated British advocates of a proposal 'à la Briand', but desire for some sort of friendly agreement with the US." Gilbert Murray argued that the LNU should support the pact because it represented a clear choice by the United States, pushed by the U.S. peace movement, to engage in further initiatives for peace after the Coolidge Conference's failure.[39]

British peace groups, indeed, saw that any "outlawry of war" pact would have little material meaning. A *No More War* editorial asserted

> There may be a gain for pacifists from a propaganda standpoint if the British Government finally agrees to sign a treaty based on the Kellogg proposals for outlawing war, [but], It must be realised that a declaration in favour of the outlawry of war, unless it is supported by constructive preparation for the settlement of international questions by pacific means, is a purely negative thing which may mean hardly anything at all.[40]

Nevertheless, if such a pact could force the British government to improve relations with the United States, bring the United States closer to League arbitration mechanisms, and especially pave the way for disarmament, it would be worthwhile. Consequently, the LNU (as well as other peace groups) "did not encourage over-close scrutiny of the proposals or hairsplitting discussions about their practical effect."[41]

The British government was decidedly cool about a pact to renounce war despite the fact that there were clear benefits to be obtained from improving Anglo-American relations. In September 1927 the League As-

[39] WIL, *Monthly News Sheet*, Vol. XI., No. 6, October 1923, p. 2; According to A. J. P. Taylor, Leon Trotsky predicted that the next major war would be fought between Britain and the United States. See also B. J. C. McKercher, "The British Diplomatic Service in the United States and the Chamberlain Foreign Office's Perceptions of Domestic America, 1924–1927: Images, Reality, and Diplomacy," in B. J. C. McKercher and D. J. Moss, eds., *Shadow and Substance in British Policy, 1895–1939* (Edmondton: The University of Alberta Press, 1984), pp. 238–39; A. J. P. Taylor, *English History, 1914–1945* (Oxford: Clarendon, 1956), p. 255; and Jason Tomes, "Austen Chamberlain and the Kellogg Pact," *Millennium* 18 (Spring 1989): 7, 8; Birn, *League of Nations Union*, pp. 82–83; LNU-GC Minutes, 9th Annual Meeting, June 20–22 1928, BLPES.

[40] *No More War,* June 1928, p. 4. See also Birn, *League of Nations Union*, p. 82.

[41] Birn, *League of Nations Union*, p. 83.

sembly attempted to incorporate some of Kellogg's ideas in a resolution "declaring that all wars of aggression are, and shall always be, prohibited and that every pacific means must be employed to settle disputes of every description which may arise between States." Foreign Office diplomats called the resolution "nonsensical" and yet "harmless," two adjectives that indicate the tone of the initial British response to the Kellogg–Briand negotiations.[42]

But this tone soon changed to one of worry. Austen Chamberlain and the Foreign Office kept a close watch on the progress of the bilateral pact idea between France and the United States and noted with some alarm the indications that Kellogg would attempt to turn the pact into a multilateral treaty. After the failed Geneva Naval Conference, the British were wary of allowing the Coolidge administration credit for the idea: Robert Vansittart, head of the Foreign Office's American Department, complained to the French, "It would seem to clothe the idea as a Franco-American initiative, the credit of which will be shared in probably unequal proportions." For Chamberlain the most worrisome aspect of a multilateral pact, however, was once again its effects on Britain's ability to preserve its freedom of action in defending trade routes and in putting down rebellion within the Empire. Thus, beginning in the fall of 1927, he began to try to shape events to suit British interests as the government then conceived them, casting doubt on the negotiations in a calculated speech in the House of Commons that stressed the difficulties of defining the aggressor in any type of outlawry scheme. For a time, the path appeared to be clear: Esme Howard, British Ambassador to the United States, sent a welcome press report to Chamberlain several days later stating that "the President . . . sees no shortcut to peace. The idea of outlawing war was a thing to be approached with fear and trembling; the utmost caution was necessary; the road to peace was long and arduous."[43]

Most government officials agreed with Chamberlain that the Pact posed dangers for British imperial and trade interests. Yet official discussions demonstrated that British interests were multiple and potentially contradictory. Esme Howard contended, for example, that signing the Kellogg Pact would bring the United States back "into the circle of nations striving for an era of peace" and warned that rejecting the U.S. overtures could set

---

[42] FO371/12675/W9221/61/98, 23 September 1927, PRO.

[43] FO371/12789, A68/1/45, received 4 January 1928. Many U.S. newspapers (e.g., the *New York World, Washington Post,* and the *New York American*) took note of and agreed with Chamberlain's speech, although the *New York Times* said that nations must take risks to advance the cause of peace. Howard to Chamberlain, 2 December 1927; FO371/12041, PRO.

back the "tide" of cooperation between the United States and the rest of the world.[44]

Others in the government noted that the pact also posed a conflict for the peace movement. This conflict—between fulfilling the movement's goals of bettering relations with the United States and furthering the development of League arbitration mechanisms—might be exploited. Cecil Hurst, the government's legal expert, thought Baldwin and Chamberlain could wait before making a definite move: "Public opinion in this country might not quite understand a hasty rejection of what the pacifist-minded section of the people of this country will regard as an American olive branch, but they will understand a desire on the part of H. M. Government to make their policy conform to the results of the work undertaken under the auspices of the League."[45] Hurst recognized the fact that, other things being equal, the peace movement's first choice for arbitration agreements would not take the form of a treaty renouncing war. Rather, it called for ways to lessen tensions wherever possible, but always preferred for this to be accomplished through established League institutions.

However, the Conservatives' initially negative reaction to the proposed treaty provided yet another reason for the British movement to criticize the Baldwin government for stalling on any arbitration and disarmament initiative that came its way and galvanized the movement to obtain widespread support for the Pact. The British WIL, in a response typical of peace groups, "warmly welcomed" the U.S. proposal, organized a mass demonstration in support of "outlawry," and deplored the Baldwin government's actions on arbitration in Geneva: "Over and over again in the debates we have heard the British delegation ask to have a resolution modified and toned down, thus weakening its moral effect on the countries who are feared to be a danger to peace." Peace groups thus began to incorporate the Kellogg proposals more explicitly into their campaigns for compulsory arbitration and disarmament. By April 13, when the U.S. draft treaty was formally presented to Britain (as well as Japan, Germany, and Italy), influential members of the Foreign Office were arguing for speedier British action on the U.S. proposals: G. W. Villiers, of the Foreign Office's Western Department, commented, "I sincerely trust that we shall accept the American proposals: the peace feeling in this country is very strong and there will be great trouble if we reject it." Sir William Tyrrell, the Foreign Office Permanent Undersecretary, saw the necessity of achiev-

[44] Memo from Sir Esme Howard, FO371/12790, 2 March 1928, PRO.
[45] Memo from Sir Esme Howard, FO371/12790, 2 March 1928, PRO; FO371/12789/A68/1/45, rec'd 4 January 1928, PRO.

ing agreement on British policy: "I would urge that we should lose no time in doing so in view of the popular agitation which is developing here in favour of whole-hearted indiscriminate acceptance of the American proposals."[46]

But the Foreign Office, and especially Chamberlain, was determined to make reservations for British "vital interests." In particular, officials wanted to be able to respond to insurrection in Egypt but could not say so directly because Britain had granted Egypt nominal independence in 1922. British officials assumed, given the Monroe Doctrine, that the United States would likewise reserve for itself "freedom of action" in Latin America and hoped this would provide an out. But U.S. Secretary of State Kellogg was determined to push the pact through without any troublesome clarifications or dilutions, and the issue of reservations became the central sticking point in the Anglo-American negotiations.

British officials knew that taking a position in favor of reservations involved political risk: Robert Vansittart, then head of the Foreign Office's American Department, considered the pros and cons, complaining, "If we [reserve freedom of action], there would almost certainly be a howl, the proposal would almost certainly break down, and we should have another Geneva, for which we should be blamed not only in America, but also possibly or probably by a good deal of uninstructed electors here. . . . On the other hand if we do not reserve it, we should be committed to the very thing we were determined to avoid 18 months ago" at Geneva. Vansittart was further annoyed that the United States acted without official consultation, even though the British had kept tabs on Kellogg's intentions: "the U.S.G. have played on us the same opening gambit as when they invited us to Geneva: the press is full of it before we have even seen the terms or had time to think."[47]

The government's insistence on reservations angered peace groups, particularly those critical of both the U.S. Monroe Doctrine and British imperial interests. The organizations affiliated with the National Council for Prevention of War (NCPW) pressed it to "take the lead" in expressing the peace movement's "desire for a cordial British response" and to "convey to the American public that British public opinion was largely opposed to [British] Government policy." *No More War* argued, "If the British proposal is accepted, it means that the world would be parcelled out into huge spheres of influence between half a dozen Powers, and a new imperialism

[46] WIL, British Section, Annual Council Meeting Report, February 1928; *Pax International* 2 (November 1927), and 3 (April 1928), BLPES; FO371/12790/A2542/1/45, 13 April 1928, PRO.

[47] Ibid., FO371/12789, rec'd 4 January 1928, PRO.

would be established that must finally lead to war and the destruction of the League." Even the LNU "scorned Chamberlain's efforts to pin reservations" to the proposals; the Pact was needed because "it represented progress, badly-needed motion" forward. Gilbert Murray, chair of the LNU's Executive Committee (and professor of classics at Oxford), argued at the LNU General Council meeting that reservations could not contradict the spirit and letter of the Pact: "So that when the thing is signed I think it will be practically impossible to interpret either the Monroe Doctrine or [the British] Reservation 10 in any sense which is really contrary to the new Treaty."[48]

In early May 1928 Chamberlain made it known that he recognized the "widespread public interest" aroused by the U.S. démarche and that he was confident it would "lead to a successful agreement in due course." Two days later, the Cabinet decided to accept the U.S. draft Treaty, but only if subject to "a clear statement of significance." Chamberlain acknowledged, "The suggestion for the conclusion of a treaty for the renunciation of war as an instrument of national policy has evoked widespread interest in this country, and His Majesty's Government will support the movement to the utmost of their power."[49] Britain sent its formal reply to the United States on May 19, stating its readiness to cooperate in such a pact and engage in negotiations to that end. But Chamberlain made a final attempt to reserve British freedom of action by including a paragraph stating

> there are certain regions of the world the welfare and integrity of which constitute a special and vital interest for our peace and safety. . . . Their protection against attack is to the British Empire a measure of self-defence. It must be clearly understood that His Majesty's Government . . . accept the new Treaty upon the distinct understanding that it does not prejudice their freedom of action in this respect."[50]

The government then began to interpret its interests once again, developing a military-security rationale for supporting the pact. The *New York Times* in April outlined a traditionalist explanation for the British "change of heart" on the Kellogg treaty:

[48] NPC/NPCW Minutes, Special council meeting, 1 November 1928, BLPES; "The Kellogg Proposals for the Outlawry of War, A Declaration of the Movement's Policy," *No More War,* July–August 1928, p. 5; Birn, *League of Nations War,* p. 83; LNU-GC Minutes, 9th Annual Meeting, 20–22 June 1928, BLPES.

[49] FO371/12790, 2 May 1928, PRO; FO371/12791; 9 May 1928; Chamberlain's reply to Mr. Houghton (U.S. Ambassador), FO371/12792, 19 May 1928, PRO.

[50] Richardson, *Evolution,* p. 162; Tomes, "Austen Chamberlain and the Kellog Pact," pp. 13–14.

The principal reason for this change of heart is highly interesting. . . . Britain sees [in the treaty] . . . a heaven-sent opportunity to associate the United States not nominally but with effect with the League peace purpose. . . . If a nation which is a member of the League becomes also a signatory of a multilateral compact oulawing war and then is guilty of aggression against another, it will have offended against the United States as well as its fellow-members of the League by so doing, and America would thus have little or no reason to quarrel with the means adopted by the League to bring it to terms by a blockade or other measures.[51]

A June 8 Cabinet memo clarified this logic. According to the memo, if the Kellogg Treaty were to be

concluded along the lines of the present draft, the U.S. would be precluded from going to war with us on account of blockade measures taken by this country against a third party provided, of course, that the British Empire was clearly not itself the disturber of the peace. From our point of view, the above represents one of the most important advantages to be derived from the conclusion of the Renunciation of War Treaty.

Thus, the Kellogg Pact could resolve on British terms one of the thorniest issues between the United States and Britain since the onset of World War I, that of conflict resulting from the use of the blockade. Indeed, Robert Craigie, the new head of the Foreign Office's American Department and the author of the memo, went on to note the potential effect of the Kellogg treaty on subsequent Anglo-American negotiations: "while, therefore, to us the existence of the proposed Kellogg Treaty would render the negotiation of an Anglo-American blockade agreement less interesting, in the U.S. the opposite effect may be produced." According to the British logic, a neutral United States would no longer be able to shield maritime trade routes from belligerent action.[52]

The Foreign Office was still not entirely comfortable with the U.S. version of the treaty, however. At the same time as it put forth the new security rationale for the pact, William Tyrrell requested one of the British diplomats in the United States to obtain, "privately and confidentially" an indication of what the United States thought of the British reply (subjecting the pact to a "statement of significance" regarding special interests):

[51] *New York Times*, 14 April 1928.
[52] FO371, 12795, 8 June 1928, PRO. See also McKercher, "British Diplomatic Service in the United States," 222.

Enquiry should however only be made if you are reasonably satisfied [the] response is likely to be favorable. . . . For your own information I may say we are especially anxious that, whatever attitude [the] U.S. Government towards paragraph 10 of British note may be [regarding "special regions"], nothing should be included in their reply which by disturbing [a] section of public opinion here may render agreement on this point more difficult to reach.[53]

The Foreign Office also sent a telegram to Tokyo on the same day asking the British embassy to "ascertain discreetly" why the Japanese did not feel it necessary to make a reservation similar to that of the British: "It will occur to you that (the) Japanese position in Manchuria presents many aspects of similarity with ours in Egypt." The Foreign Office was thus willing to acknowledge Japanese "interests" in Manchuria to gain an ally in the Kellogg treaty negotiations.[54]

Kellogg, however, ignored Paragraph 10 in his reply to the British Note, and Chamberlain decided it was best not to press the point in public correspondence. The matter continued to generate disagreement: the final draft included no specific reservations, and whereas Kellogg insisted that only the final wording could be considered binding, Chamberlain contended that, as part of the pre-pact official correspondence, the British note provided for the necessary reservations. Once both sides agreed to sign, however, neither side insisted on resolving the dispute.[55]

The Kellogg Pact, like the Locarno Treaties, represented a second-best option for peace groups. British groups campaigned in favor of the Pact not because they saw it as a panacea for war, but rather because they believed that the pledge to renounce war pushed states one step further toward a commitment to arbitration, in addition to reinforcing the foundation for disarmament. Moreover, the defeat of reservations represented a step toward dismantling Great Power prerogatives in favor of a norm of equality among states.

For the government, the Kellogg Pact negotiations resulted in two unanticipated consequences. In the short term, the pact put the Conservative government on the defensive. When in 1929 it lost power to a new Labour government, again headed by Ramsay MacDonald, Chamberlain was "seen as the opponent of general disarmament and arbitration, and the champion of the old diplomacy, balance of power politics and special

---

[53] FO371/12793, 8 June 1928, PRO.
[54] FO371/12793, 8 June 1928, F.O. to Mr. Dormer in Tokyo.
[55] Tomes, "Austen Chamberlain and the Kellog Pact," pp. 14–21.

alliances."[56] Thus in the short term, Chamberlain and Baldwin's claims in favor of British prerogatives backfired. In the longer term, however, the Pact would become the basis for a series of arguments put forth by both peace groups and governments in the coming years. Peace activists used the Pact to justify disarmament and peaceful conflict resolution, whereas government officials used the Pact as the basis for claims in favor of assistance in collective action against aggression. Chamberlain himself cited the Pact in calling for a collective League response to Italian aggression in Abyssinia in 1935. Both usages departed from traditional norms and placed constraints on individual states' prerogatives. Thus the Kellogg–Briand Pact should not be seen as the embodiment of simple idealism.

Following the Kellogg–Briand pact, the event of the 1920s that gave the most encouragement to peace groups was Britain's signing the Optional Clause of the Permanent Court of International Justice in 1929 under the second Labour Government of Ramsay MacDonald. This clause committed Britain to compulsory arbitration of all "justiciable" disputes under the League of Nations. The Conservatives had long opposed signing the clause, but because British positions led to charges of unnecessary intransigeance during the Coolidge conference and Kellogg Pact negotiations, the new Labour government gained the approval of peace groups by signing quickly. The British signature was largely due to the efforts of Arthur Henderson, long a peace movement supporter. Henderson fended off arguments against the Optional Clause (or for signing only with explicit reservations regarding British prerogatives in "areas of vital interest") on the part of the Foreign Office, Dominions, and Chiefs of Staff. He candidly labeled their reservations vestiges of an imperialism completely at odds with Labour's stated policy. In so doing, he recognized the problem of the declining legitimacy of Empire that plagued security debates from the Covenant to the Kellogg Pact:

> I would emphasise the extreme undesirability of asserting the so-called British Monroe Doctrine in any explicit form by way of reservation. To assert it as our predecessors did in connexion with the Kellogg Pact, by reference to certain unnamed regions, is plainly inconsistent with the repeated declarations, and the whole internationalist outlook, of the Labour Party. To assert it, on the other hand, with Egypt specifically named, would be to advertise the fact that our legal status in Egypt was untenable.[57]

[56] Ibid., p. 23.
[57] Minute by Henderson, 24 July 1929, Records of Cabinet Ad Hoc Committees, Cab. 27/392, quoted in Carlton, *MacDonald versus Henderson*, p. 76.

The Optional Clause, the hopes engendered in economic conferences for revising reparations, and the inclusion of Germany in 1926 in the League of Nations, indicated the strength of peace movement claims in favor of equality of status, restraints on state powers to engage in war, and universal (and democratic) participation in global international organization. These moves directly set the imperialist and Great Power rationales for security policy against the equal rights rationale. Support for equal rights, whether based on a critique of either war-as-imperialism or war-as-power politics, united peace groups for the next several years in a sustained campaign for general disarmament.

From the realist vantage point, early efforts to achieve naval disarmament (at Washington in 1921–1922) represented unwelcome budgetary necessity and were complicated by insistence from peace groups on tangible weapons cuts and an equitable agreement.[58] If the United States persisted in challenging British supremacy on the seas (for no good reason, according to the British Admiralty and Cabinet), then Britain must agree to negotiations to find some acceptable means of asserting its naval prerogatives. Likewise, Britain had to decide whether or not to renew the Anglo-Japanese naval alliance; one way or another, Japan must be kept in its proper place as a second-rate power and Britain must continue to court it as an ally. For the Lloyd-George government multilateral negotiations were an acceptable means of fulfilling the first half of this goal, but it was preferable not to complicate negotiations by the constant need to justify British positions in public.

The draft Geneva Protocol of 1923, which would have "filled the gaps" in the Covenant by instituting compulsory arbitration and specifying the conditions under which the League would apply economic and military sanctions, was an exercise in futility that happily failed, in no small part because of the efforts of the British government. Conversely, the Locarno Treaties of October 1925, signed by Britain, Germany, France, and Belgium, constituted "a simple and revealing illustration of the working of power politics," fulfilling "the British traditionalist *desiderata* in an almost ideal fashion."[59] Bypassing the League of Nations, Locarno forged a pragmatic arrangement to guarantee the eastern border of France against German attack, an agreement that entailed limited, and therefore acceptable, British obligations on the Continent. Realism took a step backward with

[58] Kaufmann, *Arms Control*, pp. 33–36.
[59] E. H. Carr, *The Twenty Years' Crisis, 1919–1939: An Introduction to the Study of International Relations,* 2d ed. (New York: Harper & Row, 1964), p. 105; Arnold Wolfers, *Britain and France between Two Wars* (New York: Harcourt, Brace, 1940, 2d ed. 1966), p. 257.

the Geneva (Coolidge) Naval Conference of 1926, which accomplished nothing and left bitter feeling and hints of a "war scare" between the United States and Britain. (On the other hand, realist international relations theory could use this failure as an example of the impossibility of success in arms control negotiations when allegedly vital interests are at stake.) Following on the heels of the Coolidge Conference, the 1928 Kellogg–Briand Pact, or "Pact of Paris," represented the height of interwar folly. Spurred on by peace groups' demands, the Pact's provision to "outlaw aggressive war" stoked the vain popular hope that war could be put to an end once and for all and injured any prospect of educating public opinion about the necessity of preparedness.

Yet this narrative misses both the normative contestation of the period and the contradictions and unnecessary intransigeance inherent in "realist" British policy. The normative delegitimization of traditional security discourse and practice took hold during the Geneva Protocol and Locarno debates and turned to direct opposition during the Coolidge Naval Conference. The Kellogg–Briand Pact represented an uneasy reconstruction of security norms to emphasize international responsibility in resolving conflicts and delegitimize "self-help" in the form of "offensive war." Yet the unsettled issue of British reservations about its empire indicated that norms guiding British policy could be fluid. The next chapter narrates the implications of this state of affairs for the crises and tragedies of the 1930s.

CHAPTER FOUR

Normative Struggle and the
British Peace Movement in the 1930s

The impression of Neville Chamberlain returning from Munich, proclaiming to cheering throngs that he had achieved "peace in our time" and "peace with honor," indelibly marks any discussion of British appeasement and interwar politics. In Parliament, joyful MPs rose to their feet to give the prime minister a standing ovation. The majority of the press hailed the four-power accord; the *Times* said "No conqueror returning from victory on the battlefield has come home adorned with nobler laurels than Mr. Chamberlain from Munich."[1] Many pacifists (but not socialists or the League of Nations Union) joined in the celebratory wave of relief.

Several possible narratives exist to describe and explain how social forces participated in the events that led to this drama. The traditional narrative in international relations suggests that pacifists, peace groups, or "public opinion," motivated by moralistic beliefs and weak-kneed sympathy for Germany, interfered with prudent foreign policy imperatives. Munich, after all, was preceded by the Peace Ballot of 1935 and the Disarmament Conference of 1932–1934, both offering proof that peace movement groups fostered a naive belief in the power of the League of Nations to avert war. The League of Nations failed disastrously, especially in its attempt to restrain Italian ambitions in Abyssinia. Peace activists' interference was also a primary cause of Britain's woefully inadequate state

---

[1] Quoted in Roger Eatwell, "Munich, Public Opinion, and Popular Front," *Journal of Contemporary History* 6 (1971): 122.

of military preparedness in the late 1930s. The "consistent opposition of . . . the idealists of the League of Nations Union and other pacifist organizations towards rearmament" effectively neutralized Britain, preventing it from building adequate military forces until it was too late to stem German military power and thus German territorial conquests.[2] Consequently, Neville Chamberlain's government had no choice but to pursue a policy of political appeasement.

The debate in Britain over appeasement has evolved through several phases, each in turn revealing evidence that pokes holes in the traditional international relations narrative about the role played by peace movements, but not challenging the narrative head-on. The primary line of division is between those who believe that World War II was "evitable" and those who adhere to structural explanations and conclude that the war was unavoidable. Historians have developed sophisticated arguments in favor of one or the other of these two lines of argument. But international relations theory remains schizophrenic. It traditionally leans toward structural explanations of conflict (present in most balance-of-power theories), yet simultaneously tends to consider that World War II, more so than World War I, was a war that could have been avoided if only the Allied powers had observed rigorously throughout the interwar period the requirement of self-preservation through adequate military might and demonstrations of strength. If the war was avoidable, then particular actors must bear responsibility for its outbreak, giving rise to what Donald Cameron Watt has called "the sin theory of international relations."[3]

In the traditional view, the events of the 1920s provided the foundation on which the path toward appeasement was set. The decade ended on a dangerous note, although the severity of the danger was not yet apparent. The 1930s opened inauspiciously with the London Naval Conference, the third in a series of four interwar naval conferences. Peace movement insistence on agreement to redress the failure of the Coolidge Conference, especially strong on the part of women's groups, placed unwelcome constraints on the government's negotiating position. But imprudent foreign policy reached its apex at the 1932 World Disarmament Conference, the event peace groups had long awaited to connect and resolve the various aspects of the problem of armaments under the League of Nations.

[2] Stephen Roskill, *Hankey, Man of Secrets,* iii (London: Collins, 1970–74), p. 382; quoted in Donald Birn, *The League of Nations Union, 1918–1945* (Oxford: Oxford University Press, 1981), pp. 4–5. It is incorrect, as Birn and others point out, to say that the LNU was either pacifist or consistently opposed to rearmament throughout the interwar period.

[3] Donald Cameron Watt, "The Historiography of Appeasement," in Chris Cook and Alan Sked, eds., *Crisis and Controversy: Essays in Honour of A. J. P. Taylor* (London: Macmillan, 1976), p. 111.

Moving from the Kellogg–Briand Pact to these two conferences left the movement completely unprepared to address in a responsible manner the successive international crises that immediately began to demand the attention of British foreign policy: the Japanese invasion of Manchuria in 1932, Adolf Hitler's accession to power in 1933, the Italian invasion of Abyssinia in 1935, German remilitarization of the Rhineland in 1936, and finally the apex of political appeasement, ceding the Sudetenland to Germany at Munich in September 1938. (The Spanish Civil War of 1936–1939 is of less concern to many proponents of realpolitik, although it proved to be a crisis of enormous significance for most peace movement groups and an epiphany for many on the Left).[4] Manchuria and Abyssinia demonstrated once and for all the futility of relying on the international polity to stop aggression. The political appeasement put into play at Munich and World War II itself were the inevitable results of a sequence of failed utopian projects of disarmament and arbitration that idealists attempted to enact through the chimera of global international organization.

Thus if the conventional narrative views the 1920s as the era of unbounded idealism, the 1930s represents its unraveling. The traditional narrative of the 1930s takes the peace movement to task for blindly continuing to promote disarmament, especially during the League's World Disarmament Conference of 1932–1934, when it should have become apparent that any further arms reductions were foolish given the increasingly volatile international situation. Criticisms of the actions of peace movement later in the decade concern its neglect in confronting the potential necessity of sanctions (military and economic) and therefore its failure to think through a coherent policy in the event that war could not be averted. "Lessons" for prudent policy follow: disarmament is futile, states must not engage in multilateral agreements that will inhibit future "freedom of action," and restraints on state prerogatives are dangerous.

Again, however, a different narrative is possible. There is no doubt that the succession of crises that was the 1930s—Manchuria, the failure of the World Disarmament Conference, Abyssinia, the Spanish Civil War, Munich—epitomize tragedy in world politics. But this is not necessarily because "realist" policy was ignored or because of "structural inevitability." Rather, it is unclear whether a prudential policy along realpolitik lines was possible during the decade. At a minimum, any realistic policy would have to call into question some elements of Britain's position in the world, including its role as head of an increasingly restive and expensive Empire.

---

[4] See Fenner Brockway, *Inside the Left* (London: Allen & Unwin, 1947), pp. 294–305.

Two problems with the traditional narrative are, first, that peace groups did not remain oblivious to events in Europe and the Far East, but viewed them with increasing alarm. They did not recalibrate their position in favor of disarmament, at least not during the early 1930s while the Disarmament Conference was in session. They soldiered on in their efforts, in many cases not out of any "modernist" belief in "liberal progress," but rather despite their lack of hope in progress, because they saw little alternative to their reasoning that a *sauve qui peut* arms race would lead to tragedy, especially when any modern defense posture included "bombing aeroplanes" and "poison gases." Fear of the horrors resulting from bombing and chemical weapons was as potent in the 1920s and 1930s as the fear of nuclear weapons would be a generation later. Dystopic, rather than utopian, literature abounded, and all peace groups conducted studies, wrote articles and disseminated tracts against the "menace from the air."[5] No More War's 1925 scenario of the effects of an air war was illustrative:

> Aeroplanes, manageable through wireless . . . will throw bombs on enemy cities, chiefly on the industrial centres. Of these bombs, which will be filled with poison gas, about twelve will be sufficient to destroy all human, animal and vegetable life in cities like Paris, or Berlin, within a few minutes . . . there does not exist any effective protection against these gases. . . . There is no defence in such a war . . . the nations will have to choose either total disarmament or total destruction.[6]

Peace groups saw the Disarmament Conference as the sole forum capable of addressing and potentially eliminating the twin problems of bombing and chemical weapons.

Second, there was no clear official alternative in the early (or late) 1930s to peace movement positions. Tory governments, as well as the National government of Ramsay MacDonald, looked askance on peace group claims and demands, but they (as well as the 1929 Labour government) more often than not advocated passivity rather than action. However, this lack of coherence was a product of the increasingly apparent contradictions in the governments' construction of British "interests," rather than emanating either from individual officials' lack of ability or deference to peace movements.

---

[5] M. Keith Booker, *The Dystopian Impulse in Modern Literature: Fiction as Social Criticism* (Westport, Conn.: Greenwood Press, 1994); Peter Edgerly Firchon, *The End of Utopia: A Study of Aldous Huxley's* Brave New World (London: Associated University Presses, 1984); Phyllis Lassner, *British Women Writers of World War II: Battlegrounds of Their Own* (New York: St. Martin's Press, 1998).

[6] *No More War,* February 1925.

The following narrative outlines the growing fissures in British policy and the way in which peace groups exploited these fissures to delegitimize further individualistic security norms. The London Naval Conference represented a move toward normative consensus after the failures of the mid-1920s, but the World Disarmament Conference of 1932 exposed once again the difficulties of promoting a norm of equality of status. Even prior to the advent of National Socialism in Germany, such a norm had to contend with the contradictions inherent in British "interests." Abyssinia promoted the legitimacy of collective action, even though the British and French governments eventually backed down from plans for a strong collective response. Abyssinia also reinforced the normative illegitimacy of imperial conquest, further exposing the contradictions inherent in official British goals and delegitimizing the British double-standard on imperial possessions. These events formed the basis of the peace movement's stance—ranging from lukewarm support of avoiding war to outright opposition to annexation—to Munich.

NORMS OF PARITY, EQUALITY, AND DISARMAMENT: THE LONDON NAVAL CONFERENCE AND THE WORLD DISARMAMENT CONFERENCE

After 1929, Britain's signature to the Optional Clause for compulsory arbitration and the existence in power of a Labour government committed to internationalism revitalized peace groups' claim that substantive progress on disarmament had become possible. Peace groups were aware that first the Baldwin, then the MacDonald governments had taken up once again negotiations on naval disarmament with the United States, at least in part to appease peace sentiment after the Coolidge Conference's failure. Peace groups used this opening on naval questions, as well as progress toward negotiating a draft Disarmament Convention in Geneva, to press their demands for disarmament. Even the No More War Movement, which had called the Geneva Conference a "sham," expressed enthusiasm about the preparations for the London Conference.[7]

Women's groups took the lead in articulating the views of peace movements on disarmament for the London Naval Conference of 1930 and the World Disarmament Conference, which finally opened in February 1932. After the Equal Franchise Act of July 1928 gave the vote to over four and three-quarters million women (just in time for the 1929 elections), women's groups immediately played up their newfound political power. Eigh-

---

[7] No More War Movement, 8th Annual Conference Minutes, 16–17 November 1929.

teen women's groups, including the Women's International League, (WIL) formed the British Peace Crusade, which claimed to represent over two million women, to campaign for successful reductions at the London Naval Conference; the British women formed the core of the international Women's Peace Crusade, a coalition of American, French, Japanese, and British women's groups. Women's political power temporarily muted charges of feminine "idealism." Even the hawkish Secretary to the Cabinet, Sir Maurice Hankey, reminded MacDonald several times not to ignore the women's request for a deputation with representatives from governments participating in the Conference. Women's group representatives eventually met with foreign ministers and defense officials, including MacDonald, Hankey, and U.S. Secretary of State Stimson, in February 1930.[8] Margery Corbett-Ashby used the occasion to place women's voices within the bounds of "practical politics" and refute charges of feminist idealism while reminding government officials of women's newfound political power:

the deputation is memorable because it is introducing women as a new factor in international politics. They come here because they feel that women are not only idealists; they will represent in politics a very practical force. . . . If little is accomplished by this Conference there will be an enormous disappointment throughout all the countries which will have quite a definite effect on politics, and indeed we believe that Governments will be selected who can accomplish the practical reduction of armaments and the definite and constructive steps towards peace.[9]

The demands of Women's organizations and other peace groups were based on the twin claims that disarmament was now more than ever a practical possibility (forty-two states had signed the Optional Clause to require compulsory arbitration of disputes) and that the Conference provided an opportunity for states to affirm the principle of parity while building on the successes of the Washington Naval Treaty.

Peace groups evaluated the London Conference on the basis of these claims. The London accord expanded the categories of weapons addressed by the Washington Treaty of 1922 and repaired part of the failure and ill-feeling resulting from the Coolidge Conference of 1927: it ex-

---

[8] Keith Middlemas and John Barnes, *Baldwin: A Biography* (London: Macmillan, 1969), p. 509. Letter from Edith Zangiwill to MacDonald, 27 January 1930, and the transcript of the women's deputation, 6 February 1930. CAB 21/341, PRO.

[9] Women's Peace Crusade deputation, 6 February 1930, CAB 21/341.

tended the former's holiday on battleship construction until 1936 and set by category ceilings on the numbers of cruisers, destroyers, and submarines for Britain, the United States, and Japan. Peace movement sentiment was favorable with reservations: it was satisfied with that part of the agreement that furthered the principle of parity by placing controls on the arms race in cruisers. However, foreshadowing reactions to post–World War II arms control talks, it expressed keen disappointment that the agreed-upon ceiling would permit a net buildup, rather than reduction, of actual numbers of ships.[10] Consequently peace groups made clear that they viewed any agreement at the London Naval Conference as a prelude to further success at the general disarmament conference being planned by the League Preparatory Commission.

The World Disarmament Conference opened in Geneva in February 1932, and women's groups again took the lead by presenting millions of disarmament petitions with great fanfare to Arthur Henderson, the Conference president. Peace group representatives gave speeches under official auspices in a scene that, according to Philip Noel-Baker, had "no precedent in the history of diplomatic or other international Congresses." The campaign for disarmament leading up to the Conference had generated impressive programmatic and normative unity among peace groups as well as extensive mass participation. The churches (especially Anglican and Non-conformist), universities, technical schools and colleges, many local peace groups and chambers of commerce, women's groups, the cooperative movement, and (with Henderson's assistance) the trade unions participated in peace group disarmament campaigns. The combined WIL and National Peace Council (NPC) 1925 arbitration petition gathered 488,000 signatures, and the WIL campaign for disarmament by mutual agreement, aided by other peace groups, amassed over two million. Most groups also peaked in numbers in the late 1920s and early 1930s. The League of Nations Union (LNU), by far the largest peace group, claimed over 400,000 dues-paying members at this time; its total membership (the figure reported by the LNU itself) was over 1 million.[11]

---

[10] See B. J. C. McKercher, "Of Horns and Teeth: The Preparatory Commission and the World Disarmament Conference, 1926–1934," in *Restraints on War: Arms Control and Disarmament in British Foreign Policy* (Westport, Conn.: Praeger, 1992); Brian Bond, *British Military Policy between the Wars* (Oxford: Clarendon, 1980); Robert Kaufman, *Arms Control in the Pre-Nuclear Era* (New York: Columbia University Press, 1990); NPC, *Peace Year Book 1931,* (London: NPC 1932) pp. 30–33; Philip Noel-Baker, *The First World Disarmament Conference, 1932–1933, and Why It Failed* (Oxford: Pergamon Press, 1979); NPC, *Peace Year Book 1931,* p. 32.

[11] NPC Minutes, 11 November 1925, BLPES; NPC, *Peace Year Book 1933* (London: NPC 1934), p. 111; Birn, *League of Nations Union,* p. 93; Martin Ceadel, "The Peace Movement between the Wars: Problems of Definition," in Richard Taylor and Nigel Young, eds., *Campaigns*

In the traditional international relations narrative, these events served primarily to feed, in the famous words of John Wheeler-Bennett, the "pipe dream of peace."[12] But a more contextualized interpretation views peace movement actions in a different light. Peace groups were determined not to let the opportunity for equality of status and tangible disarmament (especially of the "air weapon") slip by after more than a decade of disarmament campaigns and worked feverishly to ensure the Conference took place. But Japanese aggression against China and Hitler's accession to the chancellorship in Germany troubled peace groups and the government alike. Whereas these events provided the context for the government to fall back on rearmament and scrap the Ten Year rule, for peace groups they reinforced claims on the destructiveness of bombing, the dangers of the arms trade, and the probable justification rearmament would give to Germany against its enforced inferiority.

Peace movement demands in preparation for the Conference coalesced around the "Budapest proposals" of the International Federation of League of Nations Societies, initiated by the LNU and pushed through by Cecil, which called for abolishing the weapons forbidden to Germany and instituting a program of budgetary limitation. These demands, in essence, resuscitated peace movement claims promoting the principle of equality of status, or "parity" in armaments, by prohibiting the categories of "aggressive" weapons forbidden to Germany by the Treaty of Versailles: tanks, heavy mobile guns, bombers, submarines, and chemical weapons. The Budapest Proposals also added the demand for a 25 percent budgetary cut in arms expenditures worldwide to advance the principle of "international equality," not by increasing numbers of weapons already reduced under the Peace Treaties, but through the "proportionate reduction" of the arms of other states. The LNU lobbied hard for solidarity on this program. In one of its most unified moments, almost all peace groups agreed to support the proposals, although many pacifist groups continued to demand that Britain "lead by example" through unilateral arms reductions.[13]

In addition to the principle of equality, the peace movement continued to advance claims restricting states' military power, especially through "the suppression of military aviation" as "one of the first and most consequential steps to be taken" in disarmament. "All societies interested in peace in-

---

for Peace: British Peace Movements in the Twentieth Century (Manchester: Manchester University Press, 1987).

[12] John Wheeler-Bennett, *The Pipe Dream of Peace* (New York: Morrow, 1935).

[13] Twelfth Annual Meeting of the LNU General Council, June 24–26 1931, LNU-GC Minutes, BLPES; NPC *Peace Year Book 1932* (London: NPC, 1933).

cluding Churches, Women's Societies, League of Nation Societies as well as the direct Pacifist bodies" agreed on abolishing the bomber and other air weapons.[14]

Demanding adherence to the norms of equality of status and controls on states' power and prerogatives to prepare for war signified more for peace groups than merely reducing the numbers of weapons (and thereby hindering the means to wage war). Some groups such as the LNU recognized that adherence to the norm of equality of status would also remove the bases for Germany's post-Versailles grievances and eliminate any justifiable rationale for German rearmament. Moreover, the LNU's inclusion of budgetary limitation, while open to the criticism that it lacked a verifiable means of implementation, was in part designed to put Germany on guard. France and Britain both detected anomalies in Germany's military appropriations figures in the early 1930s. For example, one report noted that according to German figures, trench mortars in Germany cost one hundred twenty times as much as British trench mortars. These anomalies increased suspicions that Germany was actively violating the provisions of the Versailles Treaties either by procuring greater numbers of weapons than it admitted or by producing weapons listed in the "forbidden" categories. Cecil and others argued that budgetary limitation would curtail Germany's ability to carry out such violations successfully.[15]

But for most peace movement members the demand for equality of status focused attention on the British government's consistent claim that it should be exempted from further arms reductions because of the exigencies of maintaining the Empire. The British government's position through the first year of the Conference was that it supported cuts by others but was "unable to offer further reductions" itself.[16] Peace groups condemned this position unanimously and often. For the LNU and church leadership, this criticism stemmed primarily from a strong adherence to the principle of equal rights and responsibilities, but for socialists, pacifists, and many in the rank and file, it also emanated from a critique of Britain's imperial policies.

While peace groups consolidated their position on disarmament in the early 1930s (despite continued debate and disagreement over proposals for an international police force, unilateral disarmament, and sanctions),

[14] Cecil statement, FO371/15708/W14278/47/98, 10 December 1931.

[15] Edward W. Bennett, *German Rearmament and the West, 1932–1933* (Princeton: Princeton University Press, 1979), pp. 80–81; Cecil to Ramsay MacDonald, 14 September 1932, Cecil papers, 51081, British Library.

[16] Foreign Office comparison of Cecil and Cabinet views on disarmament, January 1932, Simon papers, FO800, PRO.

the British government over and over put off developing a "constructive" disarmament policy. When Labour acceded to power in 1929, Britain took the lead in developing the draft disarmament treaty at Geneva, largely because Arthur Henderson became Foreign Minister and Cecil served as the Labour government's delegate to the drafting committee. The draft document, completed at the end of 1930, represented a compromise among British, French, and peace movement positions. It called for budgetary limitation, a permanent disarmament commission, the method of naval limitation agreed to at the London Conference, the principle of limiting land, sea, and air effectives, and the renunciation of chemical and bacteriological warfare—all in accord with peace movement demands. To placate the French, the draft did not count reserves as part of a country's land armies.[17] However, in October 1931, four months before the General Conference began, MacDonald's Labour government fell from power because of the worsening economic crisis, and a coalition of Conservatives under Baldwin's leadership, pro-MacDonald Labourites, and a rump of disaffected Liberals created a "National" government. Although MacDonald remained premier, real power resided with Baldwin, and Arthur Henderson reluctantly led the majority of Labour into opposition to the new government. Disagreement exists over the degree to which the change in government caused a substantial alteration in British disarmament policy and attitudes toward the League Conference. As prime minister, MacDonald, never an ardent advocate of disarmament, retained ultimate control of policy, but Arthur Henderson, a Labour activist with strong ties to peace movement elites, was replaced in the Foreign Office by John Simon, a Liberal with mixed sympathies. Henderson, however, became the Conference's President in Geneva.[18]

Although the change in government may not have represented a fundamental change in British disarmament policy, it did coincide with an increasingly passive position on disarmament that manifested itself publicly as a combination of inactivity and confusion. This confusion left the door open to more coherent peace movement claims as well as public frustration at official inaction and vacillations. In late 1931 and early 1932, as Conference preparations came to a close, the government essentially found itself hoping the Conference would be canceled but unwilling, be-

[17] McKercher, "Of Horns and Teeth," 260; Wheeler-Bennett, *The Pipe Dream of Peace,* p. 4; NPC, *Peace Year Book 1932,* pp. 36–39.
[18] David Carlton, *MacDonald versus Henderson: The Foreign Policy of the Second Labour Government* (London: Macmillan, 1970); Wheeler-Bennett, *Pipe Dream of Peace,* p. 7; Philip Noel-Baker, *The First World Disarmament Conference, 1932–33, and Why It Failed* (New York: Pergamon Press, 1979), pp. 72–73; McKercher, "Of Horns and Teeth," p. 262.

cause of the possibility of a public backlash, to take the lead in postponing.[19] The government continued to hold that while Britain should be exempt from further arms reductions others should continue to make progress on the issue.[20] Some Foreign Office diplomats recognized that seizing the initiative would gain the favor of peace movements.[21] They also wished to show good faith to the United States to gain the latter's favor at the forthcoming Lausanne Conference on international reparations, and some Cabinet officials shared the general fear of the bomber and thus wished to find a means to control "military aviation." But the government worried that a strong pro-disarmament stance might force it to take specific steps that it would be unwilling to carry out. Further disarmament would hinder Britain's ability to police sea trade routes, maintain Far Eastern military bases, and put down troublesome colonial uprisings. Foreign Office discussions thus tended to leave the issue of British policy at the Disarmament Conference unresolved, with some diplomats arguing for a bold course, others for caution.[22]

Alexander Cadogan, in a telling memorandum, likened the government's inaction on disarmament to its previous stance on the Geneva Protocol. Reminding his foreign office colleagues of the relationship between the Protocol and disarmament, he recounted how the government had over time agreed to many of the Protocol's provisions, including its ban on aggressive war and the compulsory arbitration of disputes:

a very large part of the Protocol has already been wrung from us since 1924. If, in 1924, we could have offered spontaneously what we have now been forced to give with not too good a grace, we might almost have secured a Disarmament Conference in that year. . . . We have done this before, we have said "thus far and no further," and only some years after have we discovered that, while asseverating our complete immobility, we have been pushed several miles further along the road. Might it be better to try to ascertain how much further advance is expected of us so that we may weigh carefully whether it would not be better to cover the remaining distance of our own free will (if we can), rather than be dragged unwillingly along.[23]

[19] Simon to MacDonald, 30 November 1931; Simon to Cecil, 28 December 1931, Simon papers, FO800, PRO.

[20] FO371/15707, Fall 1931, PRO.

[21] Leeper memo, 17 December 1931, FO371/15708, PRO.

[22] Leeper and Cadogan comments, 15 December, 1931, FO371/15708/W14304/47/98, PRO.

[23] Cadogan memo, "Disarmament: Historical Review of the Obligations of Great Britain in the Matter of 'Security,'" 13 March 1931, FO371/15704, PRO.

Nevertheless, the government's policy continued in a state of paralysis that officials themselves criticized. Cecil had finally agreed after much pressure from Simon to lead the British delegation at Geneva, but deplored the recommendations of a multiparty committee convened to develop a nonpartisan policy. These recommendations rejected any responsibility for disarmament by Britain and thus promoted an attitude that, according to Cecil, "would . . . be absolutely hopeless at the Conference." Simon admitted to Baldwin his own confusion regarding British policy, acknowledging "I confess that I do not see daylight at present on disarmament policy at all."[24]

Simon temporarily validated peace movement claims by making a well-received speech at the opening of the Conference calling for "qualitative disarmament," prohibiting "offensive" weaponry, and establishing a Permanent Disarmament Commission. Yet he, MacDonald, and Baldwin did not follow with concrete proposals, and peace groups questioned the government's sincerity. The impatience of the movement's rank and file continued to grow, peaking when U.S. President Herbert Hoover made his proposals for reducing "offensive armaments" by one third.[25]

The Cabinet had been aware that Hoover might be considering a disarmament scheme along the lines of the international League of Nations associations' Budapest proposals (a 25 percent reduction of arms expenditures worldwide), although it initially developed no counter plan. Instead Simon, meeting the criticisms of those in the Cabinet reluctant to engage in further arms limitation, clarified the government's position with a speech on July 7. Although Britain would retain proposals to abolish bombers and submarines, the government refused to reduce British strength in battleships and reserved the right to retain bombers for "police" purposes in the colonies. Peace groups were outraged. Resolutions and condemnations poured in from all over the country. In a typical example, WIL wrote to MacDonald, "the only step that would be of any practical value would be the abolition of all military and naval planes that could be used as bombers and the complete prohibition of bombing from the air in all circumstances and places." WIL's Annual Report for 1933 noted the "widespread protest in the press and elsewhere" incited by the British reservation on bombing, and credited WIL in organizing demands to withdraw it.[26]

---

[24] Cecil to Simon, 30 November 1931, Simon papers; Simon to Prime Minister Baldwin, Simon papers (undated), FO800, PRO.

[25] Gilbert Murray (of the LNU) to Simon, 9 January 1932, Simon papers, FO800, PRO.

[26] Howard Smith to Air Ministry, 21 October 1931, FO371/15706/W12055/47/98; Air Ministry report, 31 October 1931, FO371/15707/W12525/47/98, PRO; On Simon's reception of the Hoover proposals, see also McKercher, "Of Horns and Teeth," p. 267, and Noel-

Simon then began to argue for a change in British policy, contending that the situation would be serious if the government continued to argue along the "old lines" and not put forward a constructive proposal. "At home the Government will be exposed to ever-increasing criticism for their failure to make the Disarmament Conference a success." He also criticized the military for their rejection of a comprehensive plan and argued it was essential to "show that we are contributing to disarmament and convince both our own people and other nations of our sincerity." The Foreign Office also noted the force of the equality of status claim: "The resolutions received here show that [abolition of the classes of weapons forbidden to Germany] is becoming more and more the objective of Disarmament propaganda in this country." Two major peace movement deputations, one from all the major churches (except the Roman Catholic) and another organized by the LNU, went to the Foreign Office to press their case, the first arguing that, "The situation is critical, and there is much unrest in church circles that nothing adequate is being done to voice opinion . . . ." Another church official, A. S. Duncan-Jones, added, "I have never known Church opinion of all grades and kinds so agreed and so deeply stirred since 1914." Robert Vansittart, Permanent Undersecretary at the Foreign Office, in helping to prepare government officials for the meetings with peace groups, commented, "There are points in this which it will indeed be hard for the Prime Minister to answer, but the deputations can be assured of general sympathy, and points of embarrassment could be met by reference to the impending—as we hope— conversations between the Four Powers which HMG have taken the initiative in proposing."[27]

The Cabinet continued through the fall to argue the pros and cons of a more aggressive disarmament policy, including abolishing the bomber. Maurice Hankey acknowledged in a memo to the prime minister that any treaty prohibiting bombing would be circumvented if bombers' "technical efficiency" were kept alive by permitting bombing in colonial territories. On the other hand, for Hankey, any accord to eliminate bombing would bring a great disadvantage. Both the United Kingdom and France would be prohibited from using "aircraft for the control of tribesmen."[28]

Baker, *First World Disarmament Conference,* pp. 105–7; The condemnations are in FO371/16451, PRO; K. E. Innes to Ramsay MacDonald for the WIL Executive Committee, 11 July 1932, FO371/16451, PRO; WIL, 18th Annual Report, March 1933–Feb. 1934, BLPES.

[27] Simon to Ramsay MacDonald, 25 July 1932, Simon papers, FO800, PRO; Nevile Butler to Sir Walford Selby, 28 September 1932; W10953/130/98, 1 October 1932; W10844/130/98, PRO; A. S. Duncan-Jones, Chichester Deanery, 5 October 1932, FO371/16439/W11047/13098, PRO; 1 October 1932, FO371/16439, W10953/130/98, PRO.

[28] Hankey to Prime Minister, 11 December 1932, Simon papers, FO800, PRO.

But by November of 1932 a number of British officials, including Simon, MacDonald, and Stanley Baldwin, began to give publicly the outlines of a more aggressive disarmament plan. In a famous November 12 speech that shocked the House of Commons, Baldwin gave an indication of the Cabinet's proposals, calling for air disarmament because "the bomber will always get through" since there was no effective defense against it. British officials also began to push France to agree to negotiations with Germany, who had quit the Conference during the summer of 1932 in protest over the major powers' refusal to grant it parity in armaments.[29]

Simon and Baldwin then followed these steps by formulating an alternative British plan to reactivate the Conference. The plan granted Germany "qualitative" equality, prohibited chemical weapons, set limits on certain classes of ships (in accordance with the London Treaty), and advocated abolishing the submarine. It also called for abolishing bombing but continued to reserve the right, which the NPC called "deplorable," for "the use of such machines as are necessary for police purposes in outlying places."[30] However, the British Disarmament Convention was not put forth at the Conference until March 1933, six weeks after Hitler's accession to the German chancellorship.

The Government's position, relying primarily on its perceived need to preserve military control of its colonies, was increasingly exposed and delegitimized by peace groups. The government's initial position reserving the right to build and use bombers hindered the promotion of a humanitarian ethical stance. Its modification of this rationale, however, showed that the government did not accept the norm of equality of status on either the political front (colonies demanding self-determination) or the military front (vis-à-vis other powers). Peace groups, therefore, continued to question the government's ability to construct British interests in terms that were normatively coherent and ethically acceptable.

The Japanese bombing of Shanghai in January 1931 and eventual annexation of Manchuria the following May, however, posed major threats to the Disarmament Conference. These occured even before Germany quit the Conference (and later the League of Nations itself). Both the Sino-Japanese and the German crises are traditionally seen as exemplifying the ineffectiveness and naïveté of peace movements. With Shanghai and Manchuria, however, the peace movement rank and file reacted immediately. The LNU membership pressured its more cautious leadership to take a strong position in favor of British and League of Nations condem-

[29] Middlemas and Barnes, *Baldwin*, pp. 735–36; Noel-Baker, *First World Disarmament Conference*, pp. 119–20; Bennett, *German Rearmament and the West*, pp. 230–72.

[30] NPC, *Peace Year Book 1933*, pp. 69–70.

nation of Japanese actions. More important, Shanghai and Manchuria, and later Spain and Abyssinia, magnified the worries of peace groups about bombers and validated claims underlying the call for their abolition. The Women's International League for Peace and Freedom (WILPF) monthly *Pax International* editorialized later in 1938 that "the bombardment of open Spanish and Chinese cities" continued to rouse "indignation, horror and protest," justifying WILPF's longstanding position in favor of abolishing military aircraft and internationalizing civil aviation. During the early 1930s, the Sino-Japanese conflict also reinforced demands to curtail the arms trade. Groups and individuals pointed out that the government's arms exports favored Japan, assisting its violation of international law and worsening the destruction of Chinese cities. For example, one letter to the Foreign Office asserted that Britain exported four times more munitions to Japan than to China. The Foreign Office found the writer's figures to be "about right," but excused the imbalance, even though the government had ratified the Arms Traffic Convention of 1925, to ensure "that (other) Powers may not get a market at our expense."[31]

For the government Manchuria did not initially cause a significant change in disarmament policy. But it did provide the rationale for service chiefs to argue in favor of scrapping the Ten Year Rule (the Cabinet's guideline for military appropriations, originally formulated in 1919 but renewed periodically throughout the 1920s, that there would be no major war for ten years). Shanghai and Manchuria "gave the British military the opening they required to bring the Ten Year Rule into question. . . . the realization of the vulnerability to attack of British interests in the Far East was dramatically brought home." Again, the government's concern was to protect trading interests and concessions and preserve imperial possessions.[32]

It was not until 1933 that the government began to see Germany as the main threat to peace and as a reason to rearm.[33] Hitler represented a serious worry in 1933 for the government and peace groups alike. But because their respective claims regarding the necessity and purposes of disarmament differed, so did their application of these claims to Germany.

Peace groups continued to argue in favor of granting Germany parity in armaments, less as a good in its own right than as a means to blunt any justification for German rearmament. Peace groups had long argued in

[31] Birn, *League of Nations Union,* chap. 5; *Pax International* (July 1938), p. 1; Women's Co-operative Guild resolution, 15 July 1932, FO371/16451; Henry T. Gillett to FO, 9 June 1932, FO371/16451, PRO.

[32] Robert Paul Shay, Jr., *British Rearmament in the Thirties: Politics and Profits* (Princeton: Princeton University Press, 1977), p. 20.

[33] Shay, *British Rearmament in the Thirties;* Bennett, *German Rearmament and the West.*

the name of "realism" that inaction on equality of status did nothing to increase security. Kathleen Innes of the WIL Executive wrote to Simon, "It is realised here that Germany cannot be forbidden for ever to have armaments which are retained by other countries on the ground that they are necessary to legitimate defence," and to MacDonald, "If tanks up to 20 tons are really defensive weapons and save the lives of infantrymen, why were they forbidden to Germany?" The Quakers pressed the point by highlighting what they saw as the alternative to granting the equality of status claim: "we would express our astonishment that the Great Powers appear to prefer the re-armament of Germany to a continuance of her present state of disarmament, although the latter could be secured by their own agreement to abandon the aggressive weapons forbidden to her."[34]

Following the lead of Cecil and the LNU, peace groups increasingly turned from "quantitative" equality to "qualitative" equality as they desperately searched for a way to salvage something from the Conference. Peace groups had long claimed that the refusal of Britain and of the League of Nations to grant equality in armaments to Germany further marginalized moderate forces in Germany; they continued to argue that even if numerical equality was impossible, it would be difficult for Germany to refuse to acknowledge steps toward recognition of the principle.[35]

Consequently, peace groups continued in their demands because they feared a renewed arms race that they saw as the alternative to recognizing some semblance of equality. But few, if any, believed that a successful disarmament agreement, let alone "progressive peace," was attainable after this time. When the World Alliance for International Friendship through the Churches asked its member organizations in 1934 for their confidential views on the future of the Disarmament Conference, not a single reply expressed hope for success. The British Library of Information in New York reported to the Foreign Office that "the fact that these opinions were expressed by people whom normally one regards as unduly optimistic and who are in close touch with the peace movements in the various countries adds greatly to their significance." Moreover, many in the peace movement became increasingly bitter over their belief that the government, by its passivity and insistence on reservations, had squandered the opportunity for disarmament when it might have been more easily attained.[36]

---

[34] Innes to Simon, 11 July 1932, and Innes to MacDonald, 11 July 1932; FO371/16451, PRO; F. E. Pollard, Chair, to Simon, 7 February 1934, Society of Friends, London, from FO371/W415.

[35] Memo, Cecil conversation with Benes, 4 July 1931, FO371/15705; Cecil memo, 13 March 1931; and Henderson minute, 25 March 1931, FO371/15703, PRO.

[36] 6 June 1934, FO371/18548; See also Birn, *League of Nations Union*, pp. 109–11; Noel-Baker, *First World Disarmament Conference*.

From this point on, questions of rearmament and sanctions occupied peace movement relations with the government. In the end these two issues also divided the movement itself. The New Commonwealth Society, created by David Davies to promote an international air force, and the Peace Pledge Union, which originated in a 1934 postcard campaign to record pledges never to participate in war or war preparations, epitomized this eventual split. Yet disarmament by no means disappeared from the peace movement's agenda. Although in 1935 the government published a Defence White Paper announcing plans for rearmament, Stanley Baldwin publicly proclaimed there would be "no great armaments," much to the relief of all peace groups, including the LNU. When rearmament began, despite lukewarm support from the LNU and Labour, it did so in the context of a society deeply divided over the legitimacy of the need for new weapons, the principles behind acquiring them, and the stated and potential purposes of the program.

THE LATE 1930S: LAYING THE GROUND FOR NORMATIVE INFLUENCE BEYOND APPEASEMENT

From the 1940s to the present, appeasement has remained a fertile topic for interpretation and reinterpretation. Although periodic updates on appeasement historiography appear,[37] no one has resolved the question of whether or to what degree the peace movement "caused" or contributed to appeasement policies. But as Robert Beck points out, international relations theorizing about appeasement has not kept pace with historiographical developments, resulting in the perpetuation of truisms that may not prove valid.[38]

Appeasement historiography (as discussed in Chapter 1) moved from attempts to apportion blame to various political or social factions (Conservatives, Chamberlain, Labour, the peace movement, public opinion, "pacifists," or "League" opinion) in the immediate post–World War II period to a greater focus on structural factors, both economic and political.

---

[37] Especially on the fifty-year anniversary of Munich. See Robert J. Beck, "Munich's Lessons Reconsidered," *International Security* 14 (Fall 1989): 161–91; J. L. Richardson, "New Perspectives on Appeasement: Some Implications for International Relations," *World Politics* XL (April 1988): 289–316; Donald Cameron Watt, "1939 Revisited: On Theories of the Origins of Wars," *International Affairs* 65 (Autumn 1989): 407–13; and Michael Howard, "1989: A Farewell to Arms?" *International Affairs* 65 (Summer 1989).

[38] Beck, "Munich's Lessons." On appeasement and international relations, see also R. Barry Jones, "The Study of 'Appeasement' and the Study of International Relations," *British Journal of International Studies* 1 (April 1975): 68–76.

Thus Walter Lippmann blamed pacifists; Frank Owen, Michael Foot, and Peter Howard Chamberlain's Tory Cabinet; Martin Gilbert and Richard Gott likewise (followed by Gilbert's reversal several years later); and Corelli Barnett "all the customary groups" of the the peace movement. A. J. P. Taylor first reversed the blame thesis to focus on structural factors, followed by Paul Kennedy. More recently, historians continue to debate the structuralist explanation, constructing historiographies to assess the state of the field. Simultaneously, a group of historians sympathetic to the 1930s Conservatives developed a quasi-structuralist argument that emphasizes the multiple constraints placed on Chamberlain's policies.[39]

Nevertheless, efforts to assign responsibility for appeasement still touch a raw nerve, even among historians. Academic controversies indicate that moving the discussion of appeasement away from individual and toward structural analysis has not resolved the issue of culpability. Despite "years of British historiographical controversy and writing on the nature of appeasement," British historian Donald Cameron Watt complains that the "sin theory of British foreign policy in which the evil and indefensibility of 'appeasement' is taken as given" is still present.[40]

It is certainly true that some peace movement activists warned against appeasement early on, while others looked the other way at, or even excused, Nazi foreign policies.[41] The peace movement thus represented a microcosm of British society—each political party as well as literary and

---

[39] Walter Lippmann, *U.S. Foreign Policy: Shield of the Republic* (Boston: Little, Brown, 1943); Michael Foot and Frank Owen ("Cato"), *Guilty Men* (New York: Frederick Stokes, 1960); Martin Gilbert and Richard Gott, *The Appeasers* (Boston: Houghton Mifflin, 1963); Martin Gilbert, *Roots of Appeasement* (London: Weidenfeld & Nicholson, 1966); Telford Taylor, *Munich: The Price of Peace* (Garden City, N.Y.: Doubleday, 1979); Corelli Barnett, *The Collapse of British Power* (London: Eyre Methuen, 1972); A. J. P. Taylor, *The Origins of the Second World War* (New York: Atheneum, 1966); Paul M. Kennedy, "Idealists and Realists: British Views of Germany, 1864–1939," *Transactions of the Royal Historical Society*, Fifth Series, 25 (London: Royal Historial Society, 1975): 132–36; "'Appeasement' and British Defence Policy in the Interwar years," *British Journal of International Studies* 4 (1978): 161–77; and "Appeasement," in Gordon Martel, ed., *The Origins of the Second World War Reconsidered: The A. J. P. Taylor Debate after Twenty-Five Years* (Boston: Allen & Unwin, 1986); On the structuralist debate see Paul Schroeder, "Munich and the British Tradition," *Historical Journal* 19 (1976): 223–43; and Anthony Adamthwaite, "War Origins Again," *Journal of Modern History* 56 (March 1984): 100–104. For a review of "conservative" theorizing, see Watt, "The Historiography of Appeasement."

[40] Donald Cameron Watt, "Wimp or Tyrant: Twilight of the Truth," *History Today* 40 (February 1990): 53–54.

[41] Ceadel, *Pacifism in Britain;* David Lufkowitz, "British Pacifists and Appeasement: The Peace Pledge Union," *Journal of Contemporary History* 9 (1974): 413–40; and Bill Hetherington's articles on the Peace Pledge Union in *The Pacifist:* "Origins of World War 2," 26 (November 1988): 10–12.

artistic elites contained opposing views of national socialism. Yet despite the increasing divisions between pacifists and liberal internationalists within the peace movement and the pro-Nazi sentiments of a few, neither side provided normative legitimacy to the actions of Neville Chamberlain's government from 1937 to 1939. Led by the LNU, internationalists grew increasingly vocal in opposing the government's appeasement policy and refusal to back collective security through the League. Most pacifists, despite their determination not to be involved in war preparations, opposed the appeasement of Italy in 1937–1938, condemned Hitler's racist domestic policies, condemned German and Italian assistance to General Franco's forces in Spain, and expressed unease about Germany's foreign policy intentions. The common denominator between pacifists and internationalists was their work in favor of strengthening multilateral means of conflict resolution: internationalists through collective security; pacifists through a multilateral conference to rectify what they saw as a double standard established at Versailles by Britain and France on the question of colonies, self-determination, and access to raw materials.

The problem with the "political" policy of appeasement (as distinguished from the "economic" appeasement supported by pacifist sections of the movement especially) concerned the principle of condemning aggression. Merely "giving in" to dictators violated this principle; and although some pacifists were willing to placate Hitler's Germany to "preserve the peace," most in the movement were uncomfortable with such a stance.[42] Strict pacifists, generally accused of ignoring violence and constructing utopian views of the world, saw the options for action as an anguishing choice among evils. According to one:

> The pacifist attitude was—amongst people that I knew—"yes these things are dreadful and shocking and if we are to be genuine pacifists we are going to probably have to face the fact we may be done over by the Gestapo ourselves." [But war would be] Armageddon utterly and completely. Almost as we now think about nuclear warfare. . . . This is the point to remember, it was not that we wanted to capitulate to nazism, it wasn't that. We thought that even nazism was the lesser of two evils.[43]

[42] On the different meanings of the term *appeasement,* see Keith Robbins, *Appeasement* (London: Basil Blackwell, 1988); for a good discussion of what the peace movement meant by "economic appeasement," see Barry Buzan, "The British Peace Movement from 1919 to 1939," Ph.D. dissertation, London School of Economics, 1973; Hetherington, "Origins of World War 2"; Lufkowitz, "British Pacifists."

[43] Transcript, interview with John Marshall, "The Anti-War Movement since 1914," 10307/5/1, recorded 1988, Imperial War Museum.

Pacifists could not sweep aside claims about the indiscriminate destruction caused by "modern" means of warfare that had formed the basis of their disarmament demands for more than a decade. Nor could they dismiss claims regarding international economic inequalities and the need to eliminate double standards. Vera Brittain reiterated, "Though Germany is now the undoubted cause of the present political neurosis, we regard her as only one amongst many powers who are mutually to blame." She explained many pacifists' initial support of the Munich settlement: "Let us admit—and British pacifists are the first to do so—that the Munich settlement is an inglorious peace, purchased at the expense of a small power whose sacrifices left her greater neighbours free to make none." But, while an "honourable settlement at a reasonable price" might have been made in 1933, "by 1938 the time had gone by. England was faced, not with the alternative between good and evil, but with the alternative between one evil and another."[44]

The real differences within the peace movement concerned not whether to condemn aggression, but rather how an aggressor should be punished. The locus of disagreement centered on the actual implications of a policy of collective security enacted through the League of Nations. The left-pacifist No More War Movement, for example, deplored the consolidation of Hitler's power in Germany during the mid-1930s, yet believed (along with its successor, the Peace Pledge Union) that "collective security" was merely a cover for imperialist interests; at the same time many other groups solidified throughout the 1930s their claim that collective security was the only way to provide for states to be treated equally while guarding against aggression.

Growing divisions within the peace movement eventually allowed the government a freer hand in determining independently its perceptions of British interests. These divisions also enabled the government to attempt to divide the movement further. But the government did not take the offensive until the enormous success of the 1934–1935 Peace Ballot forced it to take note of pro-collective security sentiment within the movement.

The success of the National Declaration, commonly known as the Peace Ballot, had the effect not only of rejuvenating the movement after the Disarmament Conference's collapse, but also of reorienting many peace activists toward a stronger collective security policy. The Ballot was an amazingly well-organized amateur poll on armaments and collective security spearheaded by the LNU. A considerable section of the peace move-

[44] Vera Brittain, "Pacifism after Munich," in *Testament of a Generation: The Journalism of Vera Brittain and Winifred Holtby* (London: Virapo, 1985), pp. 228–30.

ment, including women's groups and the churches, actively participated. The LNU assembled half a million volunteers to distribute and collect ballots; an estimated 38.2 percent of the British electorate voted in the poll. The Ballot resulted in 87 percent of participants approving of "economic and non-military measures" to stop an aggressor and 59 percent approving of military force "if necessary." Over 11 million people, or 96 percent of those polled, wanted Britain to remain a member of the League of Nations.[45]

For Martin Ceadel, "The Peace Ballot can . . . be interpreted as a collective manifestation of the 'trouble making' concern for morality in foreign policy." But the Ballot, in fact, was much more. It (as intended by its organizers) forced people both in and out of the peace movement to clarify their stance on sanctions and collective security. The dean of Chichester pointed out during a deputation to the government that many people, especially in the churches, who had thought themselves strict pacifists, found that under certain circumstances they would support multilateral economic, and even military, sanctions against an aggressor.[46] Before 1935, primarily the LNU advocated such policies, although already in 1934, the strictly antimilitarist and antisanctions No More War Movement warned "The Peace Movement generally is more and more committing itself to the working out of a 'collective peace system' on the basis of 'pooled security'."[47] In deciding to work for the Ballot effort, however, groups such as WIL also began to gather under the collective security banner, whereas pacifist groups such as the No More War Movement (NMWM) opposed the Ballot on the grounds that it promoted the use of force.

As Ceadel and others point out, the Ballot has often been misinterpreted as proof of the British public's embrace of pacifism. But this was not the interpretation of the government. By its own admission, the government attempted to throw cold water on the Ballot, denouncing it as an incitement to open opposition to its security policy. (Foreign Secretary John Simon in a November 1934 speech in the House of Commons even ac-

[45] Martin Ceadel, "The First British Referendum: The Peace Ballot, 1934–35," *English Historical Review,* XCV (October 1980): 810–39; Dame Adelaide Livingstone, *The Peace Ballot: The Official History* (London: Victor Gollancz, 1935); Birn, *League of Nations Union;* University Group on Defence Policy, "Who Was for Munich?"; and Daniel Waley, *British Public Opinion and the Abyssinian War, 1935–36* (London: Maurice Temple Smith, 1975); University Group on Defence Policy, p. 14.

[46] Ceadel, "The First British Referendum"; Peace Ballot deputation, 23 July 1935, Prem1/178, PRO.

[47] It went on to argue it was "of the utmost importance" for the NMWM to "maintain itself as the one Pacifist organization that offers unqualified opposition to participation in war." No More War Movement Annual Report, 1933–34, London.

cused the normally noncontroversial LNU of socialist bias.) [48] The peace
movement's mobilization of pro-League sentiment also impressed the
government, and it began to formulate its Abyssinian policy accordingly.

The final Ballot results were tabulated during June of 1935, at the same
time as Italian designs on Abyssinia were growing increasingly evident and
ominous. The LNU had allowed early results to dribble out from November 1934 through May 1935, heightening the suspense for the final Ballot
rally in late June.[49] Prime Minister Baldwin, Foreign Secretary Samuel
Hoare, and Minister for League of Nations affairs Anthony Eden all began
to refer to peace opinion as one of the most important factors to take into
account in determining British policy.

As Italy's intentions toward Abyssinia became clearer in August 1935,
Foreign Secretary Samuel Hoare put out feelers to party leaders and other
prominent politicians to obtain their sense of what options British policy
should pursue. Hoare, at times joined by Eden, held talks with Conservatives Austen Chamberlain and Winston Churchill, David Lloyd-George,
the Liberal former Prime Minister, George Lansbury, leader of the Labour
Party, and Lord Robert Cecil for the LNU, which, therefore, was represented equally with the major political parties. All stressed the importance
of firm action through the League of Nations: their rationale (except in
the case of Churchill) concerned the strength of public support for collective League action against aggression.[50]

Austen Chamberlain (who learned the power of peace opinion from the
Coolidge and Kellogg negotiations), agreed with Hoare that "the League
should work on the line of least resistance." But he insisted that "economic
sanctions of some kind were inevitable. British public opinion would not
be satisfied by a policy of inaction or despair. If we edged out of collective
action of this kind, a great wave of opinion would sweep the Government
out of power." Britain should make as much use as possible of the Kellogg
Pact, but the government had to recognize that such action would not "be
altogether adequate in the face of the demands of British public opinion."
Chamberlain thus advocated an export embargo to Italy. Likewise, Lloyd-
George agreed with Chamberlain that the League machinery had to be
"tried out": he, too, "made it clear to us that any failure on our part to go
to this point" (of collective action through sanctions) "would bring down
upon our heads the overwhelming mass of public opinion." According to
Hoare, "this view is confirmed by the Press Department, the foreign editor

[48] Ceadel, "The First British Referendum," 824.
[49] Ibid., pp. 827–29.
[50] CAB 21/412, 21 August 1935, PRO.

of the "Yorkshire Post" declaring that 75% of the north of England is behind the Covenant, and even the "Morning Post" is growing very restive at
Italian arrogance."[51] Government and party officials, therefore, did not
argue that collective machinery was utopian or naive at this time. Rather,
official views of necessary action tended to merge with the demands of a
significant section of the peace movement.

Lord Cecil during his interview "stated that so far as the League of Nations Union was concerned, they were entirely behind the Government in
the action they had taken, both at Geneva and at Paris. We could be sure
of their continued support in any efforts which we made to carry out the
Covenant." Cecil, however, wanted a public statement of the government's
intended actions. George Lansbury also requested a public declaration of
the government's adherence to its League obligations. "Neither he nor his
followers, with very few exceptions, contemplated unilateral action, and
by collective action they meant in particular Anglo-French action." The
League's collective action machinery had to be tried, therefore; if it failed,
then and only then "the time would have arrived for scrapping the existing machinery of the League and for attempting some new plan of international co-operation."[52]

The government also began to use arguments regarding the boundaries
set by public opinion in its negotiations with Italy. As early as February,
John Simon warned the Italian Ambassador, Signor Grandi, "of the increasing interest of British public opinion in the situation *and in Italian intentions.*" This was the first serious official intimation to the Italian Ambassador of British concerns, although similar warnings had been conveyed
orally on several earlier occasions. From April on, throughout the summer
of 1935, Simon, Hoare, and Vansittart met numerous times with the Italian ambassador: "on virtually every occasion Signor Grandi was warned,
and warned seriously, of the dangers of Italian policy, both with regard to
its inevitable repercussions on British public opinion, and consequently
on Anglo-Italian relations, and with reference to its effect on the European situation and the League of Nations." As one Foreign Office official
put it, "We had a very vocal and humanitarian element in our public opinion who would not conceal their feelings."[53]

Eric Drummond, the former General Secretary of the League of Nations who in 1935 was the British ambassador to Italy, also added to this

[51] 20 August 1935, CAB 21/412, PRO; CAB 21/412, 21 August 1935, PRO.

[52] CAB 21/412, 21 August 1935, PRO.

[53] G. H. Thompson memo, 14 October 1935, CAB 21/421. This memo outlined the
chronology of official British actions from the spring of 1935 to the League Assembly of September 1935, defending the Government's actions retrospectively.

procession of warnings. He met with Mussolini himself at least twice in 1935, since the British were determined to make "persistent efforts" to inform the Italian government of the British stance. Mussolini argued that "collective security should be confined to Europe," but Drummond warned of "the dangers of a policy which would not be understood by British public opinion" and stressed "If [Mussolini] weakened or destroyed the League, then he would be destroying the whole existing political system."[54]

Foreign Secretary Samuel Hoare followed these warnings with a strong speech in favor of collective security at the annual League Assembly in September 1935. At that time, Hoare declared that Britain stood for "steady and collective resistance to all acts of unprovoked aggression. The attitude of the British nation in the last few weeks has clearly demonstrated the fact that this is no variable and unreliable sentiment but a principle of international conduct to which they and their Government hold with firm, enduring and universal persistence."[55] As a result, when Italy invaded Abyssinia one month later, Anthony Eden, the minister responsible for League affairs, took the lead in developing a policy of limited sanctions—an export embargo on certain metals and commodities in addition to an imports embargo—through the League of Nations.

The LNU, WILPF, and many local groups led public opinion in applauding the sanctions policy and encouraging stricter punishment of Italy, including an oil embargo. Many influential players in the government itself worked to institute sanctions on oil, which were agreed to in principle by the League on November 6. These sanctions, however, were never implemented. The French stalled and eventually refused to go along with an oil embargo, the United States could not be counted on, and the British were reluctant to go it alone, although Hoare, in attempting to persuade the French, lamented, "Of all the members of the League we were the only great oil-producing Power that had not informed Geneva of our acceptance of the embargo."[56]

Despite these measures, the differences between the government's interpretation of sufficient collective measures and that of the peace movement (and by now, public opinion at large) remained considerable. The ill-fated Hoare–Laval Pact highlighted the gap. In November and December of 1935, Samuel Hoare and his French counterpart, Pierre Laval, agreed on an initially secret diplomatic effort to appease Mussolini by giv-

[54] G. H. Thompson memo, 14 October 1935, CAB 21/421.

[55] Cecil Memorandum, 19 April 1936, FO371/20472; Daniel Waley, *British Public Opinion and the Abyssinian War, 1935–36* (London: Maurice Temple Smith, 1975), p. 31.

[56] Hoare to G. Clerk, CAB 21/421 (J8593/1/1), 28 November 1935, PRO.

ing Italy control over two-thirds of Abyssinian territory. This proposal would have effectively ended Abyssinia's status as a sovereign nation and legitimized Italian aggression. But when the pact became public, it produced a virtually unanimous and spontaneous outcry within the peace movement and among the press and public at large. Principles of collective security and resistance to aggression had become vital matters of debate. The government backed down and sacrificed Foreign Secretary Samuel Hoare to save face, though his resignation caused the prime minister to complain that "the League of Nations Union have done a great deal of their propaganda in making people believe they could rely upon collective security."[57]

Sanctions, however, caused bitter debates in the more pacifist movement groups. The number of pacifists pledging not to assist in war preparations of any kind was rapidly expanding—the Peace Pledge Union, founded in 1934, claimed 100,000 signatories by 1936. Many pacifists refused to acquiesce to sanctions against Italy, in spite of their sympathy for the Abyssinian cause, because of their claim that economic sanctions inexorably led to military ones (and hence to war). Consequently the umbrella National Peace Council, despite strong resolutions in favor of collective measures and strengthening the League, found itself unable to decide for or against a sanctions policy.[58]

Because of French and British disinclination to alienate Italy and British hesitation over pressing the French, the National Government's pro-League stance disintegrated quickly. The government thus interpreted its foray into collective security as a failure and concluded by November 1936 that its official policy of promoting collective security through the League should end. Stanley Baldwin, in another famous speech of the interwar period, demonstrated the government's change of policy by declaring, "I am not going to get this country into a war with anybody for the League of Nations or anybody else or for anything else."[59] The government increas-

[57] On the Hoare–Laval Pact, see Waley, *British Public Opinion;* R. A. C. Parker, "Great Britain, France, and the Ethiopian Crisis, 1935–1936," *English Historical Review* 89 (April 1974): 293–332; James C. Robertson, "The Hoare–Laval Plan," *Journal of Contemporary History* 10 (July 1975): 433–64; and Norton Medlicott, "The Hoare–Laval Pact Reconsidered," in David Dilks, ed., *Retreat from Power: Studies in Britain's Foreign Policy of the Twentieth Century* (London: Macmillan, 1981), pp. 118–38. On the public outcry, see *Headway,* Dec. 1935, Jan. 1936; Waley, *British Public Opinion.* Official quote from Prem1/193, 23 November 1936, PRO. The pact originated not with Hoare, but rather with Robert Vansittart, though the former was forced to resign. Keith Robbins, *Appeasement* (London: Blackwell, 1988), pp. 54–55.

[58] For Peace Pledge Union figures, see Bill Hetherington, *Resisting War* (London: PPU, 1986). On sanctions, see Lufkowitz, "British Pacifists and Appeasement"; NPC Council Minutes, 19 September 1935, BLPES.

[59] NPC Council Minutes, 19 September 1935, BLPES.

ingly used its relations with peace groups to exploit the split within the movement, hoping to receive support from the pacifist camp.

Yet even pacifist groups increasingly distanced themselves from the government's brand of appeasement diplomacy. This became evident in their insistence on defining economic, rather than political, appeasement and their continued promotion of League institutions to resolve disputes. Pacifist groups, through deputations sent to Whitehall, attempted to outline their concerns about government policy and to promote multilateral alternatives, particularly an economic conference to resolve long-standing German complaints of ill treatment. The deputations chastised Britain for keeping its Empire while maintaining to Germany and Italy that colonies were of no economic value. They thus proposed an "all-round revision of the peace settlement" of 1919 as a means of redressing the British double standard.[60]

In 1938 pacifists' demands for a norm of equality of status caused even more acute differences with the government. The entire peace movement bitterly criticized Neville Chamberlain's decision to recognize the Italian conquest of Abyssinia. The move, long debated within the government, represented a clear violation of the principles of self-determination and the condemnation of aggression. WIL reminded Chamberlain that he had previously stated that, at a minimum, "an agreement with Italy could only follow when she evacuated her volunteers from Spain" and emphasized its position that "the recognition of the annexation of Ethiopia would be a disastrous blow to the Covenant and the system of international law." Again, resolutions opposing government policy poured into the Foreign Office. Anthony Eden, who had replaced Hoare as foreign secretary, validated for peace groups their claims that recognition was not only unnecessary but also counterproductive when he resigned from the government over the issue in February 1938.[61]

Immediately preceeding the Munich agreement of September 1938, peace groups representing all tendencies—internationalist, socialist, and pacifist—drew the line at any chipping off the block of Czech sovereignty. They pleaded with the government not only to ensure the maintenance of peace, but also not to permit territorial concessions to Germany. As resolutions from peace groups poured in, the Foreign Office belatedly noted, "Public opinion has certainly stiffened a great deal against Germany in the last week." The International Peace Campaign (created in 1936 by Cecil

[60] First and Second Deputations on Economic Appeasement, Prem1/212, March 22, 1937; Prem 1/213, October, 1937, PRO.

[61] WIL, Annual Council Meeting Minutes, London, 193(8), BLPES. Eden was supported by 71 percent of the public. Beck, "Munich's Lessons Reconsidered," 181.

to stir up public opinion in continental countries and unite it with pro-League opinion in Britain) organized a resolution on September 11, 1938, from groups holding "very varying political opinions" condemning what it termed the government's policy of avoiding the risk of war at all costs and urging a firm line toward German designs on Czechoslovakia. Other peace groups combined conflicting goals in their petitions: WIL urged in a typical resolution on September 8, "a maximum effort for appeasement coupled with a clearly worded determination to resist aggression." Nevertheless, WIL and others made clear they approved of no settlement that would accede to any demand for Czechoslovakia to cede its Sudeten fringe to Germany.[62]

Thus the normative goals underlying the settlement with Germany and the point at which the line against aggressors was drawn differed for the peace movement and the government. After Munich, reactions ranged from unease to condemnation. While pacifists such as Vera Brittain viewed the accord as the lesser of (at least) two evils and the Peace Pledge Union gave it conditional support, the LNU condemned the agreement and WIL editorialized, "the 'peace' proclaimed at Munich is not the peace we have always fought for. . . . It cannot be called peace because it is not founded on justice."[63]

If the peace movement's reaction to Munich was a microcosm of that of the public at large, the quick reversal in support for the agreement is not surprising. Yet the government still hoped to keep the pacifist section of the movement on its side, accepting a deputation from pacifist and centrist groups who were thought to be "disposed rather to support than to criticize" Chamberlain's actions at Munich. Joseph Ball, the Conservative Party's chief researcher, advised Chamberlain to meet with these groups, who gathered over one million signatures for "A New Peace Conference" because "it might help to widen the gulf between them and the militant sanctionist, anti-Munich" section of the peace movement.[64]

The government believed its real difficulty lay with the still strong pro-League bloc that continued to push for new pledges in favor of collective security. Yet it also realized that dialogue with the pacifists was tendentious. Even pacifists, despite their initial support, were not satisfied with Munich. Many continued to favor a vaguely defined "third way" between appeasement and war. A long list of prominent personages linked to the

[62] 6 September 1938, FO371/21780/C9443/6490/18, PRO.
[63] Brittain, *Testament; Pax International,* October 1938, p. 1.
[64] Richardson, "New Perspectives on Appeasement," and Beck, "Munich's Lessons Reconsidered," discuss historians' puzzlement over this "change" in opinion; Joseph Ball to Cecil Syers, 1 February 1939, Prem 1/320, PRO.

movement, including bishops of England, heads of other denominations, and heads of prominent colleges and universities, spearheaded a proposal for a "New Peace Conference," which called again for a multilateral solution to European tensions, equal access to raw materials, and steps toward the "emancipation of colonies."[65] This proposal underscored the differing normative claims of peace groups and of the government.

A major dilemma for the argument that the public (and the peace movement) wished to avoid war with Germany at all costs is the fact that pacifist, public and parliamentary approbation of the Munich accord was anxious and short-lived. Michael Foot, in his pseudonymously written denunciation of the "Guilty Men" in the Chamberlain Cabinet he believed responsible for appeasing Hitler, likened the euphoria that greeted Chamberlain's original plan to avoid war by going to Munich to the hysteria of a madman:

> On a hot summer afternoon several hundred years ago a Balkan peasant arose from the stone he was squatting upon and began to dance.
>
> Quickly the villagers ran to the spot. They gaped at the remarkable spectacle of a man twirling and gyrating all by himself in the sunlight. They giggled.
>
> But presently the man's dance became more frantic. His eyes began to stare. Foam drooled from his lips and nostrils.
>
> The peasants watching him began to tap their feet in sympathy. Soon they began to dance too.
>
> They streamed across the countryside in a frenzy, dancing all the way. Wherever they went, others joined the dance.
>
> The dance mania spread all over Europe, from country to country. Women gashed themselves with knives as they capered. Men dashed their heads against walls. When the madness spread across the sea to England, over five hundred deaths were reported as a result of the dancing. The hysteria did not depart from Europe for many months. . . .
>
> At about half past four on a warm autumn afternoon September 28, 1938, an exhibition of hysteria, the result of which was also destined to spread over the whole face of Europe, took place in the British House of Commons.[66]

A great deal of uncertainty and unease underlay the cathartic reception of Chamberlain's plan, and the outpouring of relief on his return proved

---

[65] Joseph Ball to Cecil Syers, 1 February 1939, Prem 1/320, PRO.
[66] Michael Foot ("Cato"), *Guilty Men,* pp. 51–53.

temporary. In the months prior to Munich, the government distributed gas masks throughout the country and broadcast plans to evacuate children from London in the event of war. The September 1938 Munich accord meant, in its most immediate sense, that these preparations could be stopped or at least put on hold. Yet the public remained wary of Hitler and suspicious of Munich. Paul Kennedy dates the British public opinion's "vital change in mood" from "the anger and disgust produced in Britain by news of the Kristallnacht (9 November 1938)" and "Hitler's rabid speeches of late 1938 in which he . . . proclaimed the Munich settlement as a victory for brute force—exactly the opposite of what the prime minister was saying." But Anthony Adamthwaite reaches back further to the year before Munich: "The evidence indicates that in the early months of 1938 a majority may have been opposed to official [appeasement] policy." This led, for Adamthwaite, to successful government control of the press and suppression of anti-appeasement opinion.[67]

Another problematic simplifying assumption in international relations theory is that unrealistic faith in collective security through the League of Nations prevented a stronger line toward dictators, "causing" appeasement. Yet it was that component of the peace movement which was most uncritical of the League and of its alleged ability to control conflict that was also the most unequivocally opposed to the Munich accords. The LNU bitterly opposed conceding the Sudetenland to Germany, issuing the following statement on September 23, before the final accord was reached:

> The League of Nations Union has repeatedly during the past months urged His Majesty's Government to ensure peace by accompanying its efforts at appeasement with an unequivocal declaration that it would oppose any attempt to settle the Sudeten problem by force. The Government has chosen a different procedure. By hesitation when firmness was required, and by last minute concessions to threats they have brought discredit upon this country, without making peace secure.[68]

Moreover, Britain's insistence on fulfilling the twin goals of controlling its far-flung Empire while maintaining peace in Europe represented an ex-

---

[67] Kennedy, "'Appeasement,'" p. 147; see also Roger Eatwell, "Munich, Public Opinion, and Popular Front," *Journal of Contemporary History* 6 (1971): 138–39; Anthony Adamthwaite, "The British Government and the Media," *Journal of Contemporary History* 18 (1983): 291–92; see also Richard Cockett, *Twilight of Truth: Chamberlain, Appeasement and the Manipulation of the Press* (London: Weidenfeld & Nicolson, 1989).

[68] LNU-Executive Committee Minutes, Special Meeting, 23 September 1938, BLPES.

tremely significant complicating factor for the argument that pacifism or faith in collective security caused appeasement. Those in the peace movement's pacifist and left wings who did not voice strong opposition to Munich believed that the British Empire had backed itself into a corner trying to enact a double standard: Britain not only refused to give up its colonial possessions, but also used brutal methods itself to control rebellion in Egypt and India. Hence Vera Brittain's caustic words:

> In England we are always completely innocent of aggressive intentions. When we decide, with expressions of profound reluctance, to embark upon a heavy armaments programme, it is never in order to outpace an ambitious neighbor, nor even to hold those vast possessions which we acquired so comfortably when there was no League of Nations or organized pacifist opinion to interfere in our military adventures. With impeccable altruism we build tanks and bombing aeroplanes to defend the cause of peace.[69]

Britain thus had to rectify its own behavior to convince Germany (and pacifists) that the British position on German territorial conquest was both serious and defensible. If realism is prudence, then either a stronger policy of collective security (according to the LNU's logic) or a willingness to let go of imperial bonds (according to pacifists and the Left) might well have been the most pragmatic option for British policy.

Historical scholarship has recast the problem of British rearmament in terms of similar difficult choices. Any decision to rearm brought with it a host of related dilemmas: which branch of the service to prioritize (during the interwar period, governments consciously gave preference to the air force over the army and the navy), which area(s) of the world to defend (China, India, Egypt, France, Central Europe) and against whom (insurrection by colonial peoples, Japan, Italy, Germany, the Soviet Union). The depression, compounded by the business sector's insistence on laissez-faire economic policies, complicated the government's difficulties in answering these questions, restricting the amount and control of available resources even further. From this vantage point, the domestic economic situation emptied of any real meaning the debate over whether Britain could have rearmed at a pace sufficient to keep German aggression at bay. As Paul Kennedy pointed out, "Britain could either possess adequate de-

---

[69] Vera Brittain, "World Review of Reviews," May 1937, repr. in *Testament*, p. 223.

fences and be bankrupt, or remain solvent yet strategically vulnerable, *but she could not achieve her aims in both areas.*"[70]

This narrative presents an interpretation of peace movement claims and demands in the 1930s that differs considerably from the traditional view. The problem in the interwar period was not that "realist" policy was forsaken for "idealist" or "utopian" dreams. Rather, it is unclear that any policy line articulated during the period was "realistic" in the sense of being both practicable and likely to have the desired effects.

A working collective security system was indeed probably too much to hope for in either the 1920s or the 1930s. Likewise it might have been unrealistic to suppose that British decision makers would dismember the Empire either to streamline defense requirements or to support norms of social, political, and economic equality. But if these solutions were "utopian," so was the "realpolitik" solution of early, "sufficient" rearmament to keep German aggression at bay. Likewise, in the late 1930s the attempt to "balance" Italy against Germany was based on a utopian myth. Although the realist view is that Britain could not afford to alienate Italy because its forces were inadequate to defend the Mediterranean, the situation would have been different if policing the Empire had not occupied the bulk of the British military. Moreover, if this was the only pragmatic option from 1936 to 1938, it represents a major instance in which realism failed.

The temptation to resort to a purported "realistic" appraisal of the interwar situation is thus unsatisfactory. Competing claims existed about each of these "solutions" to conflict, and these claims were constructed and deconstructed during the interwar period in a great competition for normative legitimacy. The peace movement was an active participant in this process, promoting equality of status, restraints on war, and widespread participation as replacements for arms races and Great Power machinations.

The predominant narrative in international relations results from the fact that one set of claims—that of a constructed "realpolitik"—was labeled legitimate by scholars after World War II. The peace movement's claims in favor of restraints on war, multilateral arbitration, and participation helped little in its short-run attempts to promote equality of status while condemning aggression. But understanding the claims of peace

---

[70] Brian Bond, *British Military Policy between the Two World Wars* (Oxford: Clarendon, 1980), p. 8; Kennedy, "'Appeasement,'" 167. For a cultural interpretation of British military policy, see Elizabeth Kier, *Imagining War: French and British Military Doctrine between the Wars* (Princeton: Princeton University Press, 1997).

groups should affect our interpretation of the interwar British peace movement in two ways. First, it complicates notions of idealism and realism to the degree that they become of little use at all. Second, it misses the longer-term struggle for legitimacy of the claims about international relations and the norms of behavior that peace groups attempted to promote. This longer-term struggle became embodied in the conflicting goals and purposes of the United Nations after 1945, examined in Chapter 7.

Reinterpreting the U.S.
Peace Movement in the 1920s

"Now, what are we going to do with the leadership of the world presently when it clearly falls into our hands? And how can we join hands with the English for the highest uses of democracy?" The first half of this quotation, in the traditional realist narrative, expresses the central conundrum for the United States during the interwar period: the problem of how to maintain the belief in an inevitable U.S. "manifest destiny" of world leadership given a profound ambivalence about whether and how to engineer opportunities to attain that status. The second half, however, is equally interesting, because Americans during the interwar period seemed to experience a love–hate relationship with their former colonizers across the Atlantic. The sense of shared principles and destiny peaked in the late 1930s with Clarence Streit's *Union Now,* a book advocating Anglo-American leadership of a federal union of democratic states. The book became a best-seller in 1939 and was reprinted fourteen times in the next two years.[1]

But a general unease with everything "European" (the British were included in this appellation) also permeated the American consciousness during the period, particularly among those who became known as "isolationists." The Big Navy supporters, for example, openly talked of the possibility of war with Britain during the 1920s. Distrust of Britain also reached

[1] Letter from W. H. Page to President Wilson and Colonel House, 23 October 1913, quoted by Sir A. Geddes (British Ambassador to the U.S.) to the Marquess Curzon of Kedleston (British Foreign Secretary), 21 September 1921, CAB 21/218/154143, PRO; Robert Divine, *Second Chance: The Triumph of Internationalism in America during World War II* (New York: Atheneum, 1967), pp. 38–39.

high into official U.S. circles. One British ambassador remarked that U.S. opinion favored "the effective co-operation of the English-speaking peoples," while American diplomats complained of Britons' "almost diabolical cunning." (The British attributed this complaint to their belief that "most of the United States diplomatic failures have occurred in negotiations with Great Britain.")[2]

Because of these two tendencies—one wishing to right the ills of the world and the other suspicious of the peoples in it, not only the British but humanity at large—United States foreign policy has long been labeled dichotomously as either "internationalist" or "isolationist." "Isolationism," that is, withdrawal from world affairs and international responsibilities, marked, in the traditional narrative, the U.S. condition during the interwar period. With U.S. entry into World War II, the United States finally saw the wisdom of "internationalism." In this narrative, internationalism connotes the willingness to take on the responsibility of world leadership. Because this responsibility includes managing instability, the traditional definition of internationalism connotes the willingness to intervene militarily abroad.

But "internationalism" possessed another meaning during the interwar period than it does today. At the very least, the interwar period witnessed a struggle between multiple meanings of "internationalism," each of which vied for legitimacy and dominance. For liberal internationalists, the United States should play according to the rules of international law. Inherent in liberals' view of internationalism was a tension, never completely resolved, between a U.S. role of "first among equals" and participation according to rules that, if enacted, would require the United States to submit to compulsory arbitration and to disarm in a manner more in keeping with a norm of equality of status. For pacifists and radical activists, internationalism meant U.S. participation in world affairs to delegitimize imperialism and balance-of-power politics and to encourage a humanitarian involvement in improving the economic well-being and independence of the world's peoples. In this definition, U.S. participation in international institutions was not to take the form of "management" of either world security or the world political economy. Most important, pacifists and radicals attempted to legitimize a form of internationalism that opposed military intervention abroad.

The U.S. peace movement aspired to work with its British counterpart during the interwar period to realize the agreed-upon elements of an "in-

[2] A. Geddes to the Marquess Curzon of Kedleston, 21 September 1921, CAB 21/218/ 154143, PRO.

ternationalist" vision of political practice. In this vision, norms of universal participation and equality of status underlay mechanisms of conflict resolution. In this aspiration, the peace movement differed from the U.S. government, which saw Britain as both ally and competitor, from the "Union Now" enthusiasts, who envisioned a world order based on Anglo-American *noblesse oblige* (although some gravitated toward this stance), and the U.S. isolationists, whose critique of European balance-of-power politics led to a stance of political and social autarky.

The peace movement, as in Britain, worked to further disarmament, arbitration, and participation. In more embryonic form, peace groups also promoted demands for a more equitable distribution of economic benefits internationally and for attention to humanitarian concerns and human rights. But because the United States had not joined the League of Nations, debates over separate U.S. participation in the World Court and World Disarmament Conference assumed a unique importance, and the significance of U.S. participation in multilateral fora such as the naval disarmament conferences increased.

Moreover, foreign policy in the United States did not hold the privileged position it was accorded in Britain, where, by the end of the nineteenth century, diplomacy had developed into "high politics" distinct from domestic economic and social issues. As the *Detroit Free Press* editorialized in 1928, "There is nothing sacred about foreign policies, any more than there is about the tariff or prohibition or any other matter on which the nation is called to express an opinion."[3] The political culture encouraged a more relaxed attitude to unofficial social group input, opening the way for different voices to be heard on foreign policy. Whereas British officials apparently considered unofficial attempts to influence security policy to pose a serious challenge to the successful conduct of state affairs, U.S. officials were less in the habit of restricting information and access. The reaction of U.S. journalists to a press conference given in 1924 by Austen Chamberlain, then British foreign secretary, illustrates the point:

Chamberlain held an amusing official interview with the American correspondents the other day. He wasn't to be quoted, and of course he said next to nothing not already covered. . . . He started out by saying that MacDonald had created this precedent . . . that he was very sorry and would on no account have seen any journalists except that he didn't like to break a Foreign Office precedent even though a new one. He nearly

[3] 14 September 1928, reprinted in "Digest of American Editorial Comment," compiled by the League of Nations Non-Partisan Association, 811.43, League of Nations Non-Partisan Association file, RG59.

fainted when someone asked him if he would see the American correspondents regularly.[4]

This more relaxed attitude did not, however, automatically give the peace
movement a privileged position in U.S. politics. Peace group claims, once
again, competed not only with those of U.S. government officials, but also
with those of the countermovement that promoted a Big Navy and an au-
tarkic, unilateralist U.S. stance in the world.

Finally, the U.S. political system was at the root of a major difference
during the interwar period: the constant and often bitter struggle between
the executive and the legislative branches to control foreign policy. The
Senate jealously guarded its power to ratify and abrogate treaties and de-
clare war, and the executive strove to wrest control of the foreign policy-
making process from the hands of Congress. The resulting debates pitted
the peace movement on both sides: successive presidents approved of
peace movement demands during the World Court debates, since U.S.
membership would have mitigated the Senate's power to interpret treaties
and agreements, while Senate isolationists allied with center-pacifist peace
groups to demand controls on executive power, epitomized by the neutrality legislation of the late 1930s.

Despite these differences, the U.S. peace movement, like the British, was
tarred with the brush of appeasement. For the U.S. movement, however,
the primary bogey became isolationism. In the post–World War II era,
especially after the United States solidified its predominance in the bi-
polar world order, the argument persisted that the United States shut itself off from world affairs and responsibilities during the interwar period
because of the machinations of "isolationists" who included major sectors
of the peace movement. This narrative equated interwar peace activism
with isolationism.[5]

Ironically, the traditional narrative in international relations sees the
isolationism of the 1920s, in the form of the U.S. rejection of League of
Nations membership and its consistent refusal to join the World Court, as
proof, if not of outright utopianism, at least of a pervasive and dangerous
*un*realism. Thus adherence to international institutions, labeled idealist in
the British context, becomes a test of realistic policy in the United States
once its alleged Wilsonian origins are forgotten. The Kellogg–Briand Pact

[4] John L. Balderston (*New York World*) to Herbert Bayard Swope and Secretary of State
Hughes, 23 December 1924, 411.3B1/269, RG59.
[5] For a refutation of this view as applied to congressional opponents of involvement in
war, see Robert David Johnson, *The Peace Progressives and American Foreign Relations* (Cambridge: Harvard University Press, 1995).

in this narrative plays a dual role, as a poor second to a more grounded official policy that would reflect recognition of U.S. international responsibilities, and as a utopian panacea promoted by peace groups.

Two alternative interpretations that pose problems for the traditional narrative exist for the U.S. case, but they have not modified significantly the prevailing "realist" dogma. William Appleman Williams argued from the Left that the United States, long a Great Power (and an imperial one) with entrenched and far-flung economic interests and a liberal free-trade ideology, was never in fact isolationist. Taking off from Williams's point of departure, the corporatist view has drawn attention to business and government relationships in driving foreign policy during the period and provides a stronger contemporary challenge to the isolationist narrative.[6] Nevertheless, diplomatic history continues to be criticized for adhering too closely to the prevailing dogma. A second narrative separates interwar liberal internationalists from pacifists and those on the left. In this narrative the "militant internationalists" of the League of Nations Association finally succeeded, after a difficult struggle, in squashing nondiscriminatory neutrality, thereby paving the way for the United States' rational and prudent participation in international affairs.[7]

Yet another narrative takes into account social struggle and debate and best represents the normative contestation of the period. In this narrative the definition of "internationalism" is contested. The U.S. peace movement during the period promoted norms that, in its view, formed the components of a more comprehensive internationalist stance. Liberal internationalists, pacifists, women, radical activists, and religious groups united in promoting three types of norms: placing constraints on states' rights to prepare for and wage war; enabling new forms of international organiza-

---

[6] William A. Williams, "The Legend of Isolationism in the 1920s," *Science and Society* 18 (Winter 1954): 1–20; Michael J. Hogan, "Corporatism," in Michael J. Hogan and Thomas G. Patterson, eds., *Explaining the History of American Foreign Relations* (Cambridge University Press, repr. 1974); Thomas J. McCormick, "Drift or Mastery? A Corporatist Synthesis for American Diplomatic History," *Reviews in American History* 10 (December 1982): 318–30. See also Beth McKillen, "The Corporatist Model, World War I, and the Public Debate over the League of Nations," *Diplomatic History* 15 (Spring 1991): 171–97. Craig Murphy makes an argument along similar lines linking the "businessman's peace movement" to the development of global international organization (*International Organization and Industrial Change: Global Governance since 1950* [New York: Oxford University Press, 1994]).

[7] Bruce Cumings, "'Revising Postrevisionism,' or, the Poverty of Theory in Diplomatic History," *Diplomatic History* 17 (Fall 1993): 539–70; and Elizabeth McKillen, "Historical Contingency and the Peace Progressives," *Diplomatic History* 20 (Winter 1996): 123, n. 5; Robert Accinelli, "Militant Internationalists: The League of Nations Association, the Peace Movement, and U.S. Foreign Policy, 1934–1938," *Diplomatic History* 4 (1980): 19–38; Divine, *Second Chance.*

tion to take collective responsibility for conflict resolution; and demanding rights of participation in decisions regarding war and peace. Their demands remained by and large consistent through the 1920s and 1930s. All peace groups saw themselves as forces favoring and promoting U.S. participation in the world and as fighters against isolationism. Peace groups, in this view, were capable of fostering both noninterventionist and internationalist norms.

NORMATIVE POSSIBILITIES: THE WASHINGTON NAVAL CONFERENCE AND THE FIRST WORLD COURT CAMPAIGN

As in Britain, peace movement efforts in the United States moved from disarmament to arbitration and back. Both represented aspects of the normative goals of placing constraints on state military power and of constructing cooperative forms of conflict resolution. Disarmament and arbitration, especially through the World Court, thus represented mutually reinforcing objectives that emanated from the same underlying assumptions.

In the United States, as in Britain, a terror of the power of newly developed "bombing planes," chemical and poison gases, and submarines fed a widespread demand for disarmament during the interwar period. Given the geographic distance of the United States from the European theater, this fear was somewhat less immediate. But the U.S. public's determination to avoid the evils of the "European situation" combined with the fear of air power to encourage widespread suspicion of armaments. In addition to arms races, this suspicion extended to unregulated armaments manufacture and trade. In the United States, peace groups and much of the public believed World War I to be the outcome not only of secret treaties and arms races, but also of a conspiracy by weapons manufacturers to incite conflict.[8] Disarmament would, according to this logic, diminish the influence of weapons manufacturers as well as prevent future arms races. Peace groups consequently worked to achieve disarmament through campaigns directed at reducing naval spending and countering the "Big Navy" forces, exposing the conspiratorial dealings of armament manufacturers and exporters, and promoting U.S. participation in multilateral and international disarmament conferences. On some occasions the U.S. peace movement helped to initiate multilateral conferences, as in the case of the

---

[8] Frederick Libby, *To End War* (Nyack, N.Y.: Fellowship Publications, 1969); Dorothy Detzer, *Appointment on the Hill* (New York: Holt, 1948).

Washington Naval Conference of 1921–1922; on others they seized on moves by governments or the British peace movement, as in the cases of the Coolidge Naval Conference and the World Disarmament Conference.

The Washington Naval Conference was the product of a convergence of both interests and claims on the part of the U.S. peace movement and the U.S. government. On the part of governments, the conference did not represent a strong desire for disarmament. The Harding administration saw naval negotiations as a way to neutralize Japanese power in the Pacific and end the Anglo-Japanese alliance of 1902; the British hoped to institute controls over the challenges posed by both rivals to their supremacy on the seas, and the Japanese coveted explicit recognition of their status as a great naval power along with an implicit acquiescence in their plans for expansion in the Pacific. Economic considerations also clearly played a role: domestic publics were eager to return to peacetime military budgets.[9]

For peace groups, however, an international naval conference represented the means to further claims that would redefine the terms of two important security debates that took place between 1919 and 1921. These debates concerned first, the choice left by Woodrow Wilson between membership in the League of Nations and building "a navy second to none," and second, the debate over military appropriations.

At the end of his presidency Woodrow Wilson, playing on the opposite poles in societal debates over security, drew rigid boundaries around the security options available to the United States: either the United States would join the League of Nations, thereby ensuring its security through collective mechanisms, or it would rely on self-help and embark on a large-scale naval building program.[10] Peace groups rejected a choice framed in these terms. Despite their agreement on the need for international institutionalized cooperation, peace groups divided over support for the League: many pacifists who had worked with internationalists to develop plans for an international organization refused to endorse the final treaty. Their reservations concerned not the League, internationalism, multilateralism, or institutionalization per se, but rather the issues of the morality and efficacy of sanctions, acceptable standards for genuine

[9] Robert Kaufman, *Arms Control in the Pre-Nuclear Era* (New York: Columbia University Press, 1990); Thomas H. Buckley, *The United States and the Washington Conference, 1921–1922* (Knoxville: University of Tennessee Press, 1970); C. Leonard Hoag, *Preface to Preparedness: The Washington Disarmament Conference and Public Opinion* (Washington, D.C.: American Council on Public Affairs, 1941).

[10] Kaufman, *Arms Control*, pp. 24–26; Charles Chatfield, *For Peace and Justice: Pacifism in America, 1914–1941* (Knoxville: University of Tennessee Press, 1971), p. 147; Buckley, *The U.S. and the Washington Conference*, pp. 7–8.

democratic representation, and the relative weight of sanctions versus the "rule of law" in the final Covenant. Following the Senate's rejection of the Covenant in March of 1920, peace groups revitalized their efforts in favor of U.S. participation in related international fora that did not carry the stigma of Versailles.

The issue of military appropriations was the major focus of armaments debates in the United States during the 1920s. In the transition from the Wilson to the Harding administrations, "Big Navy" supporters pushed their agenda at the highest levels, including through Wilson's Secretary of the Navy, Josephus Daniels. Peace groups rejected unequivocally Wilson's alternative to the League, a navy "second to none," and constantly campaigned for reduced military budgets. But they also refused to be satisfied in 1920 and 1921 with proposals to slash the naval budget almost in half. Even after rejection of Versailles might have rendered "budgetary disarmament" a second-best option, peace groups continued to press for a multilateral solution to the problem of armaments. The peace movement fought against the Big Navy proposals while congressional progressives and peace movement activists attempted to tie specific naval appropriations to an international conference. In both the House and the Senate, disarmament advocates attempted unsuccessfully to obtain a freeze on funds for new construction "until the President sent out invitations for a naval conference."[11]

When Republican Senator William Borah of Idaho first submitted a resolution in December 1920, nine months after the Senate rejected U.S. membership in the League of Nations, urging President Warren Harding to engage in discussions with Britain and Japan to reduce naval building programs by half each year for five years, the peace movement swung into action to promote the idea of a disarmament conference. (Borah, dubbed at various times a progressive, conservative, and isolationist, remains an enigma whose motivations on disarmament and neutrality are still debated by historians. His eccentricity caused many peace activists to deem him unreliable; others, however, actively encouraged his assistance in placing peace concerns on the Congressional agenda.) Individual peace groups immediately began to discuss how to turn the resolution into tangible form. Women's groups took advantage of women's recent enfranchisement by participating in hearings held by the House Committee on Military Affairs and the Committee on Foreign Affairs and formed the Women's Committee for World Disarmament. By March of 1921, peace groups had formed a clearinghouse to coordinate efforts toward "an in-

---

[11] Kaufman, *Arms Control*, pp. 27–29.

ternational conference," and by April they were consulting with Borah to determine when to reintroduce his resolution, which had been attached as an amendment to the failed Naval Appropriation Bill. This turned into the peace movement's first large-scale campaign in the post–World War I era. The Quakers and the Foreign Policy Association formed the nucleus of the campaign, illustrating the early cooperation between the pacifist, left, and liberal internationalist sections of the movement.[12]

President Harding initially favored increases in naval appropriations, although he maintained a thoroughly noncommittal attitude toward proposals for multilateral arms negotiations. The administration then decided not to consider a multilateral conference until after U.S. naval building programs were completed. But the Senate passed a newly submitted Borah amendment to the Naval appropriations bill in May 1921, and during May and June the State Department reported receiving thousands of letters calling for an international disarmament conference;[13] peace movement records indicate the total number of letters, petitions, and telegrams reached six million by the end of the campaign.

At this point the administration began to reformulate its position to take advantage of the growing demand for U.S. participation in a multilateral disarmament conference. Harding initiated private correspondence with the other naval powers in early July to explore the idea of a conference, but still planned to wait to issue formal invitations until after Congress passed the Naval Bill, with the expected addition of the Borah resolution.[14] At the same time, Secretary of State Hughes used public opinion as a lever to compel Britain to drop its insistence on a preliminary conference to discuss "political" questions in the Far East. "If it were now announced that [a] conference on limitation of armament was to be postponed until [the] disposition of Far Eastern problems . . . there would undoubtedly be unpleasant reaction of American opinion and considerable feeling that limitation of armament had been sidetracked." The British gave in to the U.S. demand from the fear that refusal "would invite a suspicion of 'secret diplomacy' and of preferential dealings," and the administration issued formal invitations in August.[15]

But the peace movement's demands were not contained by holding an inclusive conference. Peace groups decided to reorganize the clearing-

---

[12] WILPF-US Section Records, Executive Meeting, 9 April 1921 (Series A,2), SCPC; Chatfield, *For Peace and Justice,* p. 149.

[13] 25 May and 8 June 1921, 500.A4/6, RG59.

[14] Harding correspondence, 8 July 1921, RG59.

[15] Hughes Telegram to U.S. Embassy, London, 13 July 1921, RG59, 500.A4/10; reply from Harvey to Hughes, 15 and 19 July 1921, 500.A4/21; telegram from U.S. Embassy, London, 3 August 1921, quoting lead editorial from London *Chronicle.*

house into a Council for Limitation of Armaments to maintain the commitment to a conference and increase the expectation of successful results. The new umbrella group included the Women's International League for Peace and Freedom (WILPF), League of Women Voters, FOR, Friends, Foreign Policy Association, the National Grange, the National Education Association, the Church Peace Union, the American Farm Bureau Federation, and the International Association of Machinists. The Council's stated purpose was to "unite and make articulate through the member organizations the overwhelming sentiment of the people of the United States in favor of reduction of armaments" and to coordinate member organizations' efforts by suggesting lines of action and facilitating information. The Council agreed to mute temporarily any discussion of the divisive issue of U.S. membership in the League of Nations to concentrate on disarmament.[16] It also called on the administration to appoint a woman and a labor representative as delegates to the Conference to ensure that it would not be taken over by the military.

Secretary of State Hughes developed a counterplan to keep both military personnel and representatives of "any particular class or organization" off the official governmental commission, while creating "an advisory, technical or expert delegation which could assist the real commission and . . . this association would have representatives of the Army and Navy, Labor, finance, women, etc."[17] This represented an early example of the way in which successive U.S. administrations responded, apparently willingly, to components of peace movement demands while placing controls on the overall decision-making process. The U.S. government did not mind including representatives that peace groups favored, but this inclusion guaranteed little in the way of results.

The administration, however, was not able to control the activity or momentum generated by the peace movement. George Wickersham warned Secretary of State Hughes, "there is no doubt that a lot of societies are proposing to camp out in Washington . . . [some] are more clamorous and more intent upon having 'open covenants openly arrived at'."[18] The new Council set up shop two blocks away from the conference proceedings in Washington. Its fora and press releases became the basis of peace group debates and public information, attended and used by journalists as well as peace activists and interested professionals. The Council thus became a

[16] National Council for the Limitation of Armaments, "Bulletin," vol. 1, no. 1, October 11, 1921; NCLA Press Release, 16 October 1921.
[17] Hughes to U.S. Embassy in London, 23 August 1921, 500.A4002/1a, RG59.
[18] Wickersham to Hughes, 10 October 1921, 500.A4./447, RG59.

recognized voice of the U.S. peace movement during and after the Washington Conference.

The conference resulted in a "holiday" on battleship/construction and an agreement to scrap a number of ships. This represented a moderately successful and important beginning for peace groups in the realization of their demands. Nevertheless, as in Britain, peace groups in the United States used the naval treaty to reinforce their demands for further measures of disarmament. The National Council for Prevention of War (NCPW) endorsed "the limitation of naval armaments as proposed by Secretary Hughes as a step" in the direction of promoting peace, but added "that the world-wide limitation of armies is as important as the limitation of navies. . . . We endorse the calling of other conferences following this to carry on what is here begun."[19]

Peace groups also immediately transferred their claims regarding the means to prevent war to the debate over U.S. participation in the Permanent Court of International Justice, known as the World Court. For peace groups, adherence to the Court provided a link between the U.S. and international arbitral machinery and would send a signal of American willingness to be a responsible international actor and participate more broadly in international organization. It was also "inextricably bound up with American relations towards the League of Nations and, in particular, the prospects of eventual membership."[20] Pre–World War I legal internationalists (many American and many Republican) developed the idea of creating an international arbitral court, but "legal" and "liberal" internationalists, women's groups, the churches, and pacifists all united on the need for joining the Court on the grounds that U.S. participation would go far to substitute "law for war in the settlement of international differences." Some groups thus supported U.S. membership in the Court to pave the way for eventual League membership. Other groups, such as the WILPF, which was in the midst of its "New Peace" campaign, supported U.S. membership to strengthen compulsory arbitration while creating a League more attuned to economic disparities and humanitarian needs. WILPF wanted action in eliminating inter-Allied reparations, making "reasonable" German reparations, providing humanitarian relief to former enemy populations in Europe, and ensuring that a future League would incorporate more "democratic" procedures.[21]

[19] NCPW Platform, adopted 29 November 1921, NCPW Minutes, SCPC.

[20] Michael Dunne, "Isolationism of a Kind: Two Generations of World Court Historiography in the United States," *Journal of American Studies* 21 (December 1987): 345.

[21] NCPW Executive Board Minutes, 29 November 1921, SCPC; WILPF file, A., RG59.

All factions of the movement worked actively on pro-Court campaigns from 1922 to the final defeat during the Roosevelt administration in 1935. Peace groups clearly distinguished themselves from isolationists and isolationism on the Court issue, but could never overcome isolationist Senators' determination to block U.S. adherence. William Borah, an ally on disarmament from the time of the Washington Naval Conference, became an early foe on the issue of U.S. participation in League-related institutions, including the World Court. Senate isolationists consistently defeated successive administrations' attempts to secure U.S. adherence with conditions acceptable to its international partners. Jealous of preserving their decision-making prerogative in matters of foreign affairs, isolationist senators successfully argued that the Court would hinder the unfettered pursuit of U.S. security interests.[22]

Thus for the peace movement, naval disarmament and World Court arbitration represented differing facets of the same normative project. The coherence of this project, despite differences of emphasis, remained constant through the debates of the early 1920s.

Successive administrations, however, put forth a normative program that at first diverged but eventually paralleled that of the peace movement, demonstrating the flexibility of interpretations of U.S. interests. The Harding administration in 1921 and 1922 initially waffled on the question of U.S. membership in the World Court, despite the presence of liberal internationalist Charles Evans Hughes as secretary of state. But even Hughes felt that the obstacles preventing Senate ratification—notably the Court's ties to the League—might be insuperable. He met with a delegation from the Federal Council of Churches (FCC) in early May to discuss the Court issue, using the occasion to explain the "difficulties in the way of adherence," although he assured FCC representatives of his "personal sympathy with all that pertains to the establishment of judicial methods for the settlement of international disputes."[23] After Harding and Hughes eventually decided that World Court membership was both possible and in the interest of the Executive Branch, successive administrations no longer questioned U.S. participation.

Peace groups had already agreed that World Court adherence would take precedence over other issues as their major objective after the Washington Naval Conference. The National Council for the Limitation of Armaments, created to demand results from the naval conference, quickly broadened

---

[22] For an early critique, see Denna Frank Fleming, *The United States and the World Court* (New York: Doubleday, 1945).

[23] Hughes to W. H. P. Faunce of Brown University, 4 May 1922, RG59, 500.C114/176.

its issue base to take a position in favor of World Court membership. Its first platform called for "definite steps . . . before this [naval] conference adjourns towards the constitution of world machinery for the maintenance of peace," including "representation on the part of the United States in the existing World Court." The NCPW designed this language to oppose calls to create a new arbitral body separate from the Court. Individual member groups followed through on this platform. Groups also linked the success of the Washington Naval Conference with continued U.S. obligations in world affairs. The Women's Pro-League Council, for example, called for U.S. participation in the Court given that "The success of the Disarmament Conference has revivified the popular realization of our international responsibility." Peace groups thus banded together in May and June of 1922 to organize a "national expression of sentiment" to show President Harding that the public was ready for "the next step" in U.S. participation in world affairs, namely, membership in the Court. Resolutions poured into the offices of both Harding and Hughes from a wide variety of individuals and groups, including the World Alliance for Promoting Friendship through the Churches, the National Council for Limitation of Armament, the National Catholic Welfare Council, and the Carnegie Endowment.[24]

By the fall, Hughes began to assert, "I think a way will be found to enable this Government to give its support to the International Court of Justice" if the United States could participate in the election of judges without becoming a League member. During the winter, Hughes recommended favorable action to Harding, arguing "if you see your way clear to put it before the Senate, it would give you, in my opinion, an impregnable position on this important question . . . and silence a great deal of the criticism that is heard with respect to our attitude toward international cooperation." He also added that, given a Harding speech in which he favored U.S. participation on the condition that the U.S. be allowed to participate in the selection of judges, a move by the administration to secure membership "is generally expected . . . the preponderant opinion in this country has not only favored the policy of judicial settlement of justiciable international disputes through arbitral tribunals specially established, but it has also strongly desired that a permanent court of international justice should be established and maintained." Thus when the White House officially appealed to the Senate on February 24, 1923, requesting its consent to U.S. adherence to the Court Protocol, Harding asserted, "Indeed,

[24] NCPW Executive Board Minutes, 29 November 1921, SCPC; Harriet B. Laidlaw to Hughes, 4 May 1922, RG59, 500.C114. RG59, 500.C114, May and June 1922; NCPW Executive Board Minutes, 6 June 1922, SCPC.

our Nation had a conspicuous place in the advocacy of such an agency of peace and international adjustment, and our deliberate public opinion of to-day is overwhelmingly in favor of our full participation, and the attending obligations of maintenance and the furtherance of its prestige. It is for this reason that I am now asking for the consent of the Senate to our adhesion to the protocol."[25]

From this point on successive U.S. administrations, both Republican and Democratic, maintained a position in favor of U.S. adherence to the Court. They no longer questioned a construction of interests that viewed the country's participation in international judicial machinery as facilitating increased Executive Branch decision-making powers. Soon after Calvin Coolidge's election to office in 1925, for example, both he and his secretary of state Frank Kellogg made public statements in support of U.S. adherence. Coolidge demonstrated his conversion as a true believer in the Court by putting forth a dramatic vision of international justice:

> We cannot barter away our independence or our sovereignty, but we ought to engage in no refinement of logic, no sophistries, and no subterfuges to argue away the undoubted duty of this country by reason of the might of its numbers, the power of its resources, and its position of leadership in the world, actively and comprehensively to signify its approval and to bear its full share of the responsibility of a candid and disinterested attempt at the establishment of a tribunal for the administration of even-handed justice between nation and nation.[26]

Peace groups welcomed the Executive Branch's embrace of World Court membership, even though Coolidge's justifications blending notions of duty and responsibilities with reminders of U.S. might and position left significant room for normative disagreement.

Normative Compromise: Arbitration and Outlawry

Coolidge and Kellogg's support for U.S. adherence tended to become active "particularly when pushed by obvious expressions of public opinion,"

---

[25] Hughes to George G. Wilson, 7 November 1922, RG59, 500.C114/207; Hughes to Harding, 17 February 1923, RG59, 500.C114/225a and 219a; Harding message, 24 February 1923, RG59, 500.C114/219a (also Senate Document No.309, 67th Congress, 4th Session).

[26] L. Ethan Ellis, *Frank B. Kellogg and American Foreign Relations, 1925–1929* (New Brunswick: Rutgers University Press, 1961), p. 226; Fleming, *U.S. and the World Court*, p. 48.

in 1925–1926 and 1928. The NCPW appointed influential activist Laura Puffer Morgan as its World Court strategist in September 1924, and peace groups again organized campaigns in the spring and summer of 1925. The question of "outlawry" of war had by then become tied up with that of international legal arbitration machinery, with activists opposed to or critical of the League promoting outlawry, and peace groups supportive of the League favoring participation in the World Court. Peace movement representatives from both sides met in July 1925 to work out their differences and "secure unity on a large program." Twenty-six groups signed a compromise proposal to submit to the Senate that tied U.S. adherence to the World Court to the concept of outlawry. The proposal called for "the immediate entrance of the United States into the Permanent Court of International Justice on a basis of the Harding-Hughes-Coolidge reservations, with the understanding that if the nations of Europe, within a specified time, do not call an international conference for the purpose of negotiating a general treaty outlawing war as a crime under the law of nations, the United States may in its discretion withdraw its adherence to the Court." Peace groups thus construed their campaign in terms supportive of administration goals. When the Senate once again put Court membership on its legislative calendar, the League of Nations Non-Partisan Association (LNNPA) wrote to Kellogg and Coolidge, "We are trying in every way— through our World Court meetings, Resolutions, organization work, and a quite widespread distribution of literature—to hold up your hands in the matter of the passage of the World Court Resolution on December 17."[27]

The Senate approved Court membership in January 1926. But the vote came with stringent reservations that other League members and the League Council could not accept. These included the stipulation, made with an eye toward preserving the freedom to intervene in Latin America, that the United States retain the right to veto consideration of any issue in which it might have an interest, even if it were not a party to the dispute in question. The League Council thus convened a conference of Court members which accepted three of the Senate's reservations and placed "counter-reservations" on provisions that would place U.S participation in arbitration subject to Senate approval. Peace groups responded by issuing a statement for U.S. consumption that insisted on placing "emphasis on the relative unimportance of technicalities as compared with the issues of war and peace" and pushed for reconsideration by the Senate. Peace

[27] Ellis, *Frank B. Kellog,* p. 231; NCPW Executive Board Minutes, 19 September 1924, SCPC; Denys P. Myers of the World Peace Foundation to Everett Sanders, 13 July 1925, RG59, 500.C114/410; Mrs. James Lees Laidlaw of the LNNPA to Kellogg, 21 October 1925, RG59, 500.C114/423.

groups organized a nationwide petition urging new negotiations and presented it to Coolidge. Peace groups even worked to get nationalist groups on board: the LNNPA devoted considerable resources to developing a cooperative relationship on the issue with the American Legion, and the latter finally agreed to support U.S. adherence.[28] But by early 1928, the peace movement had to put the issue on the back burner because of two more pressing concerns. First, the failure of the Coolidge Naval Conference compelled peace activists to confront renewed sentiment in favor of a Big Navy. Second, French Prime Minister Aristide Briand's proposal for a friendship pact with the United States temporarily reversed the relationship between Court adherence and outlawry: the latter for the first time took precedence.

Peace groups' support for the Geneva Naval Conference emerged as a natural outgrowth of their stance against the Big Navy group and in favor of international participation and multilateral solutions to conflict. Like Washington before it and London after it, the Geneva conference represented for peace groups a second-best option. Peace groups pushed for U.S. participation in various international disarmament fora: the Preparatory Commission for the World Disarmament Conference, a proposal by Ramsay MacDonald for a "second disarmament conference" to address the problem of bombers, chemical weapons, and submarines, or even "any constructive proposition for a conference on the limitation of armaments."[29]

The Coolidge administration in early 1926 agreed to participate in the League's Preparatory Commission, despite the warning by the U.S. ambassador in London, Alanson Houghton, that "the invitation itself is not extended in good faith . . . and I fear the most likely result of participation on our part would be to find ourselves faced sooner or later by an agreement which we either must sign or accept full and public responsibility for failure." Kellogg, in overruling Houghton, replied, "It is quite true we undoubtedly run some risk of being blamed for a failure but it is felt here [in the United States] we would be blamed if we did not cooperate and lend at least our moral support to the preparatory work."[30] The Coolidge administration attempted to walk a tightrope throughout its participation in

[28] NCPW, Executive Board Minutes, 22 October 1926, SCPC; Manley O. Hudson papers (Charles Bauer, Exec. Dir. of the LNNPA, to Manley O. Hudson, 29 March 1926), Box 120/9, Harvard Law Library; Fleming, *U.S. and the World Court*, p. 50.

[29] Seattle Fellowship for Peace Resolution, 26 February 1924; Federal Council of Churches letters, 7 April 1924 and 15 June 1925; both RG59, 500.A12/2; 500.A12/6; 500.A12/64; NCPW Executive Board Minutes, 6 April 1925, SCPC.

[30] Houghton to Kellogg, 22 December 1925, and Kellogg to Houghton, 2 January 1926, RG59, 500.A15/17.

the Preparatory Commission: commit itself to nothing (in particular any short-term League oversight or long-term League verification measures), but take every precaution to escape blame for a breakdown in negotiations. The United States "displayed an almost pathological aversion to enforcement measures under League auspices and a particular phobia against commitment to any form of sanctions, other than those of international good faith, for any agreements which might be arrived at." Yet at the same time the State Department stated that its "cardinal principle" at Geneva was "to avoid any situation in which we could be accused of disrupting the conference."[31] Thus when the Commission inevitably became bogged down in disagreement, Kellogg, in an attempt to push negotiations forward, gave instructions for the U.S. delegation to make a statement chastising the Commission for its lack of progress, reminding delegate Hugh Gibson to "bear in mind also that you are not addressing alone a body of men who are familiar with the whole question but are making a statement which should place clearly before the American people the position of our Delegation." At the same time, Kellogg ordered Gibson to reiterate the U.S. opposition to any "supervision and control of national armaments by an international agency, since it is felt that any limitation agreements must rest primarily upon international good faith and respect for treaties and moreover since it has been shown by the successful operation of the Washington Naval Treaty that such supervision is not necessary."[32] Thus the U.S. administration hoped to get by with platitudinous agreements in disarmament.

By late 1926 the Coolidge administration's strategy at the Preparatory Commission had begun to backfire. The administration's self-imposed constraints on participating in supervision mechanisms and other forms of international control, in addition to the interminable subcommittee debates over technical aspects of armaments, compelled Coolidge to find another forum in which he could lead the charge as peacemaker. Coolidge had mulled over the idea of another naval conference as early as 1924, prompted by congressional resolutions urging multilateral disarmament, and had Kellogg approach the British to gauge their reaction. Although Austen Chamberlain responded favorably to the idea, he was also preoccupied with the Locarno Treaties, for him the seminal achievement of his career. Moreover, immediately following Locarno, European diplomats informed the United States that the feeling abroad was that Europe could

[31] Ellis, *Frank B. Kellogg*, p. 191; memo prepared by Div. of West European Affairs, Department of State, 5 January 1927, RG59, 500.A15A/260.

[32] Gibson to Kellogg, 16 September 1926, RG59, 500.A15/367; also Kellogg to Gibson, 17 September 1926, 500.A15/367.

go it alone: the United States had not participated in Locarno and had rejected the League of Nations, which had increased in strength. Most important, war debt repayments to the United States remained a thorny issue. Consequently, Europeans made it clear that any appearance of U.S. interference in their affairs would not be looked upon kindly. Publicizing plans for a disarmament conference, especially if it were to deal with land armaments, would be construed in such terms.[33]

By 1926, however, Coolidge needed a foreign policy coup for domestic consumption. Administration officials thus began to look for a link between the Preparatory Commission and a naval arms limitation conference: if the former became mired in disagreement, Coolidge could be seen as a peacemaker (and save money) by suggesting the latter. Moreover, the administration wished to keep the discussion of naval armaments separate from negotiations over other types of forces. This stance enabled the United States to remain on the sidelines during negotiations over actual reductions at the Preparatory Commission. The United States consistently argued that because its land armaments (standing armies) had been reduced to "police force" strength (from 4 million men during the war to 118,000 men by 1926), America could offer only moral support in discussions of land force limitations.[34]

The U.S. plan was to negotiate in good faith at the Preparatory Commission until it became obvious that the Commission could not deliver immediate results. As the Assistant Secretary of State wrote to Kellog: "If we go in wholeheartedly to support the present effort to extend the principle of the Washington Treaty to non-signatory powers and the present efforts should prove abortive, we would then be in a far more advantageous position to urge the calling of a supplementary conference at Washington." When President Coolidge proposed a second naval conference in the spring of 1927, peace groups used the occasion to continue their "educational work" in favor of disarmament.[35]

Coolidge did not obtain his hoped-for public relations coup through naval negotiations. The brief 1927 Geneva conference, racked by controversy and rigid negotiating positions, brought to the fore an intransi-

[33] Memo of conversation between Austen Chamberlain and Frank Kellogg, 11 February 1925, RG59, 500.A12/38; Houghton to Kellogg, Parts One and Two, 24 October 1925, RG59, 500.A12/71; Ellis, *U.S. and the World Court*, p. 159.

[34] On Coolidge as a peacemaker, see Brian McKercher, *Esme Howard: A Diplomatic Biography* (Cambridge: Cambridge University Press, 1989), p. 303. On the U.S. position, see dispatch from State Department to the American Embassy, Paris, 20 April 1926, RG59, 500.A15/221a; Report to Kellogg from Gibson in Geneva, 10 June 1926, 500.A15/328.

[35] Assistant Secretary of State to Kellogg, 1 February 1926, RG59, 500.A15/238; NCPW Executive Board Minutes, 20 April 1927.

geance on arms reductions that peace groups began to trace to links between military authorities and armaments manufacturers.[36] This suspicion
fueled increasingly vocal demands to control arms manufacture and trade
in the 1930s.

After the Coolidge Conference's failure, peace groups in the United
States used Aristide Briand's initiative for a reformulated arbitration treaty
to promote outlawry and the World Court. Peace groups had begun to
debate the idea of outlawing war in 1922. Salmon O. Levinson, the Chicago lawyer who first articulated "outlawry," as it became known, as a plan
to codify international law in such a way as to make war illegal, first announced his plan during the Washington naval negotiations. Levinson
peddled the idea to peace groups, other "private voluntary organizations,"
government officials, and delegates to the Washington Conference. He
succeeded in gaining several adherents who were also peace movement
leaders, including the Reverend John Haynes Holmes of the Fellowship of
Reconciliation (FOR), John Dewey, and Charles Clayton Morrison, editor
of the *Christian Century*. Women's organizations also took up the idea early
on: the NCPW Press Department reported the "unanimity of action" on
the part of women's groups to pursue the question of outlawing war.[37]

Peace groups' conceptions of outlawry differed in important ways from
that of Levinson. Levinson was not a League of Nations supporter. His
plan circumvented any U.S. commitment to international institutions and
made the League superfluous. But peace groups interested in the idea of
outlawry placed it in the context of broader international responsibilities.
They linked it to a wide variety of proposals strengthening international
collaboration, including the Geneva Protocol championed by the British
peace movement. The NCPW, for example, decided to study "all proposals for the Outlawry of War, including the so-called Geneva Protocol."[38]

Moreover, for the bulk of the peace movement the concept of outlawry
took a back seat to organizing support for U.S. membership in the World
Court. When in 1927 the concepts of outlawry and "renunciation of war"
became conceptually intertwined, peace forces had seen a number of their
demands scuttled or postponed. The 1925–1926 World Court debate had
ended in defeat for peace groups because of the rigid Senate reservations
and the Coolidge administration's subsequent refusal to negotiate with the
League of Nations. On disarmament, the French and Italians had refused

[36] Detzer, *Appointment on the Hill;* Wiltz, *In Search of Peace.*
[37] Robert H. Ferrell, *Peace in Their Time: The Origins of the Kellogg–Briand Pact* (New
Haven: Yale University Press, 1952), pp. 31–32; NCPW Executive Board Minutes, 16 May
1922, SCPC.
[38] NCPW Executive Board Minutes, 6 April 1925, SCPC.

to take part in the Geneva Naval Conference, which in any case produced no substantive results except for an increase in animosity between the United States and Britain and a rise in Big Navy sentiment in the United States.[39]

In was in the midst of this atmosphere that James T. Shotwell, a leading liberal internationalist, obtained an interview with French Foreign Minister Aristide Briand. Shotwell suggested to Briand in March of 1927 that Briand propose renouncing war as an instrument of policy with the United States as a way of smoothing over France's recent refusal to participate in the Geneva Conference and to relieve tensions over war debt repayments. The proposal to renounce war would replace the soon-to-expire Root arbitration treaty between the United States and France. Briand agreed to write a letter "to the American people" in April and allowed Shotwell to write the draft.[40]

Peace groups jumped at the opportunity to recast their demands for arbitration and disarmament while realizing what they deemed to be a positive gesture in the midst of worsening relations between the United States and European states. In the process of incorporating the "renunciation of war" into their claims, peace groups agreed to reverse their hierarchy of demands. Levinson's allies in the peace movement had agreed to subvert outlawry to the World Court campaign in 1925–1926; now peace groups decided to push outlawry as a step toward realizing their objective of instituting arbitration through the World Court.

Peace groups thus placed their responses to Briand's letter in the context of U.S. participation in international arbitration machinery, focusing once again on relationships with the World Court. The American Foundation and the WILPF each backed slightly different plans, in each case providing for judicial settlement of disputes through existing World Court mechanisms. The NCPW worked with other groups, including the FCC, to promote public discussion and debate. During the summer of 1927 the NCPW outlined a national campaign to promote the Kantian idea of a series of interlocking bilateral treaties, eventually encompassing all states, to renounce war as "national policy."[41]

For the U.S. State Department, Briand's proposal had to be dealt with carefully. J. Theodore Marriner, chief of the Division of Western European

---

[39] Ellis, *U.S. and the World Court*, p. 198.

[40] Ferrell, *Peace in Their Time*, pp. 68–72; Ellis, *U.S. and the World Court;* James T. Shotwell, *War as an Instrument of National Policy and Its Renunciation in the Pact of Paris* (New York: Harcourt, Brace, 1929).

[41] WILPF, *Pax International*, December 1927; Ferrell, *Peace in Their Time*, pp. 87–88, n. 12; Shotwell, *War and National Policy*, pp. 53; NCPW Executive Board Minutes, 18 May 1927; 15 June 1927; 21 September 1927, SCPC.

Affairs, wrote a June 24 memo in which he argued that any pretense in the Briand initiative toward a "negative alliance" or an evasion of the debt settlement question must be blunted. At the same time, Marriner implied that the United States would willingly negotiate an agreement that would not give France special privileges, arguing that "if any step further . . . were required, it should be in the form of a universal undertaking not to resort to war, to which the United States would at any time be most happy to become a party."[42]

Briand sent his formal treaty proposal to the U.S. government on June 20, 1927, after Kellogg and Coolidge complained that his public appeals were contrived to bypass normal diplomatic channels. In developing a response, Kellogg and Senator Borah, a longtime advocate of outlawry but a skeptic initially concerning the Briand proposals, debated plans developed by liberal internationalists, including a draft treaty by Shotwell and the American Foundation plan to use World Court mechanisms. In the fall of 1927 President Coolidge began to send conflicting signals: he indicated he would soon engage in discussions of Briand's proposed treaty, all the while asserting he had no faith in outlawry and thought the concept was very likely unconstitutional.[43]

During this time the peace movement and the administration engaged in a struggle to control and legitimize the concept of war renunciation. While the State Department remained passive, peace groups met throughout the summer and fall of 1927 to coordinate their efforts in favor of a war renunciation treaty and demand an official U.S. reply to the French. The NCPW, women's groups and internationalists announced their displeasure at the administration's stalling tactics. The NCPW asked why the State Department was "silent on this truly great proposal," Jane Addams led a December 10 delegation to the White House to present Coolidge with a petition signed by 30,000 supporters, and liberal internationalists met with Senator Borah and State Department officials throughout the fall. Kellogg, furious at "pacifists" for what he perceived as their attempts to embarrass the State Department, and Coolidge, who had resisted Briand's appeals to public opinion, began tentative negotiations with French Ambassador Paul Claudel in November. Robert Ferrell concludes that Kellogg and Coolidge saw "that the United States Government would have to do something to mollify the American peace movement," Ethan Ellis pointed out that "Kellogg was particularly sensitive to the possibility

[42] Quoted in Ferrell, *Peace in Their Time*, pp. 106–7. Ellis, *U.S. and the World Court*, pp. 196–97, states that Marriner's memo is "the first indication of a possible multilateral approach to be found in the official documents."

[43] Ellis, *Frank B. Kellogg*, p. 197; Ferrell, *Peace in Their Time*, pp. 117–18, 129.

of adverse public opinion," and Kellogg himself admitted in a draft answer to Briand "that there is a tremendous demand in this country and probably in foreign countries for the so-called outlawry of war." Kellogg and Coolidge sent a counterproposal to the French at the end of December 1927, preempting Senator Borah's intention to introduce an outlawry measure in the Senate that would provide a new focus for public demands for action. WILPF made a point of stressing that its December 10 meeting at the White House "brought the first definite word from Mr. Coolidge that the Briand proposal would be given consideration."[44]

The administration's counteroffer embodied a multilateral treaty, but it did not include the World Court as arbitral machinery; indeed, it was careful not to specify any institutional machinery at all to ensure compliance. The peace movement thus had to make a decision, once again, whether or not to expend its efforts on a less-than-ideal proposal. Supporting the Kellogg pact required compromise for peace groups and engendered serious misgivings. One West Coast NCPW activist argued that Kellogg, in making his proposals, was really trying "to put Briand in a hole and attack the League." Nevertheless, he believed the peace movement should push forward with a national demonstration in favor of the Kellogg Outlawry of War proposals, in part to call the State Department's bluff. "If the Department of State is sincere it seems to me it would be comparatively easy to line the nation almost solidly behind it." Similarly, Denys Myers of the World Peace Foundation, in congratulating Kellogg on the conclusion of the Pact the following summer, noted the peace movement's qualified acceptance: "It may be of interest to you to have the impressions of one who comes in contact with the public in respect to the anti-war treaty. . . . Curiously, the peace people are inclined to be the most skeptical and likely to depreciate the value of the treaty. . . . The critical attitude is largely based upon the assumption that the treaty is a declaration of a moral precept and has only the value of a pledge to be good without specifications as to how to accomplish the end."[45]

The misgivings of Pacifists about the Pact increased when Secretary of State Kellogg stated his support for a new naval bill in late 1928. Kellogg's move brought the Pact the support of nationalist organizations such as the American Legion and the Daughters of the American Revolution (DAR),

---

[44] NCPW Executive Board Minutes, 19 October, 16 November, and 15 December 1927; Ferrell, *Peace in Their Time*, pp. 114–19, 80–81; 129, 141; Ellis, *Frank B. Kellogg*, p. 279, n. 4; *Pax International*, December 1927.

[45] NCPW Executive Board Minutes, 18 April 1928, letter from Dr. J. J. Hansaker, Chair of Oregon Council for Prevention of War, SCPC; Myers to Kellogg, 28 July 1928, RG59, 7110012, Antiwar/128.

but it revealed significant normative divergence between the peace movement and the government. Dorothy Detzer of the WILPF, for example, lamented, "it seems to me . . . that we had better lose the Kellogg Pact at this time if the Navy Bill is to go through and if the Pact is to be filled with reservations." Moreover, Detzer resurrected long-standing attempts to delegitimize U.S. interventions in Latin America, asserting it was "almost impossible for the Peace Movement to go in with great and wide enthusiasm when Kellogg continues his policy in Nicaragua and says that it should not at all interfere with a big Navy." Religious left-pacifists John Nevin Sayre and Kirby Page expressed the general peace movement consensus, however. These two "tepidly accepted the peace pact as a suitable framework for European-American relations, but vowed to oppose Washington's 'gun-boat imperialism' elsewhere." Denys Myers summed up the conflicting social rationales for the Pact in writing to Kellogg, "Many other people seem to think it is excellent because it is something the United States has done. Another group seem to favor it on the ground that it was about time the United States did something constructive."[46] Thus the peace movement at large believed the Kellogg–Briand Pact would serve to delegitimize unilateral military action but remained wary of the government's ability to circumscribe its normative reach.

The U.S. peace movement maintained a relatively consistent normative agenda through the 1920s. This agenda consisted of promoting multinational disarmament and arbitration, while remaining wary of the possibilities for subverting existing multilateral mechanisms for militarist and interventionist purposes, particularly in Latin America. The U.S. peace movement also demonstrated its status as a participant in security debates, although it shared this status with the right-wing countermovement, and exhibited a willingness to compromise on policy.

This willingness to compromise came to a head during the debate on the Pact of Paris. Despite its misgivings, the peace movement decided to publicize and legitimize the negotiations and the resulting Pact, believing they would lead to further U.S. participation in internationalist solutions to conflict. James Shotwell argued that the Treaty was "a point of departure"; others emphasized that the World Court had now become more

---

[46] State Department, 711.0012, Anti-War/168, National Archives; Detzer quoted in Charles DeBenedetti, *Origins of the Modern American Peace Movement, 1915–1978* (Millwood, N.Y.: KTO Press, 1978), pp. 229–30; and *Peace Reform in American History* (Bloomington: Indiana University Press, 1980), p. 121. Sayre and Page quote is in DeBenedetti, *Peace Reform*, p. 121. For the Myers quote, see Myers to Kellogg, 28 July 1928, RG59, 7110012, Antiwar/128, National Archives.

necessary than before; all agreed it required follow-up by concrete actions. The NCPW embarked on a "Pact Ratification Campaign," carried out across the country, to send letters and telegrams to Senators urging early ratification without reservations.[47]

Peace movement activists thus treated the Pact as a prelude to more substantive things to come. They played an important role in articulating the meaning of renunciation of war and in engendering support for the negotiations leading to it. But many in the movement, especially pacifists and activists on the left, understood that the Pact would have no meaning if it were not accompanied by a revision of U.S. policy in Latin America and a rejection of naval spending bills. Peace groups also realized that the Pact represented only a beginning—a symbolic commitment that needed to be followed by more concrete understandings and machinery. As Harold Josephson asserts, "most peace advocates, especially those internationalists who sought to bring U.S. policy more in line with the League of Nations and the World Court, had no illusions as to what the pact really meant. It was merely a first step, a framework for making the United States part of the collective responsibility machinery being established in Geneva." During the 1930s, as the major powers were finding existing institutional machinery both wanting and unwanted, liberal internationalists, pacifists, and the U.S. government cited the Kellogg–Briand Pact as the legal foundation that necessitated U.S. participation in international arbitration and disarmament fora—including the World Court, the 1930 London Naval Conference and 1932 World Disarmament Conference, League efforts to end the Italian invasion of Abyssinia, and revision of the League Covenant.[48] The Pact provided justification for normative claims by both the peace movement and the government during the 1930s. Chapter 6 examines these claims.

---

[47] Harold Josephson, "Outlawing War: Internationalism and the Pact of Paris," *Diplomatic History* 3 (1979): 379–80; NCPW Minutes, 21 November 1928, SCPC.
[48] Josephson, "Outlawing War," 378, 381.

The U.S. Peace Movement and Internationalism in the 1930s

In the United States the debate between isolationism and internationalism defines narratives of the 1930s. According to the dominant narrative, if 1920s isolationism was imprudent, the isolationism of the 1930s posed serious hazards to international stability. These hazards began during the World Disarmament Conference of 1932, although the desire to decrease arms spending in the aftermath of the Depression was understandable. Thus the traditional narrative sees President Hoover as forced to pursue arms reductions to trim budgets in the face of economic disaster. In this view, the pursuit of disarmament at the Geneva conference was not necessarily a manifestation of misguided utopianism; rather, it demonstrated how economic necessity can intrude to obstruct the "normal" pursuit of security. Thus, because the Depression is juxtaposed with the World Disarmament Conference, the traditional narrative exempts Hoover's policies from the march toward isolationism in the late 1930s.

The dominant narrative instead dates the "isolationist turn" from the Senate Hearings on the Munitions Industry, which began in 1934 and which more clearly connected with peace movement demands. The Senate hearings on the "merchants of death" diverted attention from the real threats to peace brewing in Europe. By erroneously blaming war on armaments manufacturers, they also encouraged U.S. society to castigate its own rather than focusing on the deeper threats coming from abroad. The claims against the arms trade became the basis for the apex of U.S. isolationism, the Neutrality Acts of 1935–1937. "Undoubtedly, the Munitions Committee's pre-August 1935 activities contributed to a climate favorable to passage of the Neutrality Act. They stimulated pacifism, and pacifism was the mother of the isolationist neutrality laws of 1935–1937."[1] Because of the United States' neutral stance in the late 1930s and hence its failure to rise to the position of world leadership that its economic and military power would predict, the interwar period as a whole represents an aberration for international relations theory that ended only with the forced American entry into World War II and its subsequent willingness to intervene militarily abroad.

However, this narrative misses the social struggle over the meaning of internationalism and lumps peace groups, congressional opponents of disarmament and arbitration, and the right-wing Big Navy supporters together in the isolationist cause. It thus confuses the limits and meaning of both isolationism and internationalism by obscuring the fact that the normative bases of internationalism in the 1920s and 1930s were consistent for peace groups. My alternative interpretation highlights this consistency. In focusing on norms, however, this interpretation also demonstrates that the normative "message" of the pacifist-socialist section of the peace movement became unclear in the late 1930s. This lack of clarity was due not to the position taken over neutrality, but to a temporary and uneasy tactical alliance with the far right to "keep America out of war." In using this slogan, the pacifist-socialist section of the movement played to a norm of U.S. retrenchment rather than a norm of U.S. equal participation. This obtained despite the fact that pacifist groups were at the forefront of pushing the United States toward a more internationalist humanitarianism to help European refugees.

The confusion of the peace movement's normative agenda enabled interventionist components of the movement to gain the upper hand in the struggle over the meaning of internationalism. The resulting identification of internationalism more specifically with military intervention abroad created a definition of the term that grew increasingly potent in the post–World War II period and continues to influence debates over U.S. foreign policy today.

PARITY VERSUS RESTRAINT: THE LONDON NAVAL CONFERENCE AND THE WORLD DISARMAMENT CONFERENCE

Peace groups' limited policy successes during the early 1930s at both the London Naval Conference and the World Disarmament Conference set the stage for the normative battle over internationalism later in the de-

---

[1] John Edward Wiltz, "The Nye Committee Revisited," *Historian* 23 (February 1961): 229.

cade. Movement groups helped to move the U.S. administration from a policy embodying a norm of "parity" at London to one that incorporated elements of the movement's cherished "equality of status" at Geneva. Both policies eventually failed, but peace groups carried on the normative struggle that they embodied throughout the decade in subsequent debates over the arms trade and neutrality.

As in Britain, the prospects for disarmament improved in the United States in the late 1920s and early 1930s. Herbert Hoover's accession to the presidency in 1928 ushered in a new era for disarmament in the United States, much as the 1929 advent of a new Labour government increased the expectations of peace groups in Britain. Hoover, a Quaker, was thought to regard multilateral disarmament as a serious and desirable option for the United States to pursue. When the Republican Party nominated Hoover as its presidential candidate, some peace group organizers found the choice "encouraging," believing Hoover to share the "Quaker outlook"; they also approved of his vice-presidential choice, Senator Curtis, who had opposed naval construction bills.[2]

But the Hoover administration was also faced with the legacy of discredit that had fallen on both the Coolidge administration in the United States and the Baldwin government in Britain for the Geneva Naval Conference's failure and the stalemate in the League Preparatory Commission for disarmament. Moreover, Hoover's vaunted desire for "peace" did not preclude increases in armaments, since he approved a new cruiser construction bill in 1929. Thus the peace movement's claims in favor of substantive disarmament remained an important aspect of its normative agenda during the London Naval Conference and the World Disarmament Conference.

The U.S. peace movement at the close of the 1920s had renewed its campaign against yet another proposed $725 million naval building program. Peace groups were especially concerned that the new naval bill would hamstring any future naval disarmament conferences by depriving the president of the authority to suspend weapons construction even if limitations were agreed upon. Thus peace groups bombarded Congress and the president with letters and telegrams demanding "treaties instead of cruisers."[3] They consequently welcomed President Hoover's decision to participate in new negotiations in 1930 to limit cruisers.

---

[2] Ronald E. Swerczek, "Hugh Gibson and Disarmament: The Diplomacy of Gradualism," in Kenneth Paul Jones, ed., *U.S. Diplomats in Europe, 1919–1941* (Santa Barbara: ABC-Clio, 1981), p.80; Kaufman, *Arms Control in the Pre-Nuclear Era* (New York: Columbia University Press, 1990),p. 113; Chatfield, *For Peace and Justice,* p. 160; NCPW Executive Board Minutes, 15 December 1927, SCPC.

[3] NCPW Executive Board Minutes, 15 December 1927, SCPC.

The London Conference discussions centered on the issue of "parity," but the term represented different normative understandings in Britain and in the United States. British peace groups in London favored parity with the United States on the grounds that British naval superiority was not needed for either imperial or security reasons and that the British government should thus demonstrate its willingness to engage in constructive measures of disarmament to ensure peace. In contrast, in the United States peace groups demanded that the government drop the concept of parity. The U. S. demand for parity had, they argued, contributed to failure at the 1926 Coolidge Naval Conference. Moreover, given that the United States was still second to Britain in naval power, the concept of parity would result in stipulating ceilings on future U.S. naval building programs rather than providing for reductions. An operating norm of parity in the U.S. would do little to hinder Big Navy programs and would do nothing to place constraints on U.S. military might.

The results of the London Conference showed that the objection of peace groups to parity were well founded. Although the major naval powers achieved the limited agreement on cruisers that had eluded them at Geneva, the agreement provided for ceilings on cruisers rather than reductions. Thus after London, the U.S. peace movement, like its British counterpart, stepped up its disarmament demands in preparation for the World Disarmament Conference in Geneva.

In the alternative narrative, the World Disarmament Conference represents an explicit move toward reconstructing security norms in favor of equality of status. It also built on the delegitimization of "offensive" war embodied in the Kellogg–Briand Pact. Moreover, the way in which the Hoover administration moved to revolutionize the Disarmament Conference was "constructed" and "legitimized" in the context of peace movement activities. The Depression, in this narrative, did not "cause" the administration to change course, but it did strengthen the peace movement's claim that the U.S. military building programs were unnecessary. The U.S. peace movement, like the British, continued to focus its demands on abolishing "aggressive" weapons and providing for equality of status in armaments. To further their demands, peace groups set up shop in Geneva in a huge coordinating effort that brought together an international coalition of women's groups, League of Nations societies, and pacifist groups, called the Interorganizational Council.[4] Despite the Depression, peace groups scraped together substantial financial resources to carry out disarmament campaigns transatlantically.

---

[4] Laura Puffer Morgan Papers, League of Nations Archives.

The debate over aggressive weapons illustrates the movement's temporary success on equality of status. The administration initially instructed its delegation in Geneva not to make distinctions between "offensive" and "defensive" armaments in conference negotiations. Hoover's ideas for the conference at first focused on a minor proposal for limiting land armies, a problem of concern to the French that would place no burden of reduction on the already small U.S. forces.[5]

Peace groups put the administration on notice during the conference preparations that they expected substantive results. For example, the Women's International League for Peace and Freedom warned Norman Davis, a U.S. conference delegate, that peace groups would be on guard: "The Women's International League is afraid of only one thing—that very little, or nothing, will be done but petty bargaining. There are thousands of people who will watch the Conference with anxious eyes, waiting for moves of statesmanlike progress. The hopes of thinking people are bound up in having definite, forward action taken in Geneva."[6] Moreover, the peace movement also demanded that the Hoover administration take the lead in proposing substantive reductions. Peace groups argued in terms of ethical necessity. They did not wish to reinforce the notion of a U.S. moral right to leadership, but rather attempted to push the United States to use its clout to ensure that "constructive" proposals would be taken seriously at the Conference.

For the diplomats on the U.S. delegation, the demands of peace groups caused frustration. Hugh Gibson, who served simultaneously as U.S. ambassador to Belgium, admitted "a certain impatience with the assumption that the leadership and even the ideas which are to lead to agreement in Europe must be supplied by the United States."[7] But delegates, including Norman Davis, a diplomat and member (although inactive) of the League of Nations Association (LNA, previously LNNPA) and the World Alliance for International Friendship through the Churches, and Mary E. Woolley, professor at Mount Holyoke College and a member of several women's peace organizations, were in greater sympathy and frequent contact with the Geneva representatives of U.S. groups. The U.S. delegation to the conference eventually proposed plans that would result in the Hoover proposals of April and June 1932.

[5] Hugh Gibson to Secretary of State Stimson, 26 March 1932. Norman Davis papers, Box 20, Library of Congress.
[6] Emily Cooper Johnson to Norman Davis, 21 January 1932, Norman Davis papers, Box 18, Library of Congress.
[7] Hugh Gibson to Secretary of State Stimson, 26 March 1932. Norman Davis papers, Box 20, Library of Congress.

In March 1932, a month after the conference opened, the U.S. delegation proposed to Washington "a new conception of security . . . a simple
and comprehensive plan for the work of the Conference unless it is to peter out. . . . Our proposal may sound paradoxical but it is to make armaments non-aggressive, that is to say, to make it impossible for them to take
the offensive with any assurance of success." The way to accmplish this was
to abolish the "types of weapons which make invasion possible, namely,
great mobile guns . . . tanks . . . and bombing planes."[8]

Hoover began to revise his positions. One month later he instructed
delegates to put forth a plan calling for general reduction of all "offensive"
weapons. Peace groups applauded the new stance, but continued to demand both reducing weapons expenditures and specific reductions in the
weapons categories forbidden to Germany. Secretary of State Stimson had
already instructed the U.S. delegation that it could consider budgetary
limitation combined with the "direct" methods of limitation advocated by
Hoover. Stimson's instructions stemmed from the fact that the administration would be blamed if the conference broke down. In June, the president fine-tuned the delegation's suggestion to put forth a surprise comprehensive plan to reduce all "offensive" armaments by one third. These
proposals revolutionized (temporarily) the conference debates. Moreover, they represented a major move toward accepting the program of action of the International Federation of League of Nations Societies, formulated at Budapest and agreed to by the major U.S. and British groups
as a starting point for comprehensive disarmament.[9]

Peace groups in the United States and Britain received the Hoover proposals with great fanfare, but they ultimately came to nought. The British
spent months debating ways to water them down. At the same time, the
delegates and peace groups at the Conference watched with worry as national socialism gained strength in Germany. Most in the peace movement
believed the conference's refusal to grant Germany equality of status in armaments increased the strength of the National Socialists and criticized
their governments for dragging the Conference on without result.

The U.S. peace movement thus adopted a new strategy to promote its
demands for multilateral disarmament along with restraints on state military power. The WILPF procured Senator Gerald P. Nye's agreement to
conduct Senate hearings on the munitions industry. These hearings generated public outrage against weapons manufacturers and encouraged

[8]   Ibid.
[9]   Fred Winkler, "The War Department and Disarmament," 1926–1935, *Historian*, 28, 3
(1966): 444–45. Telegram from Secretary of State to American Delegation, 2 April 1932,
Box 20, Norman Davis papers, Library of Congress; NCPW Executive Board Minutes, Report
of the Education Department, 21 September 1932, SCPC.

initiatives to place controls on weapons exports, initiatives that would form part of the rationale for neutrality legislation. The hearings also generated new momentum for disarmament. This momentum, in turn, was used by the U.S. Interorganizational Council to continue to press its claims in favor of disarmament at Geneva.[10]

Once again, the U.S. delegation presented the administration with a radical proposal to submit a convention to control the manufacture and trade of armaments. Peace activists claimed a measure of success:

> An immediate result of this Senate investigation was the announcement on November 13 by the Secretary of State that the United States was seeking, through the Disarmament conference, the negotiation of a convention to provide effective control of the traffic in and manufacture of arms. The continued pressure of the American peace forces for some effective action by the Disarmament Conference was undoubtedly an influence in the government's determination to accomplish this step in the disarmament program.[11]

President Roosevelt then provided limited additional support for peace movement demands by altering the previous U.S. negotiating position to permit on-site inspection of weapons facilities. Again motivated by the desire to salvage "some tangible achievement from the rubble of the Conference," the Administration, in taking this new position, overrode long-standing objections by the War Department.[12]

The debate on the international arms trade, however, did not go far at the World Disarmament Conference in Geneva, given the increasing number of crises in both Europe and the Far East. In the eyes of the peace movement, these crises made normative and material constraints on arms production and trade both more necessary and more difficult to attain internationally. They thus turned their attention to limiting U.S. participation in this production and trade.

CONSISTENCY AND CONFUSION: THE NEUTRALITY DEBATES

The United States during the interwar period is best remembered for its isolationism, that is, its attempts to seal itself off from European insecuri-

---

[10] NCPW, Executive Council Minutes on Interorganizational Council, 1934.

[11] Florence Brewer Boeckel, draft for "The Peace Movement," American Year Book, 1934, SCPC. Fred Winkler, "Disarmament and Security: The American Policy at Geneva, 1926–1935," North Dakota Quarterly 39 (Autumm 1971): 21–33.

[12] Winkler, "Disarmament and Security," 29–32; also Winkler, "The War Department and Disarmament," 426–46.

ties. Most of the literature covering security issues during the period deals with the isolationist theme. In the traditional narrative, neutrality was a deviant policy, part and parcel of an isolationism that sprang from wrongheaded views of the U.S. position in the world by domestic forces (congressional and societal). More specifically, the isolationism of the late 1930s emanated directly from the 1934 Nye Senate hearings on the munitions industry, which laid the foundation for the Neutrality Acts of 1935–1937.[13] Neutrality, although long practiced by the United States, thus took a turn in the late 1930s that caused it to bear little resemblance to the nation's earlier stance. Neutrality policy, with its refusal to recognize the U.S. obligation to lead the world, had extremely deleterious effects on international politics. Moreover, the negative connotations attached to interwar isolationism and neutrality are reflected in end-of-Cold–War debates over the question of whether or not the United States should withdraw from the military leadership of the world. Opponents of U.S. military withdrawal reject isolationism as a danger and a myth, and even proponents argue in favor of a "neo-isolationism" that attempts to distance itself from the United States stance of the 1920s and 1930s.[14]

But the label "isolationist," like the label "idealist," has proven to be overly elastic and unclear. It is applied to congressional opponents of U.S. participation in international institutions, as well as to societal proponents of those institutions who took an antiwar stance. Thomas McCormick follows the traditional narrative in linking these groups by stating succinctly, "Stimulated by the depression to look inward, Americans were more attracted to the antiwar, anti-intervention movement. Powerfully represented in Congress, these so-called isolationists shaped the neutrality laws of the mid-1930s, designed to avoid American involvement in future European wars."[15]

Yet another narrative, one that distinguishes between the claims and rationales for neutrality provisions, helps us to move away from the inconsistencies of the isolationist/internationalist dichotomy. Many peace

[13] See, for example, the early postwar literature, such as Selig Adler, *The Isolationist Impulse* (New York: Abelord Schuman, 1957); Alexander DeConde, ed., *Isolation and Security* (Durham: University of North Carolina Press, 1957); William L. Langer and S. E. Gleason, *The Challenge to Isolation, 1937–1940* (New York: Council on Foreign Relations, 1952); Manfred Jonas, *Isolationism in America, 1935–1941* (Chicago: Imprint Publications, repr. 1990); Robert E. Osgood, *Ideals and Self-Interest in American Foreign Relations* (Chicago: University of Chicago Press, 1953); Wiltz, "The Nye Committee Revisited."

[14] Robert Divine, *The Illusion of Neutrality* (Chicago: University of Chicago Press, 1962). See Stephen D. Krasner, "Realist Praxis: Neo-Isolationism and Structural Change," *Journal of International Affairs* 43 (Summer–Fall 1989): 143–60.

[15] Thomas J. McCormick, *America's Half Century: United States Foreign Policy in the Cold War* (Baltimore: Johns Hopkins University Press, 1989), p. 37.

groups, especially pacifists and radical activists, promoted neutrality because of a normative distinction between economic and military constraints. In this view, economic embargoes could encourage states to alter aggressive policies, while military sanctions would only worsen bloodshed and instability. These humanitarian arguments were reinforced by the outbreak of war in Spain and China, where bombing resulted in much loss of life and appeared to pose significant obstacles to resolving the conflicts.

These claims were extremely different in character from those of nationalist groups. Nationalists opposed any international responsibilities or participation on the part of the United States and advocated placing security in the hands of U.S. military might. Yet pacifist groups lost control of the meaning of neutrality and internationalism during the 1935–1939 period, partly because of the strength of the nationalist countermovement and its normative identification of neutrality with U.S. isolation from the European arena and because of tactical decisions by pacifists themselves to adopt slogans and alliances that reinforced the nationalists' normative agenda. The resulting normative problems facing pacifists at the outbreak of war left the door open for identifying all neutrality policies with isolationism and internationalism with military intervention and, eventually, U.S. economic hegemony.

The peace movement played an extremely significant role in the neutrality debates, but this role was not paramount. Neutrality, in the end, was a policy "constructed" from the arguments of multiple actors making very different types of claims about world politics and promoting very different normative agendas. The peace movement fostered claims that pushed the neutrality debates in two diametrically opposed ways. The pacifist and left wing of the peace movement helped to bring neutrality to the forefront of the foreign policy agenda in 1935, and consistently argued in favor of comprehensive neutrality after that time. But before 1935, pacifist groups opposed neutrality, and their demands continued to differ considerably from the provisions of the Neutrality Act of 1935. Thus they worked to revise U.S. neutrality laws. Liberal internationalists tried to instigate debate over neutrality revision as early as 1927, when they argued that revision should be based on the responsibilities the U.S. had taken on through the Pact of Paris. Ten years later, liberals played an important role in helping to articulate the Roosevelt administration's attempts to eliminate mandatory neutrality. The differences between the pacifist/left and liberal internationalists on the issue of neutrality were therefore extremely significant. Nevertheless, focusing exclusively on these differences prevents an understanding of the continuing mutual commitment to global international organization. This commitment would have a longer-term bearing on the legitimization of U.S. participation in a reconstituted League after World War II.

The debates over arbitration and disarmament—from the Washington Conference and the Pact of Paris through the World Disarmament Conference and the World Court resolutions—helped to shape the peace movement's claims and demands on neutrality legislation during the mid to late 1920s. In the late 1920s, liberal internationalists took the Kellogg Pact as a point of departure to develop the concept of "the new neutrality," a first step toward a "doctrine of collective responsibility" for the United States. James Shotwell, Manley Hudson, Quincy Wright, and others argued that signing the Pact spelled the end of U.S. neutrality as it traditionally stood. Thus the right to trade with belligerents and the protection of U.S. nationals in their dealings with belligerents, both guaranteed by U.S. neutrality laws, could no longer be justified given the new U.S. obligation not to aid aggression. Although the Pact in its final form did not include Shotwell's hoped-for definition of aggression, he attempted to popularize the idea advanced by David Mitrany in Britain that the United States should pledge not to interfere in League economic sanctions.[16] The main concern of liberal internationalists was to strengthen the League's collective security machinery by prohibiting the United States from hindering European efforts to punish an aggressor through economic sanctions. Accordingly, consciously doing nothing to hinder sanctions meant responding cooperatively to aggression for the United States.

During the early 1930s, Secretary of State Henry Stimson became a powerful ally of liberal internationalists and their interpretation of revised neutrality. Although President Hoover would not agree to an explicit restatement of U.S. neutrality policy, in August 1932 Stimson took the opportunity to make a speech before the Council on Foreign Relations outlining his personal view that the Kellogg Pact "changed the nature of international law" and made traditional neutrality "no longer viable for Pact signatories." Internationalists continued to build on this interpretation of neutrality throughout the early 1930s. President Hoover continued to avoid any formal revision of U.S. neutrality policy, but he and Stimson invoked the Kellogg Pact on a number of occasions, including the Russian-Chinese dispute in Manchuria in 1929, the Sino-Japanese war in the early 1930s, and the Chaco dispute between Bolivia and Paraguay.[17]

---

[16] Divine, *Illusion,* chap. 1; Harold Josephson, "Outlawing War: Internationalism and the Pact of Paris," *Diplomatic History* 3 (1979): 377–90; 78; 381–82.

[17] Resolution on Neutrality, League of Nations Association Convention, 1933, Manley O. Hudson papers, Harvard Law Library; Josephson, "Outlawing War," pp. 383–85.

From the time of the Kellogg Pact negotiations until the mid-1930s, pacifists tended to agree with international legal specialists' interpretation of neutrality and supported efforts to write it into legislation. For example, the American Friends Service Committee, along with the LNNPA and the National Conference on the Cause and Cure of War, supported the original Burton Resolution of December 1927, which would have embargoed armaments exports to aggressor states. Burton provided a solid link between the peace movement and Congress: he had been chair of the U.S. delegation to the 1925 Geneva conference on the arms trade and was also president of the American Peace Society. The Fellowship of Reconciliation and WILPF supported a similar resolution, by Senator Capper, "to make the peace pact effective." This resolution would have authorized the president to embargo weapons to aggressors, with the added provision that trade between U.S. citizens and aggressor states would not be protected.[18]

The U.S. response to the Sino-Japanese conflict in 1931–1932, the disintegration of the World Disarmament Conference in 1934, and the Nye Committee investigations into the munitions industry caused an epiphany on neutrality for many pacifists. During the initial Sino-Japanese conflict, pacifists at first supported more militant action against Japan than did internationalists. James G. MacDonald of the Foreign Policy Association was "shocked and horrified by the willingness of so-called radicals and pacifists to jump into the use of sanctions almost without thinking." The peace movement as a whole carefully watched the series of aggressions against Manchuria in late 1931 and throughout 1932, and soon "Peace advocates were as nearly united as they ever became in favor of cooperation with the League of Nations in vigorous diplomatic sanctions," a stance that precluded strict neutrality on the part of the United States. Laura Puffer Morgan of the National Council on Prevention of War (NCPW), for example, negotiated with Representative Hull on his resolution to make illegal any commercial and financial transactions with a violator of the Pact of Paris (i.e., an aggressor).[19]

Moreover, "nearly every major peace organization in the country went on record" in favor of the Borah resolution of January 1933. That resolution, formulated in consultation with the Hoover administration, gave the president discretion in embargoing armaments to a belligerent, provided that other arms-producing nations cooperated in the effort. Both

---

[18] Divine, *Illusion*, pp. 7–12, 13–15; Josephson, "Outlawing War," pp. 380–82; Chatfield, *For Peace and Justice*, p. 232.

[19] Quotes from Chatfield, *For Peace and Justice*, pp. 224–26; NCPW Executive Board Minutes, 16 December 1931, SCPC.

the FOR and the WILPF, among others, supported the resolution. The Borah resolution passed in the House in April 1933, during the early days of the Roosevelt administration, with the approval of pacifist groups. Even the NCPW supported this resolution over a nondiscriminatory version put forth by Senator Hiram Johnson.[20]

Pacifists, however, soon began to split on the issue of neutrality. They based their reevaluation of neutrality on claims regarding equality of status and humanitarian concerns, as well as on their criticisms of imperialist and liberal economic practices. Some pacifists feared that the League's lack of a firm response to the Sino-Japanese conflict indicated that collective sanctions would merely be applied to further imperial interests on the part of the major powers. Others were concerned that instituting sanctions against Japan would contribute to anti-Japanese racism. Moreover, the World Disarmament Conference's notable lack of achievement convinced many pacifists that if armaments could not be limited, profits from trading them must be reduced. Finally, many in the peace movement claimed that the experience of the impartial weapons embargo against Bolivia and Paraguay in the Chaco dispute, an embargo agreed to by President Roosevelt and twenty-seven other nations, provided evidence that such embargoes could indeed assist in ending hostilities.[21]

Pacifists' claims about these events, abetted by the findings of the Nye Committee, caused them to reformulate their demands on neutrality and to begin to articulate a neutral stance that would prohibit profiteering by the arms manufacturers they termed the "merchants of death." During the mid to late 1930s neutrality thus turned into a watershed issue for the U.S. peace movement. Neutrality became part of the rationale for pacifists and some activists on the Left to place nonintervention equal to or before international participation. In 1936 the NCPW recommended to its member organizations a statement announcing, "We recognize that the principles of individual governments must be directed toward the maintenance of peace before international cooperation can be effective for this purpose." Conversely, nondiscriminatory neutrality became the basis of liberal internationalists' demands that neutrality be scrapped in favor of a more active interventionist stance.[22] This marked the beginning of the process by which activists on the Left and pacifists lost control over the normative meaning of internationalism.

[20] Divine, *Illusion*, pp. 35–37; NCPW Execuitve Board Minutes, 18 November 1932, SCPC; Chatfield, *For Peace and Justice*, pp. 233–234.

[21] Divine, *Illusion*, pp. 61–62; Chatfield, *For Peace and Justice*, pp. 228–29, 234–37.

[22] NCPW Executive Board Minutes, 18 March 1936, SCPC; Robert D. Accinelli, "Militant Internationalists: The League of Nations Association, the Peace Movement, and U.S. Foreign Policy, 1934–38," *Diplomatic History* 4 (1980): 19–38.

Pacifist peace groups played an extremely significant role in promoting a policy of nondiscriminatory neutrality from 1935 to 1937. They first helped to set the agenda for mandatory neutrality legislation passed in late summer 1935. After 1932 the NCPW, through legislative activists Jeannette Rankin and Laura Puffer Morgan, and the WILPF, through Dorothy Detzer, kept watch on both discriminatory (directed against aggressors only) and nondiscriminatory (directed against all parties to a dispute) neutrality proposals as they wended their way through Congress. Simultaneously, they demanded controls on the arms trade by testifying in congressional hearings and, eventually, before the Nye Senate Hearings on Munitions.[23] Pacifists' demands on neutrality had not yet jelled into a firm stance, and they embraced both collective security and strict neutrality proposals.

President Roosevelt, too, reflected this catholic understanding of neutrality. Roosevelt frustrated Cordell Hull and other State Department advisors by approving both Norman Davis's elucidation of neutrality based on cooperation with the League and Hiram Johnson's strict nondiscriminatory neutrality amendment. Davis's proposal, made from Geneva in 1932, originated in a plan by Arthur Henderson to break the deadlock at the World Disarmament Conference by assuring the League of the United States' passive support against aggression. In 1934 and 1935, pacifists recommended that their organizations study both the Davis and nondiscriminatory neutrality proposals. In April 1935 the NCPW formally announced its revised policy on neutrality: "pending the full cooperation of the United States with other nations in establishing positive substitutes for war, measures withholding aid from all belligerents in any conflict will help to protect this country from war, and will act as a deterrent to war."[24]

Once their revised stance on neutrality was articulated, pacifist activists became more assertive in their demands for neutrality. Pacifists urged organizations in the umbrella National Peace Council (NPC) to recommend "strong pressure" on the House Foreign Affairs Committee to report out the Maverick resolution, which mandated an arms embargo on all belligerents and prohibited travel on belligerent ships. Pacifist groups also supported neutrality legislation put forth by Senators Nye and Clark in April 1935. From May through July 1935 peace groups pushed the Roosevelt administration to take action on neutrality. The National Peace

---

[23] NCPW Executive Board Minutes, Legislative Reports of 21 December 1932; 15 February 1933; 19 April 1933; 17 May 1933; 14 June 1933; 20 December 1933; also Divine, *Illusion*, pp. 29, 37.

[24] Divine, *Illusion*, pp. 48–54; NCPW Executive Board Minutes, 19 December 1934 and 24 April 1935; NCPW Executive Board Minutes, 24 April 1935.

Conference held a mass meeting in Carnegie Hall, the Federal Council of Churches (FCC) adopted a resolution in favor of strict neutrality, the NCPW began a radio broadcast series on neutrality, and the WILPF began a telegram and letter campaign to Congress to support the Maverick resolution.[25]

Senator Nye, working with peace groups, rejected the administration's efforts to negotiate a neutrality policy that provided for executive discretion. By August, it had become clear that Congress would enact some type of neutrality legislation. Senator Key Pittman, head of the Foreign Relations Committee, decided in August 1935 to introduce a strict neutrality bill "to placate public opinion." Secretary of State Hull strongly opposed mandatory neutrality, and Assistant Secretary Joseph Green worked diligently, although unsuccessfully, to reshape impartial embargo legislation into a policy more acceptable to the administration. Nevertheless Roosevelt, wanting to keep the support of isolationist senators on domestic legislation, agreed to go along with an impartial embargo after a short Senate filibuster. The first mandatory neutrality legislation, signed August 31, 1935, provided for an obligatory embargo on weapons to all belligerents and created a National Munitions Control Board, headed by the Secretary of State, to supervise and license all weapons shipments. Senators agreed with Roosevelt's wish to limit the embargo to six months (to expire February 29, 1936). They also allowed presidential discretion in defining armaments and naming belligerents.[26]

Pacifist peace groups, however, claimed that they had legitimized a broader-based neutrality law than that signed by the president. The NCPW, for example, maintained that the 1935 Act was "disappointing considering the tremendous sentiment for it in the country. Great pressure should be brought on the President to convince him of this sentiment." Pacifists thus continued to demand controls over loans and raw materials exported to belligerents. They sponsored radio broadcasts, organized petitions and public meetings, and demanded permanent legislation that would enshrine the concept of "impartial neutralism." Pacifists also expanded their base into farm and labor groups. The NCPW, for ex-

[25] NCPW Executive Board Minutes, 5 June 1935; Divine, *Illusion*, pp. 89–90, 94–95.
[26] Wayne S. Cole, "Senator Key Pittman and American Neutrality Policies, 1933–1940," *Mississippi Valley Historical Review*, 46 (March 1960): 644–62; Divine, *Illusion*, pp. 103–8, 110–12; Hull to Roosevelt, 29 August 1935, in Edgar B. Nixon, ed., *Franklin D. Roosevelt and Foreign Affairs*, Vol. II: *March 1934–August 1935* (Cambridge: Harvard University Press, 1969), pp. 630–32; Memorandum on Neutrality by Assistant Secretary of State R. Walton Moore, 27 August 1935, in Nixon, ed., *Franklin D. Roosevelt and Foreign Affairs*, II, pp. 624–28.

ample, succeeded in rallying farm conventions to pass four resolutions demanding "permanent 'mandatory neutrality' legislation." The NCPW also added a labor organizer to its staff in 1935. It claimed moderate success in achieving trade union support, ensuring that labor newsletters were filled with "column after column" of "peace news which we release weekly to the labor press." In 1936 the National Grange, the Farmer's Union, the United Mine Workers, churches, women's groups, and university groups combined with pacifist peace organizations to create the Emergency Peace Campaign (EPC) to promote neutrality as a means to peace.[27]

The traditional narrative on neutrality paints the demands of peace groups in the mid-1930s as a struggle between clear-sighted liberal internationalists and isolationist pacifists determined to keep the United States out of war at all costs.[28] Pacifists, however, despite their work to initiate, push through, and legitimate nondiscriminatory neutrality, drew a distinction between neutrality and isolationism. Some pacifists, most notably Frederick Libby of the NCPW, increasingly promoted staying out of war as a goal in and of itself, but most viewed nonintervention through mandatory neutrality as the only certain means of curbing aggressive sales of weapons and weapons materials. Controlling weapons, they claimed, in turn would assist in containing conflicts, at least in limiting their impact on civilians, and would open the way to address the underlying causes of war. In 1935 pacifist groups assessed mandatory neutrality partially through the lens of the Italo-Abyssinian conflict. Pacifists were clearly alarmed by Italy's aggression and its potential to draw the United States into war, yet justified their support of neutrality during the summer of 1935 as a means of signaling strong support for longer-term international cooperation through the League of Nations. The WILPF, NCPW, and other groups wrote to Roosevelt in late July to request an interview, arguing that the United States, in the midst of hostilities between Italy and Abyssinia, had "not yet taken a single step to revise those policies which have led to war in the past." The groups demanded a League Council meeting to develop a coordinated response, adding:

> We should like to see legislation passed in Congress, and Executive action
> taken immediately, that would place this country squarely behind the po-

[27] NCPW, Legislative Report, Executive Board Minutes, 18 March 1936, SCPC; NCPW Minutes, 21 November 1935, SCPC; Libby, *To End War* (Nyack, N.Y.: Fellowship Publications, 1969); NCPW Executive Board Minutes, 5 October 1937, SCPC; NCPW Executive Board Minutes, 17 June 1936, SCPC.

[28] Accinelli, "Militant Internationalists"; Divine, *Illusion*, and *Second Chance: The Triumph of Internationalism in America during World War II* (New York: Atheneum, 1967).

sition taken by the British Government, and give the League of Nations and the world assurance that the United States not only will not do anything to weaken the efforts of others to prevent war, but will actively assist in curbing the menace of the munitions industries by proclaiming an unequivocal disapproval of any attempts to supply arms and implements of war to nations threatening or precipitating hostilities.[29]

Pacifists pointed to evidence during the fall of 1935 that a stricter neutrality law, including an embargo on raw materials and especially oil, would hurt Italy. Thus pacifists, along with liberal internationalists, supported the Roosevelt administration's decision to encourage a "moral embargo" by U.S. merchants on trade in contraband and raw materials to the belligerents in the Italo-Abyssinian conflict. Pacifists supported the decision as a step toward a more comprehensive embargo of all war materiel, whereas liberal internationalists supported it in the hope that it would turn the tide against Italy. The moral embargo went beyond the provisions of the 1935 Neutrality Act, but its provisions were too weak to have the intended effect, and U.S. oil exports to Italy soared.[30]

Pacifists, in their claims on neutrality, were also careful to distance themselves from nationalist groups. Frederick Libby, while reaffirming his support for strict neutrality, also maintained that, "at the same time we cherish no illusions that efforts to keep out of general war are any substitute for the prevention of war through the World Court and a revised League of Nations." When President Roosevelt issued a statement approving of the legislation on the grounds that it was "an expression of the fixed desire of the Government and the people of the United States to avoid any action which might involve us in war," both pacifist and liberal internationalist groups protested. The FCC attempted to turn around this interpretation by asserting bluntly, "The churches, in supporting neutrality, are not to be understood as endorsing an isolationist policy."[31] Pacifists cooperated with liberal internationalists, many of whom were disappointed by the legislation, in sending a telegram to Roosevelt requesting him to reaffirm the U.S.'s commitment to international cooperation under the Kellogg Pact:

[29] NCPW to Marvin H. McIntyre, Assistant Secretary to the President, 26 July 1935, in Nixon, ed., *Franklin D. Roosevelt and Foreign Affairs,* II, pp. 585–86.

[30] Divine, *Illusion,* pp. 124–34.

[31] Libby quote in Divine, *Illusion,* p. 3. Libby and many pacifists wanted to "revise" the League Covenant to exempt military sanctions; Statement by Roosevelt on Approving Senate Joint Resolution 173, 31 August 1935, in Nixon, ed., *Franklin D. Roosevelt and Foreign Affairs,* II, pp. 621–22; 632–33. FCC quote in Divine, *Illusion,* p. 119.

When the National Peace Conference urged that 'The neutrality policy of the United States should be revised in order that the risk of entanglement in foreign wars may be reduced and in order that the United States may not obstruct the world community in its efforts to maintain peace' it meant the second half of the sentence as sincerely as the first. Because of the general confusion as to the purpose of the neutrality legislation we believe that it would be helpful if you were to . . . make a statement at the time you sign the neutrality bill reaffirming your policy that the United States as a signatory of the Kellogg Pact cannot be indifferent to a violation of a treaty to which it is a party, that the neutrality legislation just passed has the advantage of enabling the government to fulfill its determination to refrain from any action tending to defeat such collective effort which states may make to restore peace and that the United States will continue its policy of conferring and cooperating with the League of Nations and urging respect for the Kellogg Pact to which it is a party.[32]

The WILPF was probably the most consistent pacifist organization in supporting mandatory neutrality because of its claim that weapons supplied to belligerents, no matter what the purpose of conflict, inevitably increased bloodshed and civilian suffering. Because of this claim, Dorothy Detzer regretfully refused a request at the outbreak of the Spanish Civil War to help block the administration from invoking the arms embargo. Detzer expressed shock that the embargo was being applied unnecessarily in the case of civil war, however, and thus attempted unsuccessfully to pressure the Senate to tie an arms embargo against Spain to an arms embargo against "all the secondary supplying countries" assisting General Franco's rebels. Moreover, Detzer and the WILPF protested the administration's continued arms exports to Italy and Germany. The EPC also attempted to link its demands for neutrality to its claims regarding the economic causes of war. The EPC thus conceptualized its work in terms of "cycles." The third cycle of work was to focus on neutrality, the fourth (to take place in April and May of 1937) on a "No Foreign War Crusade," and the fifth (to begin in November 1937) on "International Economic Cooperation."[33]

In the fall and winter of 1936 the National Peace Conference, an umbrella organization in which pacifists and liberal internationalists cooper-

[32] Clark Eichelberger for the NPC to Roosevelt, 27 August 1935, signed by Carrie Chapman Catt, Frederick Libby, Ivan Lee Holt (FCC), Clarence E. Pickett (AFSC), James Shotwell, and others.

[33] Dorothy Detzer, *Appointment on the Hill* (New York: Holt, 1948), pp. 214–19; Report on EPC Steering Committee Meeting held 13 October 1936, NCPW Executive Board Minutes, 14 October 1936, SCPC.

ated, drew up draft legislation that entailed a continuation of the arms embargo plus a mandatory embargo on loans to belligerents and a discretionary ban on raw materials exports. The Roosevelt administration dropped its attempts to eliminate the mandatory arms embargo and began to focus instead on plans to accord greater discretionary power to the president. Congress extended neutrality in February 1936 in legislation that essentially continued the provisions of the 1935 Act with the addition of a prohibition on loans to belligerents. Pacifists, while obtaining financial sanctions in the new legislation, continued to demand an embargo on trade in raw materials, while liberal internationalists continued to demand that restrictions on Presidential authority be removed.[34]

For many pacifist activists, the incomplete nature of neutrality legislation remained a serious problem. Even worse in their eyes was the incorrect normative rationale that continued to be used to popularize the concept of neutrality. The NCPW's West Coast director expressed concern that "There is altogether too much isolationism in the present attitude of mind in America, and not enough of an appreciation of the necessity for international cooperation, if peace is to be attained and maintained. . . . The issue we face is not 'neutrality or war.' The third course is 'cooperation for peace.'" But pacifists, ultimately, were unable to legitimize an interpretation of neutrality that entailed links with international responsibilites for peace. The influence of pacifist groups on neutrality declined after 1937, as did pacifist-liberal internationalist cooperation in the NPC. As Frederick Libby admitted in his memoirs, "We hit the peak of our influence" between 1935 and 1937.[35]

At the same time, liberal internationalists became more aggressive in promoting an alternative discretionary neutrality policy. Their stance increased their influence with the Roosevelt administration, which actively turned to them to help set the agenda for a new policy that would give considerable powers to the president. Between 1936 and 1939, liberal internationalists worked to promote a revised neutrality policy that removed the mandatory arms embargo while incorporating the concept of "cash and carry," originally elucidated by Bernard Baruch to "preserve the profits of neutral trade while minimizing the risk of [U.S.] involvement in a major war." The plan allowed U.S. merchants to sell to belligerents any and all goods not classified as weapons, but did not permit them to be de-

[34] NCPW Executive Board Minutes, 20 January 1936; 18 March 1936; Divine, *Illusion,* pp. 135–36; Wayne Cole, "Senator Key Pittman and American Neutrality Policies, 1933–1940," *Mississippi Valley Historical Review* 46 (March 1960): 644–62, 655; Josephson, "Outlawing War," p. 386.

[35] Libby, *To End War,* chap. 16.

livered on U.S. ships or financed by U.S. banks. The Neutrality Act of 1937 incorporated some of the provisions supported by the liberal internationalists, including "cash and carry." The LNA remained disappointed, however, with the constraints still placed on the president. Pacifists' influence in restraining the administration's actions continued to wane as Roosevelt became bolder in asserting the necessity of changes along the lines preferred by liberal internationalists. The administration refused to invoke neutrality when the Sino-Japanese conflict flared anew in July 1937, a position that angered pacifists, pleased liberal internationalists, and showed the Neutrality Act to be less than mandatory after all since it relied on presidential invocation to take effect. Although the administration and liberal internationalists both supported ignoring the Act to help China resist Japanese aggression, evidence indicates that their actions unintentionally achieved the opposite goal. Nevertheless, Clark Eichelberger and the LNA helped to convince Roosevelt to give a strong endorsement of collective security at this time to demonstrate his intention to steer the country away from a mandatory arms embargo.[36] Roosevelt enunciated this stance in his famous Quarantine speech of October 5, 1937. The speech became renowned not only for indicating a change in policy (although Roosevelt continued to send conflicting signals on his support for collective military action) but also for providing the clearest break to date with the pacifist wing's normative agenda.

After the Munich accord, the LNA, joined by a number of previously "centrist" peace groups, including the World Alliance for International Friendship through the Churches, drew up a plan to authorize the president to impose arms and raw materials embargoes selectively against aggressors while removing them, with congressional approval, against victims of aggression. This plan was subsequently introduced by Senator Elbert Thomas of Utah as Senate Joint Resolution 67. Fourteen liberal internationalist groups, including the LNA and the National Conference on the Cause and Cure of War (NCCCW) led the effort to push it through Congress.[37] Soon thereafter, Roosevelt began to speak explicitly of the need for neutrality revision, and multiple plans were introduced as all sides in the congressional debate jockeyed for position.

Pacifists fought against Roosevelt and the liberal internationalists to retain an arms embargo against all belligerents. Many pacifists joined the Keep America Out of War Congress (KAOWC), spearheaded by socialist leader Norman Thomas to rejuvenate the mandatory neutrality forces.

[36] Divine, *Illusion,* pp. 165–67, 204–6; Accinelli, "Militant Internationalists," 23, 35–38.
[37] Divine, *Illusion,* pp. 239–54.

Thomas, who had supported discretionary neutrality in the Spanish Civil War, was bitterly disappointed by Roosevelt's failure to challenge nondiscriminatory neutrality in that conflict, and turned toward strict neutrality and nonintervention after 1936–1937. But some pacifists began to abandon mandatory neutrality by the fall of 1937, and the NCPW found many of its most active organizers resigning because of Frederick Libby's increasing identification of the group with keeping the country out of war at the expense of international cooperation. Laura Puffer Morgan, probably the most powerful peace group representative in Geneva during the World Disarmament Conference, tendered her resignation from the NCPW in December 1937; a number of other officers, including Mrs. Louis Brandeis, regional organizers, and organizational members, including the American Association of University Women (AAUW), the National Council of Jewish Women, and the National Women's Trade Union League, left or disaffiliated between June 1938 and January 1939. The Munich crisis exacerbated this trend: NCPW field organizer Jesse MacKnight acknowledged the increasing marginalization of the organization when he informed the board, "I cannot minimize the opposition within the ranks of the peace movement to National Council priorities and activities." He also spoke of the difficulty pro-neutrality pacifists were having in legitimizing their rationale for neutrality: "Neutrality is distinctly within the area of complex, misunderstood legislation. There is little to be gained and a great deal of harm to be achieved by continuing to use the word, Neutrality."[38]

Events in Europe thus tended to diminish the power of pacifist adherents of mandatory neutrality and turn around the anti-armaments sentiment that favored neutrality's arms embargo provisions. Pacifist groups began to find their reasons for promoting the policy less reflected in the eyes of the public than those of pro-military nationalists. Immediately after Munich, for example, public opinion supported both mandatory neutrality and President Roosevelt's $300 million proposed increase in military expenditures. This combination of positions adhered closely to the claims of the American Legion but not to those of Frederick Libby, Dorothy Detzer, or Norman Thomas. As the danger of war increased, some pacifists implicitly recognized this fact by deciding to profit from the growing resources of the nationalist groups in a last-ditch attempt to keep the country out of war. In late 1940 a tenuous, uneasy, and short-lived al-

[38] Justus D. Doenecke, "The Keep America out of War Congress, 1938–1941," *Journal of Contemporary History*, 12 (1977): 221–36; James C. Durham, "Norman Thomas as Presidential Conscience," *Presidential Studies Quarterly*, 20 (Summer 1990): 585–87; NCPW Executive Board Minutes, 15 December 1937; 15 June 1938; 19 October 1938; 16 November 1938; 18 January 1939, SCPC.

liance was born between the KAOWC (including the NCPW, WILPF, and several religious groups) and the pro-military America First Committee. The intention of groups in the alliance was to create a division of labor to keep the country out of war: the KAOWC would organize the Left, America First the Right, and the churches their own constituencies. Frederick Libby smoothed over the normative differences in writing at the time, "It seemed highly desirable to try to bridge the gulf that separates the America First Committee with its program of keeping America out of war coupled with 'impregnable defense,' and the Fellowship of Reconciliation and similar groups which couple keeping America out of war with spiritual defense."[39]

Libby provided a weak normative defense for a primarily tactical move. But this move did nothing to help pacifist groups either materially or normatively. While cooperating with one wing of the nationalist movement, pacifists were undercut by another. In early 1938 William Randolph Hearst directed that his papers give "wholehearted support" to President Roosevelt's armaments programs, while working "against the pacifist nuts" who might interfere with administration plans. Moreover, six months before Pearl Harbor, the NCPW admitted its own normative marginalization relative to that of the America First Committee: "It became evident several weeks ago that the pressure for war could be overcome only by blanketing the country with great mass meetings. . . . Since the National Council could not swing this great undertaking but the America First Committee could if convinced of its importance, [the NCPW] devoted some time to the task of making the importance of this campaign realized by the leaders of this relatively wealthy and powerful Committee."[40]

After war broke out in Europe in September 1939, liberal internationalists began a concerted drive to repeal neutrality. The LNA wrote to Roosevelt to offer its support, and the President responded by requesting that Clark Eichelberger organize a campaign to promote repeal among the public and, in effect, delegitimize neutrality. This campaign, waged under the direction of newspaper editor William Allen White, organized local offices in thirty states across the country and issued a series of press releases and radio broadcasts by prominent individuals, including religious leaders, intellectuals, and former statesmen. Support for repeal increased among the public and in Congress. Although the liberal internationalists

---

[39] NCPW Executive Board Minutes, 20 May 1941, SCPC.

[40] Rodney Carlisle, "The Foreign Policy Views of an Isolationist Press Lord: W. R. Hearst and the International Crisis, 1936–41," *Journal of Contemporary History* 9 (July 1974): 223; Langer and Gleason, *Challenge to Isolation*, pp. 36–39. NCPW Executive Board Minutes, 20 May 1941.

eventually "triumphed," Senator Key Pittman, Chair of the Foreign Relations Committee, testified to the divisiveness of the normative differences that remained when he warned in April 1939, "I fear that the divisions of opinion among the leading peace societies in the country will tend to prevent any legislation at all."[41]

A significant component of pacifists' problem in attempting to promote their version of neutrality emanated from their own tactical decisions. The actual work of pacifists on neutrality legislation embodied a reasonably coherent stance in favor of eliminating material advantages to belligerents. This stance was supported by the knowledge that, in most conflicts of the time (the Spanish Civil War, the Italo-Abyssinian conflict, the Sino-Japanese war), strict neutrality would work to the detriment of the aggressor. Moreover, pacifists' programmatic actions demonstrated the linkage they made between neutrality and an internationalist posture. The NCPW's program for 1938, for example, demanded both stronger neutrality legislation and cooperation for "peaceful change."[42] Yet pacifists lost control of the meaning of neutrality and internationalism when their tactics and publicity began to emphasize keeping out of war at the expense of international cooperation. This was best exemplified by the very name "Keep America Out of War Congress" (KAOWC) that pacifists and socialists created to demand stricter neutrality legislation. The cry to keep "America" out of war thus had the effect of providing normative support to isolationism. Pacifists' claims and demands went far beyond an isolationist stance, but the slogans of their late 1930s campaigns at times incorporated an "America first" connotation not in keeping with their program or purpose. More significant, some pacifists' tactical decision to gain public support for neutrality by focusing on the dangers of involvement in war posed a serious challenge to their own normative agenda of promoting U.S. participation in international mechanisms for creating peace and promoting humanitarianism and economic restructuring.

Yet focusing exclusively on the fractures in the peace movement generated by the neutrality debates leads to deceptive conclusions about its normative influence in legitimizing global international organization. Even in 1938, pacifists and liberal internationalists in the peace movement attempted to find common ground in pressing for international cooperation as a means of slowing, if not reversing, the march toward war. The Na-

[41] Clark M. Eichelberger, *Organizing for Peace: A Personal History of the Founding of the United Nations* (New York: Harper & Row, 1977); Divine, *Illusion*, pp. 303–5, 311, 325; Chatfield; *For Peace and Justice*, pp. 318–319.

[42] NCPW Executive Board Minutes, 15 December 1937, SCPC.

tional Peace Conference organized a Campaign for World Economic Co-operation, and the NCPW called for the United States to take the initiative in convening a world conference to establish a "fresh start on international cooperation on a universal basis." Although the idea that such a "fresh start" might be realizable during this time of tension may well appear unrealistic, it was not isolationist. It was also coupled with a campaign for U.S. "neutral mediation" in Europe, a proposal reflected in President Roosevelt's similar offers to European powers.[43]

After Pearl Harbor, the alignment of social groups promoting claims regarding U.S. foreign policy again shifted. America-Firsters then joined liberal internationalists in promoting U.S. military intervention. Many former pacifists, as well as some socialists, also joined in the war effort. Yet although the remaining pacifists and liberal internationalists disagreed on participation in the war, they immediately began to articulate, sometimes separately and sometimes in cooperation, plans for a rejuvenated global international organization to take shape in the postwar world.

---

[43] NCPW Executive Board Minutes, 15 December 1937, 15 November 1939; 19 September 1940; SCPC; William R. Rock, *Chamberlain and Roosevelt: British Foreign Policy and the United States, 1937–1940* (Columbus: Ohio State University Press, 1988); CAB documents, Chamberlain-Roosevelt correspondence, PRO.

Peace Movements and the
Construction of the United Nations

$\mathbf{B}$y the end of the interwar period, traditional wisdom claims, the League of Nations was an utter failure. The discrediting of the League and the fact that the leaders of the major powers during the war demonstrated their preference for a more "realistic" world order based on management by great power concordats might well have vitiated any possibility of global international organization after World War II. Moreover, peace movements, the long-standing societal supporters of the League, had fractured and disintegrated.

Despite their divisions and decline, however, peace movements articulated powerful normative stances during the interwar period that promoted restraints on war, delegitimized "aggressive war" and unchecked military increases, and fostered nonexclusive participation, rights, and responsibilities in international decision making. Both the British and U.S. peace movements provided influential interpretations of security in their own countries throughout the period. Peace groups, however, also played a significant role in legitimizing collective international decision-making leading up to the formative period of the United Nations. These social forces were critical in articulating a vision of post–World War II international organization that did not rely solely on Great Power machinations. The articulation of international organization promoted by this movement departed significantly from the conceptions of "Four Policemen" desired by Franklin Roosevelt and a new Concert of great powers preferred by Winston Churchill, and moved toward a more global organization founded on universalist participatory norms. It also promoted a conception of peace and security that included paying attention to human rights and humanitarian goals. The plans of peace movements for the postwar world were thus based on two types of norms: universal participation in global international organization and peace maintenance, and a "just" postwar order promoting equality of economic opportunity and group and individual rights.

This chapter takes up the question of why states bothered to create what prudential realists consider to be burdensome, multipurpose, universalist international organizations such as the League of Nations and the United Nations, a question that has not been answered adequately.[1] The question is an important one, not because the United Nations has fulfilled its promise of providing an end to "the scourge of war" or because it has succeeded in casting away balance-of-power politics. Although its lofty goals remain unfulfilled, the United Nations has acted as a focal point for struggle over the meaning of security and justice, both nationally and globally. More important, it has enabled unofficial social actors to participate in constructing norms that define the parameters of those debates.

Three loose narratives exist to describe, if not explain, the origins of the United Nations. Each imputes a particular meaning to global international organization that flows logically from the way in which its origins are constructed. International relations theory most often appeals to the "evolutionist" and the "creationist" narratives. The third narrative is the "internationalists triumphant" explanation that was first articulated by historians of internationalism.

The evolutionist narrative stems primarily from work in the field of international organization. It explains the existence of broad-based, universalist international institutions by suggesting an inevitable development from the multilateral arbitration mechanisms of the nineteenth century through the creation of the League of Nations and the United Nations in the twentieth. Followers include Inis Claude, who asserts in his classic treatise on international organization, *Swords into Plowshares:*

> Twentieth-century international organization is very largely the product of the convergence of . . . streams of development which arose in the nineteenth century. . . . Most basically, the nineteenth century contributed a broadening concept of the nature and subject matter of international relations, an evolving sense of the need for joint decisions and actions by states, a growing recognition of the potential usefulness of in-

---

[1] John Gerard Ruggie, "Multilateralism: The Anatomy of an Institution," *International Organization* 46 (Summer 1992): 576–84.

ternational machinery, and an increasingly clear awareness of the problems of achieving effective international organization.[2]

As a result, Claude argues, "It is useful to consider the nineteenth century
as the era of *preparation for* international organization." In the same vein,
Leland Goodrich wrote in 1947 that students of international organization should recognize "that the United Nations is in large measure the result of a continuous evolutionary development extending well into the
past, instead of being the product of new ideas conceived under pressure
of the recent war" and that "those social institutions which have been most
successful in achieving their purposes are those which are the product of
gradual evolutionary development." Goodrich underscores the United
Nation's ties to the League of Nations by asserting: "The student of international organization must recognize the United Nations for what it quite
properly is, a revised League, no doubt improved in some respects, possibly weaker in others, but nonetheless a League, a voluntary association
of nations, carrying on largely in the League tradition and by the League
methods."[3] Similarly, Volker Rittberger outlines a functional analysis of international organization, and historians of internationalist thought point
out that the very notion of a universalist international institution, whether
in the form of world federation or a looser mechanism, was a product of the
gradual interchange over several centuries between the ideas of philoso-
phers and moral theorists, including the Abbé de Saint-Pierre, Rousseau,
and Kant. But the primary focus of the evolutionist narrative is that states
themselves, despite the costs, have seen fit to create institutional mechanisms to restrain their war-making prerogatives.[4] In this narrative, the
meaning and significance of global international organization lie in its role
as potential "peacemaker" between state entities and developer of progressive international law.

The creationist narrative, by contrast, builds on the realist assertion of a
significant break between the interwar and post–World War II periods to
suggest the same type of separation between the League and the United

[2] Inis Claude, *Swords into Plowshares: The Problems and Progress of International Organization*
(New York: Random House, 1956), pp. 40–41.

[3] Ibid.; Leland Goodrich, "From League of Nations to United Nations," in Leland Goodrich and David A. Kay, eds., *International Organization: Politics and Process* (Madison: University of Wisconsin Press, 1973), pp. 4, 21; originally published in *International Organization* 1
(1947).

[4] Volker Rittberger, *Evolution and International Organization* (The Hague: Martinus
Nijhoff, 1973); Christian Lange, *Histoire de la doctrine pacifique* (Paris: Hachette, 1927); Beales,
The History of Peace (New York: Dial, 1931); Dorothy V. Jones, *Code of Peace: Ethics and Security
in the World of the Warlord States* (Chicago: University of Chicago Press, 1991); and Harold
Jacobson, *Networks of Interdependence*, 2d ed. (New York: McGraw-Hill, 1984), pp. 21–28.

Nations. The realist belief in a world of déjà vu does not at first glance square with creationist epistemologies. But post-interwar realist constructions of world politics lean heavily on the belief that states engineered "progress" by creating a more "realistic" world organization. In this scenario, the victorious powers of World War II learned from the interwar period that something "new"—simultaneously authoritative and realistic— had to be invented. This narrative suggests that states created a radically different world order in 1945 out of the allied collaboration during the war, one reflected by the new international organization. It stresses that the new, more "realistic" decision-making power vested in the United Nation's Security Council, with its provision for the Great Power veto, differed qualitatively from the League Council decision-making system; it also emphasizes the desire by the World War II allies not to repeat the mistakes of the League structure.[5] To the degree that this narrative deals with social forces, it focuses on the effects of the war in eradicating U.S. society's isolationism, thereby allowing predictable notions of U.S. "interests" to determine decision making.

In criticizing this narrative, I do not take issue with the contention that U.S. cooperation and leadership in the war effort helped to make the U.S. public more willing to use military force abroad. The State Department's public opinion tracking noted in 1943, for example, that the "basic attitude" on the part of Americans "favoring cooperation with other nations for maintaining future peace" had changed to extend beyond simple collaboration to support the "more explicit reference to the use of force." Yet the creationist narrative implies two corollaries that are questionable if one looks at the interwar contestation over the meaning of internationalism: (1) that isolationism denotes the lack of will to engage in specifically *military* commitments (as opposed to the lack of commitment to international cooperation on issues of economic justice or human rights, or to norms of equal status), and (2) that the debut of U.S. internationalism was due solely to the United States' involvement in war, that is, military engagement. Both corollaries result in the narrow view that internationalism can be manifested only through military commitments abroad.[6]

Some realists take a more mixed view of the meaning of the United Nation's creation. Gordon Craig and Alexander George, along with Hans

[5] F. H. Hinsley, *Power and the Pursuit of Peace* (Cambridge: Cambridge University Press, 1963), pp. 340–41. There are also elements of this perspective in Innis L. Claude, who outlines the reactions against the League in the formulation of the UN Charter *(Swords into Ploughshares: The Problems and Progress of International Organization* [New York: Random House, 1956]).

[6] Office of Public Opinion Studies (OPOS), Schuyler Foster Files, "Public Attitudes on Foreign Policy," July–September 1943, National Archives; Jonas, *Isolationism in America;* Divine, *Second Chance.*

Morgenthau, see the United Nations as a product of vestiges of idealism remaining in social forces at the end of World War II. The former, for example, argue that Roosevelt had to modify his "Four Policemen" proposal for a Concert-style Great Power directorate because of the pressure of public opinion, which was still reluctant for the United States to take on such a strongly managerial role in the world system.[7] This type of realist analysis, however, still assigns a relatively passive role to social forces. In this modified creationist variant, social forces reacted negatively (and, it is assumed, still in an isolationist manner) to the notion of a *machtpolitik* Concert system. For Craig and George, the United Nations in its ultimate form can constitute a positive force in world politics, despite its only partial deference to a system of decision making according to actual power distributions. For Morgenthau, this partial deference is a fatal flaw that dooms the United Nations to less-than-effective status as a player in world affairs. For all realist narratives of origins, however, global international organization reflects the imperative of great power "management" of international affairs and represents, at least in part, the prudential outcome of state bargaining.

The third narrative of the origins of the United Nations can be labeled the "internationalists triumphant" explanation. This narrative stems from the work of historians of internationalism during the 1935–1950 period. It focuses on domestic influences on the development of an internationalist consciousness in the United States. However, this school also zeroes in on an important break during the mid to late 1930s between liberal internationalist elites, on one hand, and more populist pacifist and radical peace groups on the other. According to this narrative, liberal internationalists, comprising pro-League of Nations academics, international law specialists, and other assorted professionals, were ineffective in promoting U.S. membership and leadership in universalist international institutions during the 1920s and early 1930s, when pacifism and isolationism prevailed. Beginning in the late 1930s and continuing throughout the war, however, liberal elites finally triumphed. Better organization and a decline in isolationism enabled the internationalist vision, which included deference to the realities of power politics, to dominate in planning for the post–World War II world order.[8]

---

[7] Gordon Craig and Alexander George, *Force and Statecraft: Diplomatic Problems of Our Time*, 2d ed. (New York: Oxford University Press, 1990). See also Hans Morgenthau, *Politics among Nations*, 6th ed., rev. Kenneth Thompson (New York: McGraw Hill, 1985).

[8] Robert A. Divine, *Second Chance: The Triumph of Internationalism in America during World War II* (New York: Atheneum, 1967); Accinelli, "Militant Internationalists"; see also Clark Eichelberger, *Organizing for Peace* (New York: Harper & Row, 1977).

In variants of both the evolutionist and liberal internationalist schools, Anne-Marie Burley (Slaughter) argues that Franklin Roosevelt's elite liberal "New Deal" architects fashioned UN agencies according to the same "general institutional design" as new domestic institutions. Craig Murphy offers a Gramscian interpretation of the marriage of liberal internationalism and the development of international organizations. And John Ruggie argues that "American exceptionalism," based on "simple geopolitical fact" and manifested in the policies of Woodrow Wilson and Franklin Roosevelt, produced twentieth-century global international organizations.[9] The United Nations in these narratives becomes an instrument of Establishment elites who foster machinery to facilitate the enlightened great power management of international affairs, assisted by liberal international monetary and financial "rules of the game" to ensure economic stability.

None of these narratives can or should be ignored, either in explaining the origins of the United Nations or in analyzing the mutual conditioning between a particular brand of historical interpretation and the development of international relations theory. The evolutionist school, for example, highlights the fact that twentieth-century institutional machinery has in fact evolved in character[10] and hints at the importance social influences played in its creation. Yet in implying that institutional machinery has a life of its own, carrying on despite failed attempts at international cooperation and significant ruptures in peaceful international relations, this school of thought ignores social agency and the necessity of legitimization. The creationist narrative, in contrast, justifiably points to the ways in which great power leaders reproduced the new postwar power distributions in the UN Security Council. Yet this narrative also reproduces the failure of much international relations theory to take sufficient account of the role of social forces and the resulting struggle over norms and legitimacy in which they engage. It thus assumes a too-significant break between pre– and post–World War II international institutions and does not address the question of why a new universalist institution was created at all, instead of the regional alliance system favored by Churchill or the Four Policemen idea articulated by Roosevelt. The internationalists

[9] Anne-Marie Burley (Slaughter), "Regulating the World: Multilateralism, International Law, and the Projection of the New Deal Regulatory State," in John Gerard Ruggie, ed., *Multilateralism Matters* (New York: Columbia University Press, 1993), p. 133; Craig N. Murphy, *International Organization and Industrial Change, Global Governance since 1850* (New York: Oxford University Press, 1994); John Gerard Ruggie, *Winning the Peace: America and World Order in the New Era* (New York: Columbia University Press, 1996), p. 25.

[10] See, for example, Volker Rittberger, *Evolution and International Organization.*

triumphant narrative highlights the split between liberal and pacifist/left/radical social forces in the United States especially, a split that had important implications for U.S. entry into World War II and often came to the fore during the the Cold War. But during World War II itself and during the construction of the United Nations, pacifist, liberal, labor, and other groups brought their work on peace, economic fairness, refugees, and rights to the debate about postwar order and global international organization. They became largely united, despite differing emphases, in their goals for the United Nations, a unity conditioned by their joint activities during the 1920s and 1930s. Both this unity and the differences it encompassed are important for understanding the form and meaning, as well as tensions, embodied in the United Nations. Despite the insightful twists on evolutionist and creationist themes that liberal internationalist narratives provide, they still privilege the role of elites rather than the contestation of social forces in legitimizing the norms that underpinned global international organization.

If social groups were significant players in the legitimization and therefore reconstruction of global international organization, then state interests are neither easily identifiable nor immutable.[11] Yet the significance of social movements in the construction of the United Nations lies just as much in the openings they provided for future normative contestation—in what was suggested yet remained unsettled—as in any partial reconfiguration of state interests.

In the alternative narrative, the agenda-setting and legitimizing roles played by interwar peace movements favored the persistence of particular norms that both influenced states' perceptions of their "interests" in international organization and affected the ongoing construction of the United Nations' goals, functions, and meaning through the present. Pacifist and centrist groups were as important in this process as liberal internationalist elites. Peace movement activities during the 1920s and 1930s represent the first stage of social agency in the construction of the United Nations. The second stage of this construction concerns the planning process initiated by the U.S. Department of State and its relationship with social groups of varying persuasions and with the British government. The third stage incorporates a dialogue and debate between the peace

[11] On this point and criticisms of it, see among others, Ruggie, *Multilateralism Matters;* Audie Klotz, *Norms and International Relations: The Struggle against Apartheid* (Ithaca: Cornell University Press; 1995); Rey Koslowski and Friedrich Kratochwil, Understanding Change in International Politics: The Soviet Empire's Demise and the International System," *International Organization* 48 (Spring 1994): 215–48; and Martha Finnemore, *National Interests in International Society* (Ithaca: Cornell University Press, 1996).

movement and the state (and State Department), beginning with preparations for the Moscow Conference of October 1943 and ending with the San Francisco Conference of April–June 1945. Again, the State Department in the United States, and to a lesser extent the Foreign Office in Britain, were forced to take into account the views of peace groups, although significant normative modifications took place from Dumbarton Oaks to San Francisco. Eventually, after 1945 liberal internationalism did in an important sense "triumph." This, in conjunction with the onslaught of the Cold War, worked to marginalize for a time social groups' participation in UN security debates. Moreover, this conjunction temporarily diminished, beginning in the late 1940s, the influence of the equality of status and humanitarian norms promoted by peace groups.

Foundations of Social Legitimization of the United Nations

Peace groups articulated plans for post–World War II international organization that were largely based on their activities and experiences as well as their perceptions of "lessons learned" during the interwar period. During the 1920s and 1930s, the peace movement worked primarily to institutionalize disarmament and obligatory arbitration mechanisms, but also spent much time and effort on humanitarian issues such as famine relief, minority rights, and the abolition of "traffic in women and children." Peace groups promoted multilateral solutions through the League of Nations for all of these problems, but in several instances also agreed to support multilateral mechanisms external to the League. In the late 1930s, when it became evident that states would no longer resort to the League and that National Socialist policies violated human rights in Germany and Austria, pacifist groups' humanitarianism focused on lifting restrictions on national immigration policies to admit greater numbers of Jewish refugees. These experiences influenced these groups' insistence on human rights provisions in the final UN Charter.

The traditional narrative of the interwar period remembers the 1920s as the heyday of internationalism and faith in the League. Yet the two primary instances of multilateral "success," the Locarno Treaties and the Pact of Paris, represent attempts by states to bypass international organization. Hence realist analysis emphasizes the limitations, if not futility, of universalist international organization by noting that states' actions during the 1920s did not match their rhetoric, which was designed to persuade naïve publics that the treaties in question did indeed support international problem-solving machinery. The crises of the 1930s, according to the traditional narrative, obviated any need for even rhetorical adherence to arbitration and disarmament under the League, and reinforced the necessity of balance-of-power politics that was practiced during World War II.

An alternative narrative acknowledges that states maneuvered to avoid the responsibilities that might have been incurred by using League mechanisms. But it also highlights officials' knowledge that arranging security through traditional methods, including alliances and secret pacts, had become illegitimate. As a result, although governments attempted to subvert the use of international institutions where it did not suit them, they had to cover their actions by creating new external multilateral mechanisms. Peace groups in turn often acquiesced in second-best options that bypassed the League, but did so as temporary measures in ways that manifested their willingness to be "realistic." Both the arguments used by governments in favor of their decisions to support multilateral treaties and negotiations and those of peace groups' continuing demands for international arbitration, disarmament, and participation, strengthened the normative legitimacy of global international organization while weakening that of the "old diplomacy."

Examples of this process during the 1920s include, in addition to the Locarno Treaties and the Pact of Paris, the drawn-out efforts of the Preparatory Commission for the Disarmament Conference. E. H. Carr and Arnold Wolfers were correct in pointing out that the Locarno Treaties bypassed and thereby weakened the League of Nations in the short run, but they overlooked the way in which the British peace movement linked the negotiations to arbitration and disarmament under the League. British groups used the treaties as a starting point to continue discussing the Geneva Protocol (which would have defined aggression and provided specific institutional mechanisms to respond to it) and the Optional Clause (which made states' acceptance of arbitration compulsory). British groups also stressed that their support of the treaties was contingent on the government's willingness to take the initiative in convening an international disarmament conference through the League.

Similarly, the Pact of Paris, or Kellogg–Briand Pact, has been disparaged for its lack of effectiveness in institutionalizing international cooperation against aggression. Nevertheless, the Pact provided the rationale for further U.S. involvement in the world at a time in which U.S. peace groups promoted an "internationalism" that denoted arbitration, military disarmament, and participation in international conferences to resolve the debt and reparations crises. These manifestations of internationalism, although not entirely selfless, still contrast markedly with later "internationalist" articulations that emphasized military engagement and market creation. For example, peace groups invoked the Kellogg–Briand Pact repeatedly from 1928 to the outbreak of war to demand movement on disarmament and U.S. participation in the World Court. Moreover, U.S. administrations invoked the Pact, although more selectively, to counter the isolationist Senate bloc and push for U.S. involvement abroad. Consequently, although the Pact itself was negotiated to avoid League responsibilities, it soon became a constant reminder of U.S. responsibilities in international politics.

The Preparatory Commission for the General Disarmament Conference likewise accomplished little. Yet peace groups' claims on the necessity of disarmament continued to justify the Commission's existence even while governments were seeking to terminate it. As early as 1926, government delegates to the Commission plotted how to rout progress on League efforts for disarmament by appointing technical committees to engage in long-term "study" of the problem. As the London *Daily Telegraph* pointed out, this course was "tantamount to the indefinite shelving of the whole disarmament question," although it also recognized that such a shelving could "cause a considerable stir in America, and bitter disappointment among large sections of American, British, and Scandinavian opinion." As a result, U.S. delegate Hugh Gibson advised Washington to avoid sidetracking the Commission despite inherent obstacles to progress, warning that, "The whole conference has now taken on the aspect of nothing more than an attempt to conciliate public opinion as no government represented here is ready to accept responsibility for an indefinite adjournment of work . . . hence the interested powers are now awaiting a pretext for breaking off work when somebody else can be made [the] scapegoat."[12] Peace groups could not compel governments to use League mechanisms properly, but their claims and demands kept alive appeals to international organization as the proper forum for resolving conflicts and worked to delegitimize bilateral and secretive diplomatic practice.

Peace groups and League officials also developed a direct relationship that bypassed individual governments. League officials early on recognized the importance of peace groups' support and worked actively to maintain and control it. This phenomenon puts a dent in evolutionist ex-

[12] John W. Wheeler-Bennett, *The Pipe Dream of Peace* (New York: Morrow, 1935); B. J. C. McKercher, "Of Horns and Teeth: The Preparatory Commission and the World Disarmament Conference, 1926–1934," in *Restraints on War: Arms Control and Disarmament in British Foreign Policy* (Westport, Conn.: Praeger, 1992); *Daily Telegraph*, 21 May 1926; telegram from Gibson to Kellogg, 23 June 1926, RG59, National Archives.

planations by underscoring the significance of social agents and social activism in legitimizing the League.

League officials worked to develop formal and informal relationships with nonofficial groups, indicating their understanding of the necessity of societal support for and involvement in League responsibilities. As early as 1921 League officials discussed how they might facilitate "practical internationalism" through service to "private international organizations." The private international organizations included, in addition to the International Federation of League of Nations Societies (IFLNS), many of the Anglo-American groups concerned with peace issues, including the Women's International League for Peace and Freedom (WILPF), the International Co-operative Women's Guild, the YWCA, the International Federation of University Women, the U.S. National Committee on the Cause and Cure of War, the U.S. League of Women Voters, and the World Alliance of Churches. Collaboration with the League most often consisted of mutual information exchanges, but at times also included representation on League commissions and committees. League officials, particularly cognizant of women's groups support, organized "systematic" contacts with national and transnational women's organizations.[13]

The League granted special status to the IFLNS, which was dominated by the League of Nations Union (LNU), since the Federation's *raison d'être* was to publicize and legitimize international cooperation through the League. Federation representatives met annually with the Assembly president to present resolutions that were then recorded in the Assembly Journal. The Federation also sent deputations to League officials during times of crisis and during the World Disarmament Conference to promote Federation demands. Conversely, the League supplied the Federation with the same information and documentation as member states. The Federation saw its mission as the broad and noble task of promoting the League: "The goal of these Associations is not merely to offer support to the existing League of Nations, but also to become familiar with it, to defend it when it is unjustly attacked, and to raise important issues." But the League also tried to rein in its supporters. The Federation submitted its meeting agendas in advance to the League's Information Section to receive opinions from interested League offices, and also consulted with the League on its propaganda programs. League officials sometimes supplied information that re-

[13] Pelt papers, P.105 (1932–1940), Section 13 (International Bureaux and Intellectual Cooperation), 35357, F.P. Walters memo, 11 April 1924, League of Nations Archives; Memo by Gabrielle Radziwill, 17 May 1934, Pelt papers, P.105.

sulted in "preventing, if possible, tendencies [that were] . . . overly radical or extremist." [14]

League officials early on saw the value of using peace groups to popularize joint demands, since League offices themselves were not authorized to propagandize their objectives or methods. Monsieur Aghinides of the Disarmament Section began in 1922 to explore mutual contacts between his office and peace groups for the express purpose of creating and sustaining propaganda campaigns carried out "avec conviction et enthousiasme" for arms reductions according to the stipulations embodied in League resolutions. Aghinides wanted to recruit the most influential national and transnational peace groups to encourage disarmament campaigns and promised regular League contacts and information in return. [15]

The relationship between the League and peace groups peaked during preparations for the World Disarmament Conference. The Conference became the focal point for the largest, best organized, and most intense transnational effort by peace movements to voice their demands during the interwar period. Peace groups cooperated with each other by organizing and sharing tasks, lobbying their own government delegations and sympathetic small state delegations and League officials, and publicizing their claims and interpretations of the proceedings in Geneva and at home. As a result of their disarmament conference campaigns, peace groups' demands and methods became increasingly dependent on the existence of global international organization.

League officials "expected that relations between private organizations and the Secretariat" would be "very active during the Disarmament Conference." They wished to "facilitate the work of these organizations as much as possible," given "that various international organizations and also several national organizations have been doing a considerable amount of propaganda work in preparation for the Conference, and that their services in this connection will also be very useful during the Conference itself." Thus immediately before and during the conference, official and unofficial League contacts with peace groups expanded greatly. The League created a Liaison Committee to streamline communication between the Political Section, the Information Section, and the International Bureaux Section and the "public and private international organizations." The Disarmament Conference also stimulated new contacts with women's organi-

[14] Translations mine (from the French). IFLNS papers, P.48/No.13 (undated), League of Nations Archives, Adrian Pelt papers, P.105; P.107.
[15] R.217/16270 (Doc.20166), 3 April 1922, League of Nations Archives.

zations. Womens groups' activities in support of the League in the year leading up to the Conference prompted both the Assembly and the Council to find ways to "extend this collaboration still further" by requesting suggestions from them on strengthening cooperation on disarmament and other League work. At least fourteen women's groups sent representatives to Geneva for the duration of the conference, and the Information Section provided them with extensive documentation.[16] During the Conference, the League Secretariat granted peace groups the right to observe proceedings and receive Conference documentation, with the understanding that the groups would attend regularly and "use systematically . . . the information gained."

The result of peace groups' interaction with the League was treatment that recognized their unique status in debates such as those over disarmament. League officials strove to "control" peace groups at the same time that they recognized the need to encourage their support. During preparations for the Disarmament Conference, for example, League officials both granted peace organizations special access and worried that their publicity might overshadow the role of governments. When it became evident that peace groups had succeeded in amassing huge numbers of pro-disarmament petitions to present to the Conference, League officials created a Petitions Committee to oversee and limit peace groups' activities.[17]

Peace groups continually pushed their claims for disarmament with League officials, the press, and member governments. Consequently, they constantly strove to expand the boundaries of their participation in the Conference and sought ways to broaden the legitimacy of their demands. The Conference rejuvenated somewhat the older, Continental-based peace groups such as the International Peace Bureau in Geneva, but the most significant organizing initiatives came from British and U.S. peace group consortiums. The International Consultative Group (ICG) became the most comprehensive and influential of these. Four types of groups combined to create the ICG, claiming to represent millions of members worldwide: the League of Nations Associations (under the rubric of the International Federation of League of Nations Societies, or IFLNS), the Women's International Organizations (the Women's Disarmament Com-

[16] Report to the Secretary-General on "Relations between the Secretariat and Private International Organizations during the Disarmament Conference," 23 December 1931 (unsigned), R2444/3071, League of Nations Archives; Pelt papers, P.105, League of Nations Archives; Report by the Secretary-General, "Collaboration of Women in the Organization of Peace," *Official Journal*, A.10, League of Nations Archives.
[17] "Report of the Petitions Committee," *Official Journal*, Conf. D. 54, 4 February 1932; R2444/3071, Federation des Institutions Internationales, memo by Bertram Pickard, 18 January 1932, League of Nations Archives.

mittee claimed 40 million members from 56 countries), the Christian International Organizations, and the Students International Organizations. The four representative groups thus claimed considerable influence. The ICG in turn provided the impetus for an American Interorganizational Council to be created with offices in New York and Geneva. A British Group, modeled after the U.S. council, formed to lobby British officials in Geneva.[18]

Peace group representatives in Geneva, through their vigorous organizational presence and personal contacts, kept their demands at the forefront of the Conference. For example, Laura Puffer Morgan, Geneva representative for the U.S. NCPW and eventually chair of the ICG, regularly informed Norman Davis, senior U.S. delegate, of peace movement positions and demands. In one instance, Morgan pressed Davis to ask President Roosevelt to reinsert a clause in a Conference resolution calling for substantial arms reductions since "We could get no support from our peace movement for a program which did not include numerical and direct reduction." Davis did the movement's bidding, although Roosevelt demurred from sending "too many messages to Europe." Morgan then informed the wider peace community in Geneva (including British groups) of the interaction.[19] Likewise, British groups sometimes met with Sir John Simon, British Foreign Minister, and Arthur Henderson, the Conference President, received a considerable amount of direct input from U.S., British, and transnational groups.

These interactions created a solid base of support for the League on the part of some peace groups and reinforced support on the part of others. For U.S. groups, participation in the Disarmament Conference debates was especially significant. Pacifist-centrist groups, in particular, whose allegiance to the League previously had been lukewarm, played important roles in the peace movement's organizational machinery set up in Geneva. For example, the NCPW, like many other peace groups, reorganized its work and offices to give priority to the Disarmament Conference and stated, "The need for immediate results in the effort toward world organization and world reduction of armaments has . . . brought about a change of emphasis in the educational work of the National Council and the

---

[18] "The International Consultative Group (for Peace and Disarmament), Its Origin, Aims, and Development," ICG papers, 341.67:06, Box 1, League of Nations Archives. Disarmament Committee of the Women's International Organizations, "A Dollar for Disarmament," (undated) flier, Laura Puffer Morgan papers, League of Nations Archives. IFLNS papers, P.41/No.6, April 14, 1932; 6 May 1932, League of Nations Archives.

[19] Morgan to Dame Adelaide Livingstone and M. Davis, 8 September 1933, 341.67:06, I61 Box VI/2, League of Nations Archives.

peace movement as a whole."[20] Increasingly, peace groups worked to strengthen global international organization to realize their demands.

Conversely, the quality of peace groups' organizational and informational work impressed League officials, government delegates, and the press, most of whom found that information generated and published by the consortiums was equal to or better than their own. Officials often came to rely on peace group activists, especially Laura Puffer Morgan of the NCPW, for both information and proposals. According to Benjamin Gerig, a former (LNA) member who at the time held a post in the League Secretariat, "Mrs. Morgan has won the respect of all, both in official and unofficial circles, who have had anything to do with the Conference. . . . [She] has taken a continuous and active part in committee work, the results of which have often been brought immediately to the attention of important, official committees of the Conference." Another activist based in Geneva noted that, "many men in Geneva were saying that Mrs. Morgan knew more about the Disarmament Conference than any other person."[21]

The cooperative mechanisms set up by peace groups enabled them to articulate their claims and demands effectively at the Conference, as well as to respond quickly to conference proceedings and external developments. Peace groups set the stage by arranging a special session at the opening of the Conference to demonstrate their ability to mobilize public opinion and to make their demands known in an extraordinary manner to governments, League bureaucrats, the press and the public at large. This opening session, although in the end scripted by League officials, featured a procession of peace groups depositing with great fanfare a total of twelve million petitions in favor of disarmament in front of League officials and government delegations. During the first year of the Conference, peace groups saw many of their demands, laid out in the Budapest Proposals, incorporated into official positions and made a point of emphasizing the commonalities between their proposals, government positions (including the Hoover proposals), and League resolutions. Peace groups also initiated widespread, rapid, and favorable responses to President Hoover's April and June 1932 proposals. Arthur Henderson responded to one peace movement supporter that he had "been receiving lately over a hundred Resolutions a day urging effective and far-reaching measures of disarmament and representing in many cases . . . large and

---

[20] NCPW Executive Board minutes, 21 September 1932, SCPC.

[21] NCPW Executive Board Minutes, 21 September 1932; 16 May 1934, SCPC; P.41/No.6, IFLNS (Disarmament Committee, 1931–33), Ruyssens to Bailey, 4 March 1932, League of Nations Archives; Gerig to NCPW; Lydia Schmidt to NCPW, NCPW Executive Board Minutes, 16 May 1934, SCPC.

important bodies of opinion throughout the world." Simultaneously, peace groups worked continually to rebut French claims rejecting the principle of equality of status. Some peace activists emphasized that the Conference itself resulted from recognizing the alternative claim that the principle of equality of status could no longer be ignored.[22]

The peace movements adopted a two-pronged strategy in the wake of the Disarmament Conference's failure to salvage what they could from their original demands. First, peace groups worked to conclude a treaty based on the generally agreed-upon points of the IFLNS's Budapest Resolution (abolition of military aviation as a step toward both greater security and equality of status, strict regulation of the international arms trade, and the foundation of a Permanent Disarmament Commission to supervise both reductions and weapons trade). Second, they directed the movement's work even more strongly toward strengthening global international organization as a viable means to work through interstate tensions. The IFLNS pushed this "Minimum Programme" beginning in February 1933. From late 1933 through 1934, when the Conference showed signs of breaking up without any measure of substantive progress, peace groups displayed as much concern over the future prospects of their brand of "internationalism" as they did over the lack of gains in arms reductions. This tendency was probably most significant for pacifist-leaning U.S. groups such as the NCPW, who notified the U.S. administration in November 1934 that the peace movement's major demands at that time were to secure ratification of the World Court protocols, obtain an official U.S. diplomatic representative to the League, and enact an educational campaign to support the League.[23]

Thus, interwar peace movements first legitimized global international institutions within and among themselves during the early 1920s. They worked to advance international mechanisms for resolving conflict through arbitration and disarmament throughout the 1920s. Their efforts to popularize, support, and make effective the World Disarmament Conference of 1932 was the defining moment of their adherence to claims that universalist international organization, based on the principle of equality of status, provided the most legitimate framework for re-

[22] IFLNS papers, P.41/No.6, Disarmament Committee files, 15 October 1933; Report of IFLNS Disarmament Committee by Malcolm Davis, Montreux, June 1933; letter to Arthur Henderson, 30 June 1932; Henderson to Captain Small, 11 July 1932; Minutes, 22 June 1932, League of Nations Archives; 26 June 1993 memo by Morgan, Laura Puffer Morgan papers, League of Nations Archives.

[23] IFLNS Disarmament Committee, P.41/No.6, 16 February 1933, League of Nations Archives; Frederick Libby to Secretary of State Cordell Hull, 14 November 1934, Laura Puffer Morgan papers, League of Nations Archives.

solving arms races and for providing an alternative to state management of conflict.

THE DECLINE OF THE LEAGUE AND THE RISE OF THE UNITED NATIONS

In the aftermath of the World Disarmament Conference, peace movements in both the United States and Britain increasingly claimed that the League in particular, and internationalism in general, provided the best means to create a viable peace. Peace groups agreed that the League should be "strengthened," although at times they still disagreed about what this would entail. The period from 1931 to 1935 marked the peak of intramovement cohesion on these demands.

In January 1934 the U.S. peace movement began its first authentic unified effort to obtain U.S. membership in the League. The LNA led the effort through its ambitious "State the Terms" campaign to demand that the Roosevelt administration state the terms on which it would join the League. Pacifist and centrist groups cooperated willingly in the campaign, which was designed "to have the widest possible appeal to peace advocates and the public."[24]

Both pacifists and liberal internationalists in the United States realized that powerful opposition to League membership remained entrenched in Congress, and both embarked on a joint legislative program to further their demands. Pacifists in the NCPW and members of the U.S. WILPF convinced Senator Gerald Nye to chair Senate investigations into the munitions industry when it became apparent that the World Disarmament Conference would founder, and these groups also persuaded the U.S. Government and the League to pursue controls on weapons manufacturers and weapons trade as the Disarmament Conference wound down. In 1934–1935 all sections of the U.S. peace movement also cooperated to launch the final push for U.S. adherence to the World Court. The NPC unified these demands through a Four-Point Legislative Program promoted by the movement. The Four-Point Program included demands for an official U.S. government statement on the terms on which it would join the League, government support for the Nye Munitions inquiry bolstered by "international and national control of the manufacture and trade in

---

[24] Florence Brewer Boeckel, "The Peace Movement," draft for the *American Year Book*, 1934, SCPC; Robert D. Accinelli, "Militant Internationalists: The League of Nations Association, the Peace Movement, and U.S. Foreign Policy, 1934–38" *Diplomatic History* 4 (1980): 10–38, 25–28.

arms," "energetic" governmental efforts for arms reduction, and "immediate ratification of the World Court Protocols."[25] In practice, however, the work for control of the arms trade and the campaign for U.S. adherence to the World Court soon overshadowed that for general U.S. membership in the League.

The British peace movement also initiated pro-League, pro-internationalist campaigns after the Disarmament Conference's failure. The NPC followed on the heels of the U.S. NCPW in calling for controls on weapons manufacture and trade, on both the national and international levels. But the movement's massive Peace Ballot campaign, organized to demonstrate the movement's claim that the League's widespread legitimacy required the British government to use it to avert or condemn conflict, had more impact. The Peace Ballot's enormous success in confirming widespread backing for the League—96 percent of respondents believed Britain "should remain a member of the League of Nations"—persuaded the government to take a leadership role in imposing international sanctions against Italy in 1935. League officials summed up the effort by calling the Ballot "a lesson and an example," with wide repercussions, "not only within the British Commonwealth but among all states friends of Great Britain" because it affirmed British citizens' "attachment to the cause of peace and their confidence in the League of Nations."[26]

By the late 1930s, U.S. and British peace movement campaigns in support of the League had met with only limited success. The U.S. "State the Terms" campaign fell short of the one million signatures hoped for. Clark Eichelberger of the LNA still approved going ahead with a congressional resolution, and the campaign lasted until Senator James Pope introduced a joint resolution calling for League membership in May 1935. Congress, through the direct efforts of James Shotwell and Clark Eichelberger, approved U.S. membership in the International Labor Organization (ILO), but rejected both the Pope resolution and adherence to the World Court.[27] The U.S. and British peace movements' efforts to institute strict controls on weapons manufacture and trade resulted on the international level in a draft convention that had little hope of being ratified. Finally, the British peace movement's early success in realizing sanctions against Italy and reversing the Hoare–Laval treaty soon came to naught as Franco-British cooperation on sanctions disintegrated.

---

[25] Accinelli, "Militant Internationalists," 25–28.
[26] Statement made by Dr. Benes to the IFLNS, 14 September 1935, Adrian Pelt papers, P.107, League of Nations Archives.
[27] Accinelli, "Militant Internationalists."

The traditional narrative on the period 1935–1939—Abyssinia, Munich, and the outbreak of the European war—is that the initial use of League sanctions first caused widespread hope, then failed miserably, resulting in severe disillusionment and irreparable divisions within peace movements. But a closer examination of the history of peace group activities, claims, and demands during these years, as well as during the war itself, points toward a more nuanced understanding of peace groups' efforts to keep alive universalist international organization as a viable and legitimate check on state power.

The first reaction of peace groups to the disappointments of 1934–1936 was to return to the question of League reform. Internationalists had long repressed debate on this topic, most likely because they did not wish to deal with the negative repercussions of a frank discussion of sanctions on their membership. By July 1936, however, when it had become clear that the limited sanctions aimed against Italy had failed to halt the aggression against Abyssinia, the IFLNS focused on reform to make the resort to sanctions obligatory. The IFLNS thus promoted a comprehensive system of graduated economic and military measures. Center-pacifist groups such as the WILPF opposed military measures, but worked to clarify procedures on international penalties short of force. Pacifist groups continued to support cooperation through the League while working for reform to address the underlying causes of aggression and eliminate all military sanctions as well as any economic sanction causing hardship to civilian populations. Peace groups' differences on this issue doomed attempts to unite on a coherent policy regarding sanctions. Yet underlying these differences was a common reliance on the principle that responding to aggression was an international responsibility and that universalist international organization was necessary to find ways to enact this principle.

From 1937 through the first years of the war, British liberal internationalists continued to urge governments to look to the League to arbitrate European tensions. Pacifists and centrists, however, increasingly turned to the idea of multilateral conferences to resolve a range of issues causing conflict. These groups' efforts rested on renewed claims that conflict stemmed from economic inequalities that could only be settled when the more affluent and powerful states—especially the United States and Britain—agreed to a fairer distribution of wealth, resources, and opportunity. British groups thus promoted "A New Peace Conference," and both U.S. and British groups attempted to secure "neutral mediation" in the European war between 1939 and 1941. In November 1939 the U.S. NCPW launched its "Peace Now" campaign, demanding the creation of a "continuing Mediation Commission" and stressing "the necessity for

America to take its rightful place in a world cooperative effort and prepare to make the economic concessions necessary." The British WILPF also called for U.S. leadership in neutral mediation efforts and praised President Roosevelt's attempts to intervene.[28]

Promoting multilateral measures outside of the League did not constitute a rejection of the institution per se; indeed, the peace movement previously had promoted the Kellogg–Briand Pact as a means of keeping alive demands to strengthen compulsory arbitration and disarmament. Although pacifists in both countries were becoming increasingly disillusioned with the League, they continued to claim that internationalism founded on universal participation and equality of status was necessary to create lasting peace. Peace groups' support of multilateral conferences external to the League indicated their practical recognition that states, that is, governments, were no longer willing to use the League to resolve conflicts or condemn aggression. Thus they sought to find other means to press their normative demands.

Thus, throughout the 1920s, peace and internationalist groups worked to keep international institutional problem-solving mechanisms on the agenda: where governments circumvented those mechanisms (such as in the naval disarmament conferences and the Kellogg-Briand Pact), peace groups agreed to support government initiatives *on the condition that* League machinery would be taken up again and reinforced. Likewise, despite the disintegration of League collective security and disarmament mechanisms in the mid to late 1930s, peace groups continued their work to legitimize multilateral forms of conflict resolution. After the failure of the 1932 World Disarmament Conference, societal groups turned their energies to attempts to reform the League. As states' unwillingness to use League mechanisms became increasingly evident, particularly in the years after the abandonment of partial sanctions against Italy in 1936, many movement groups became increasingly active in assisting refugees from Nazi Germany and in condemning the government's unwillingness to adopt more liberal immigration policies. Pacifist and Jewish groups were especially active in challenging the Administration's immigration limits for Jewish refugees.[29]

---

[28] Donald Birn, *The League of Nations Union, 1918–1945* (Oxford: Oxford University Press, 1981) pp. 202–3; "Des résolutions de l'Union pour la S.D.N.," 3 July 1936, IFLNS papers, League of Nations Archives; LNU Annual Report for year ended 31 December 1939; NCPW Executive Board Minutes, 15 November 1939, SCPC; WIL-British Section, Annual Meeting, 1940, BLPES.

[29] Dorothy Detzer, Appointment on the Hill (New York: Holt, 1948), pp. 220–52; Jacob Robinson, *Human Rights and Fundamental Freedoms in the Charter of the United Nations, A Com-*

NORMATIVE REARTICULATION: PEACE MOVEMENTS' PLANS
FOR POSTWAR INTERNATIONAL ORGANIZATION

After the outbreak of war in Europe, peace groups of all tendencies broadened their discussion of League reform to the question of how postwar international organization should be constituted. In the United States, the
Council on Foreign Relations, because of its establishment membership
and interaction with government officials, developed close ties with the
State Department postwar planning staff. Other peace groups and their
affiliates, drawn from a much wider swath of the U.S. social fabric, also
worked to gain official and public acceptance of their claims and plans in
support of global international organization. The LNA, church groups,
and women's groups led the way in initiating discussion and debate of
postwar institutions, with the additional participation of farm and labor
organizations. In Britain, the LNU, NPC, and WILPF took the lead. These
efforts, building on peace groups' promotion of the League and equality
of status before the war, kept the discussion of postwar global organization
on the public agenda. They set boundaries around the possible actions of
governments and set the stage for widespread public acceptance and legitimization of a newly constituted but still universalist international organization. They also also strove to ensure that any resulting organization
concern itself not only with peace, but also with economic distribution
and humanitarianism. Between 1939 and 1941, the phrases "an equitable
peace" and the discourse of "peace with justice" reflected this understanding of a peace that went beyond preventing aggressive war.

Most peace movement activists took it for granted that a universal membership international organization had to be reconstructed in the post–
World War II world. The LNA created a "Commission to Study the Organization of Peace" in the fall of 1939 and assembled a large number of
peace activists to conduct an "Inquiry" charged with producing reports on
all aspects of the League of Nations' activities to gauge whether or not to
demand a new organization. Yet one LNA officer admitted, "it has not
been easy to keep the writers to the central theme as to whether or not it
makes any difference if the League continues or is abandoned, and, if so,
what? There has been a tendency to concentrate on past events and future
plans, leaving out the connecting link between." The umbrella national
Peace conference (NPC) in the United States convened a Conference on
World Organization in March 1941 "in response to a feeling among the

---

mentary, Institute of Jewish Affairs of the American Jewish Congress and World Jewish Congress (New York: May 1946), pp. 3–5.

leaders in the peace movement that study should be given without delay to the kind of post-war world we want." This conference, attended by Assistant Secretary of State Adolph Berle as well as between 100 and 150 peace group delegates, brought the fractured movement together to plan for the future of global international organization. In addition, the FCC organized its well-known committee "to Study the Bases of a Just and Durable Peace"; the WILPF reoriented its program to center on "plans for a just and lasting peace" and undertook a comparative analysis of the various plans already proposed by the time of U.S. entry into the war in December 1941. Even the NCPW, which remained in the throes of an antiwar campaign until December 1941, included efforts for "post-war cooperation in a federation of nations" in its 1941 program for action. After the outbreak of war, the NCPW concentrated its work on "popularizing and discussing the many plans that are being offered by official and semiofficial bodies here and abroad."[30]

Like the U.S. LNA, the British LNU also began a comprehensive review of the League, resulting in many similar expectations about the continuation of a universalist international organization. The LNU's "Memo on the Experience of the League of Nations" asserted the claim, for example, that League institutions had not proved "unworkable" because they "did not fail when they were used." The failures of the League, according to the document, were due neither to its institutions nor to public opposition, but rather to governmental obstinacy. Consequently, the LNU used its conclusions to press for a new institution: "These lessons do not justify defeatism about the prospects of a future League." The LNU thus began its campaign for a future league in October 1939, almost immediately after the outbreak of war. Other groups in Britain also looked to the future in their quest to promote norms of equality of status, universal participation, and restraints on war. Moreover, they pushed for more explicit attention to economic and humanitarian concerns in the design of future international organization. WILPF, for example, insisted on greater recognition of economic inequalities and the need for "democratic" participation in any new world order. The NPC, whose faltering reputation was temporarily rejuvenated after its 1939 Petition for a New Peace Conference, immediately began to organize meetings and conferences on the topic of "The New World Order." The NPC held annual and biannual (when possible)

---

[30] Mrs. Harrison Thomas to Manley O. Hudson, 13 August 1943, Manley O. Hudson papers, Box 114/11, Harvard Law Library; NCPW Executive Board Minutes, 19 March 1941, SCPC. NCPW Executive Board Minutes, 20 May 1941, SCPC; NCPW Executive Board Minutes, 22 February 1941; 17 December 1941.

conferences throughout the war at Oxford, producing a series of pamphlets analyzing and debating peace aims, postwar organization, and official overtures such as the Atlantic Charter. In 1940 the NPC also organized a composite of peace groups' positions on "minimum armistice conditions," which also addressed the issue of postwar international organization. The NCPW, the WILPF, and the LNU made efforts to communicate their research and proposals to their counterparts across the Atlantic.[31]

U.S. State Department Planning for Postwar World Order

In the United States, the State Department constituted a "committee on problems of peace and reconstruction," publicly called the "Advisory Committee on Problems of Foreign Relations," in part in response to discussion about postwar order and objectives.[32] In September 1939 Secretary of State Cordell Hull began the formal process of postwar planning by appointing Leo Pasvolsky to be his Special Assistant on problems of peace. Pasvolsky thus acted as the nucleus and chief of what became the Advisory Committee, eventually an interdepartmental committee that further subdivided the massive task of postwar planning into subcommittees charged with Political Problems, Economic Problems, and Security.

The Advisory Committee was well aware that the discussion of postwar order had already begun in unofficial circles, stating that it organized in a climate in which "the policy to be pursued in relation to the future peace was being discussed in various American quarters." The Department assigned an especially influential role to elite liberal internationalists from the beginning of the planning process, first by accepting the Council on Foreign Relations' offer to contribute its research to the government. Liberal internationalists in the Council and the LNA (whose memberships

[31] Noel-Baker to Cecil, 7 December 1939; "Memo on the Experience of the League of Nations" (undated), both in Cecil papers, British Library; WIL-British Section, Annual Meetings, 1940, 1942, BLPES; Kenneth Ingram, *Fifty Years of the NPC: 1903–1958* (London: NPC), pp. 16–17, BLPES; "Peace Aims—A Summary of Unofficial British Opinion Expressed since the War," NPC papers, 16/11, 1940, BLPES; NCPW Executive Board Minutes, 22 February 1941 and 17 December 1941, SCPC; Cecil to Noel-Baker, 14 August 1942, Cecil papers, British Library.

[32] The State Department's official history of the Committee is recounted in its *Post-War Foreign Policy Preparations, 1939–1945,* by Harley A. Notter, Publication 3580, General Foreign Policy Series 15 (Washington, D.C.: GPO, 1950). Much of the following discussion stems from the account presented in this document, which Inis Claude has called "a fascinating story" (*Swords into Plowshares,* p. 63, n. 1).

overlapped) also had a conduit to official planning through the activities of Norman Davis, former U.S. delegate to several disarmament conferences and, in the late 1930s, an increasingly active member of internationalist organizations (and at the time Chair of the American Red Cross). Sumner Welles, the under Secretary of State who was known to have strong liberal internationalist sympathies, also maintained contact with the Council and LNA. In addition, James Shotwell, Manley O. Hudson, and Clark Eichelberger all played roles in the official process. The Advisory Committee purposely included "members drawn from private life," chosen "broadly to represent informed public opinion and interests."[33]

A particularly interesting facet of U.S. planners' assumptions was their emphasis on the need for arms reductions and arbitration mechanisms in any eventual postwar order. Although interwar administrations had supported, unsuccessfully, U.S. membership in the World Court, they had not provided strong leadership on the matter. Nor would it seem that an emphasis on the peaceful adjudication of disputes would be necessary in the midst of a popular war. Yet Secretary of State Hull, in a major 1942 address designed to begin to sell an eventual international organization to the U.S. public, declared that "one of the institutions which must be established and be given vitality [in the post-war order] is an international court of justice."[34]

Hull also stressed that postwar international cooperative mechanisms "must include eventual adjustment of national armaments in such a manner that the rule of law cannot be successfully challenged and that the burden of armaments may be reduced to a minimum." This emphasis concurred with the Advisory Committee's belief that a "general demand to curtail expenditures in [armaments] was likely." This assessment of the normative strength of disarmament carried over from the interwar experience, and is all the more interesting given that State Department planners made clear that they themselves did not necessarily agree that arms levels in the postwar period should be reduced. Planners themselves, conversely, claimed that the question of appropriate arms levels and "disarmament" was surrounded by uncertainty: the relationship between sufficient armaments and postwar security was apparent, but the high probability of broader societal pressures for disarmament had to be taken into account in their proposals.[35]

[33] Notter, *Post-War Foreign Policy Preparations,* pp. 19, 71–74, 80.

[34] Radio address, "The War and Human Freedom," 23 July 1942; Notter, *Post-War Foreign Policy Preparations,* pp. 93–95.

[35] Notter, *Post-War Foreign Policy Preparations,* pp. 93–95, 113–14.

The Security Sub-Committee, designed to bring the views of the military into postwar planning, also took an unusually multilateral tone in its assumptions. It accepted early on the "need for organized international action to maintain security" under the rubrique of an international association, rather than basing security on "our own efforts alone," and "assumed that necessary international political and juridical machinery for the settlement of international disputes would be established." In addition, the subcommittee assumed that states would conclude an arms treaty "to fix maximum and minimum limits for [major powers'] armaments and military forces" with the eventual "stabilization of all armaments." The subcommittee thus favored an international organization in possession of its own military forces.[36] The emphasis placed on arbitration, disarmament, and international control, especially during a period in which arms levels and expenditures enjoyed the support of large majorities of the public, suggests that the expectations engendered during the interwar period helped to shape planners' assumptions regarding public demands in the postwar period. This is especially true for disarmament, since even many internationalists had abandoned it as a goal during the late 1930s.

At the same time U.S. groups engaged in discussions of postwar international organization offered their help to the Administration. The Administration declined these offers but it remained aware of outside groups' activities. For example, although the Committee's overarching purpose was "To survey the basic principles which should underlie a desirable world order" after the war, "with primary reference to the best interests of the United States," it also recognized the need "to examine proposals and suggestions made from various sources—both official and unofficial—as regards problems of peace and reconstruction." This mandate appeared to respond to the NCPW's March 1941 conference on World Organization, which urged the president to appoint a special commission including private citizens to study "possible plans for effective international cooperation in the post-war world." Moreover, the Committee continually voiced concern over the best way to incorporate a wider selection of public views "to coordinate the work and to provide contact with private organizations actively discussing postwar problems." The Committee intended to create an Advisory Council made up of representatives from a wide variety of private organizations, in addition to Department and Congressional members, but the Council never got off the ground. In addition to labor, farm, and business groups, the Department was particularly con-

---

[36] Ibid., pp. 127–28.

cerned with the views of women's and church organizations. One of the major difficulties for the Administration and Committee was having to decide which groups to include in the proposed Council, a decision "which demanded that the greatest care be used . . . in order to avoid giving justified offense to those omitted." Roosevelt expanded considerably the list finally submitted to him by the committee, whose members then found it too unwieldy and tabled it. The intention, however, and the subsequent decision by Secretary Hull to engage in frequent informal discussions with additional interested groups, resulted in the de facto incorporation of a broad swath of unofficial views, in addition to those of liberal internationalists, into the Department's agenda. By April of 1942, the State Department committee had compiled a list of significant "private organizations" in the United States, Britain, and elsewhere who were active in postwar planning and advised Pasvolsky that "it would seem to be definitely worthwhile for the Department to maintain contact of one sort or another with most of these organizations. . . . If their enthusiasm can be discreetly guided in channels which seem to the Department to be useful and away from schemes which the Department feels are dangerous or Utopian, very helpful allies will have been won to the all-important task of gaining public support for this Government's post-war foreign policy." These organizations included the American Friends Service Committee (increasingly active in refugee assistance), Jewish and Catholic peace committees, the Commission to Study the Organization of Peace, the FCC, and the National Peace Conference in the United States, and the League of Nations Union, the New Commonwealth Institute, and the National Peace Council in Britain.[37]

The Roosevelt administration thus recognized the role of peace groups in its massive planning effort to reorganize international affairs. Britain also initiated postwar planning, although on a much smaller scale. The Foreign Office set up a "group of experts" soon after the oubreak of war to study possible peace settlements. The Royal Institute of International Affairs assisted the group in a relationship that bore many similarities to that between the U.S. State Department and the CFR. The Foreign Office was less concerned with incorporating additional views into its planning process, but the LNU sent its "Plan for a Future World Organization" to Churchill and Eden, among others, in October 1943. Cecil and Noel-

[37] Ibid., pp. 19, 20, 80, 213–15; NCPW Executive Board Minutes, 19 March 1941, SCPC; Charles W. Yost to Leo Pasvolsky, April 14, 1942, R659, Records of Leo Pasvolsky, Box 2 (1942), File 5, National Archives.

Baker pressed the Foreign Office to "do more to use the experience of people who understood the League" in planning for postwar international organization.[38]

GOVERNMENT/MOVEMENT DIALOGUE AND DEBATE

From the 1943 Moscow Conference to San Francisco in 1945, dialogue and debate on postwar order intensified. During this period, however, debates arose not only between the major powers and within official planning committees. Traditional narratives of the creation of the United Nations neglect the debates that took place between governments (especially the U.S. government) and peace movements, now perhaps more accurately labeled a "movement for international organization." The outcome of these debates was most pronounced in the general form that postwar organization eventually took, *i.e.,* a universal membership, multipurpose organization charged primarily with maintaining peace and security. Another result that grew in significance during the postwar era, however, was the embryonic attention to human rights and humanitarian issues incorporated into the UN Charter. Human rights continued to be debated and developed, especially after decolonization, and humanitarian issues again came to the forefront of security concerns half a century after the founding of the United Nations.

Both Winston Churchill and Franklin Roosevelt launched designs for a postwar system that would show more deference than the League to actual power distributions and reserve decision making for the Great Powers. Throughout 1943, Churchill made it clear to Roosevelt both privately and publicly that he prefered an alliance system comprising regional Councils, including one for Europe, one for "the Amerian Hemisphere," and one for Asia, to be overseen by a "Supreme World Council," to anchor the postwar order. Roosevelt articulated a "Four Policemen" scheme providing for a Concert-type security system, sometimes put under the umbrella of a loosely organized international institution. Some members of the British Cabinet supported Roosevelt's scheme, but the U.S. Administration appeared to vacillate in favor of Churchill's view. At one meeting of senior U.S. policymakers (including Vice President Wallace, Secretary of War

---

[38] Noel-Baker to Cecil, 1 October 1943; Cecil to Lord Cranbourne, 12 October; Cranbourne to Cecil, 4 December 1943, Cecil papers, British Library.

Stimson, Senator Connally, Under-Secretary of State Welles, and Secretary of the Interior Ickes) and Churchill, "All the American guests present said that they had been thinking on more or less the lines propounded by the Prime Minister, and thought that it was not impossible that American opinion would accept them or something like them." The initial U.S. planning subcommittee draft provided for a regional approach to conflict management, although opinion on the committee was divided.[39]

Preparations for the Moscow Conference in the summer of 1943, however, coincided with increasingly vocal demands on the part of peace groups in favor of a universalist organization. State Department planners, fearful that unofficial activity would outstrip the administration in setting the agenda for postwar order, suggested that the United States work with Britain, the Soviet Union, and China to formulate a joint declaration favoring the creation of a global international organization. Consequently, the Department's postwar planning division prepared a draft text of such an agreement, which then became the Moscow, or Four Power, Declaration. Unofficial groups widely publicized and praised Article Four of the Declaration, which promoted the creation of "a general international organization, based on the sovereign equality of all peace-loving states."[40] The Moscow Declaration, for these groups, committed the major powers to a postwar order anchored by a universalist organization.

In the United States, President Roosevelt, who had vacillated in his support of regionalism, eventually decided to push for Great Power strength within a more universalist system and advocate an organizational structure that had considerable public support.[41] Thus, although the World War II victors retained the primary decision-making power in the UN Charter, explicit plans for constructing regional spheres of influence on the one hand, or a Great Power Concert on the other, were sidetracked in favor of a structure embodying universalist (and hence, for peace groups, "internationalist") principles and understandings. In effect, the preferences of both Churchill and Roosevelt (as well as proposals debated in the Subcommittee on Political Problems) had been modified to take into account a broader normative agenda.

[39] Notter, *Post-War Foreign Policy*, p. 112, Warren F. Kimball, *The Juggler* (Princeton, 1991); *Post-War Foreign Policy*, pp. 112–13; Cecil to Noel-Baker, 27 July, 1942, Cecil papers, British Library; OPOS, Dumbarton Oaks Reports, No.1, 4 December 1944, RG59, National Archives; Memorandum of meeting with the Prime Minister, May 28, 1943, RG59, Box 19.

[40] Divine, *Second Chance*, pp. 137–38. Dorothy B. Robins, *The UN Story* (New York: American Association for the United Nations, 1950), pp. 10–11, Robins.

[41] Notter, *Post-War Foreign Policy*, pp. 112–13.

The debate between the movement and governments, however, contin-ued after Moscow. The new phase of debate focused on proposals regard-ing the content and competence of the organization, developed first at Dumbarton Oaks in the fall of 1944, then at Yalta in February 1945. The debate engendered by peace groups during and after Dumbarton Oaks had a double purpose: to reinforce claims that would encourage the in-stitutionalization of the new organization, and to criticize the specific content of official proposals for paying insufficient attention to the issues of universal participation on a basis of equality and to the human rights of both groups (through proposals for a trusteeship organization) and individuals.

Many peace groups and their affiliates supported the "broad principles" of "internationalism" underlying the Dumbarton Oaks agreements. The League of Women Voters, for example, organized an extensive effort to publicize and galvanize support for Dumbarton Oaks that the State De-partment concluded was responsible for the "markedly increasing number of comments from individuals throughout the country" endorsing the proposals. Likewise, liberal international law specialists, including the "Manley Hudson group," appealed to the public to give "unhesitating sup-port to the Dumbarton Oaks proposals." As Dorothy Robins outlines in detail, Americans United for World Organization became the most promi-nent group that emerged from Dumbarton Oaks. An umbrella inter-nationalist group led by James Shotwell and Clark Eichelberger, among others, from its creation Americans United worked closely with the State Department and coordinated discussions with the League of Women Vot-ers, peace groups, labor, business, women's groups, farmers, churches, and the National Association for the Advancement of Colored People (NAACP) to give wholehearted support to the agreements.[42]

But Dumbarton Oaks also caused consternation in many peace groups in the United States and Britain. They voiced strong concern over the pro-vision for a major power veto in the Security Council of the organization, as well as over what they perceived to be the inadequate powers accorded to the General Assembly. The Soviet Union insisted on the veto, but many groups refused to go along with it despite their attempts before the war to quell anti-Bolshevist rhetoric. When the U.S. National Peace Conference urged its twenty-five-member organizations to recognize the need for com-

---

[42] OPOS, No. 2, 11 December 1944; No. 5, 2 January 1945; Dumbarton Oaks Reports, No. 1, 4 December 1944, National Archives; and Dorothy B. Robins, *Experiment in Democracy: The Story of U.S. Citizen Organizations in Forging the Charter of the United Nations* (New York: The Parkside Press, 1971).

promise with the Soviet Union on the veto issue, six group representatives dissented. Movement groups also criticized proposals for regional military alliances that came to the fore at both Dumbarton Oaks and Yalta. The veto, in combination with talk of alliances, resurrected suspicion of great power control among many movement activists. The Second Conference for Women in New York, the churches (this time including the Catholic bishops), the LNU, and the NCPW all claimed that the Dumbarton Oaks proposals would create an "alliance of victors" that would threaten the principle of equality for small states. The Fellowship of Reconciliation asked for a return to the Atlantic Charter as a basis for postwar aims, the churches questioned whether "the traditionalism and the cynicism of Dumbarton Oaks have to be accepted as the best the nations can do," and elements of the U.S. Left (writing in *The Progressive* magazine) resented being "high-pressured into a shoddy substitute" for a more "democratic" system. These and other groups showed less willingness to compromise with the proposals of the Great Powers, and served notice publicly that they would work to revise the Dumbarton Oaks agreement. In addition to pacifists and activists clearly on the left of the political spectrum, the mainstream FCC acknowledged the administration's efforts to incorporate public views while encouraging public input to modify the proposals: "The State Department has asked the American public to discuss the pros and cons . . . While there is yet time, let us seek to modify these Proposals." The FCC approved of an organization patterned after Dumbarton Oaks, but it also criticized the regional spheres of influence plan for having "many characteristics of a military alliance." In Britain, Robert Cecil of the LNU continued to protest the idea of a Great Power directorate in discussions with Anthony Eden.[43]

The strong claims in favor of a universalist, "federalized" institution and the many open criticisms of Dumbarton Oaks and Yalta continued to frame debates on postwar international organization up to and during the San Francisco Conference. Many peace groups, especially those associated with Americans United, acquiesced in the concept of a two-tier organization with a Security Council and a General Assembly. Liberal internationalists, however, believed that the two-tier structure accorded with necessary power realities and improved on the League, while pacifists, churches

[43] "Dumbarton Oaks Reports," no. 17, 27 March 1945, Box 23, RG59, National Archives; OPOS, Box 23, Report n. 2, 11 Dec. 1944; No. 3, 18 Dec. 1944; 25 Dec. 1944, National Archives; NCPW Executive Board Minutes, SCPC; Cranbourne to Cecil, 9 August 1945, Cecil papers, British Library; OPOS, Dumbarton Oaks Reports, 4 December 1944, and No.4, 25 December 1944, RG59, National Archives; Cecil to Eden, 9 December 1944; Eden to Cecil, 22 December 1944, Cecil papers, British Library.

and groups on the left wanted to accord greater decision-making responsibilities to the Assembly. In general, the movement remained wary of great power domination through the veto, trusteeship, and military alliances.

The United States State Department continued to communicate and work with these groups in preparation for San Francisco. Recognizing their legitimizing potential, it made the unusual move of inviting representatives of forty-two groups to serve as "consultants" to the United States delegation to the Conference. These included Americans United, women's groups, the LNA, the FCC, Jewish organizations, the NAACP, and labor, church, and farm organizations previously connected to the peace movement, as well as business, civic, and veterans groups. The Administration's relationship with pacifist groups (who did not support the war) was more ambivalent. It included the American Friends Service Committee in its planning for refugee assistance (and postwar planning on humanitarian aid), and the WILPF continued to meet with then Under-Secretary of State Stettinius. Yet it did not invite exclusively pacifist organizations to be consultants, an omission that WILPF strongly criticized.[44]

The movement now included those officially designated as consultants; others involved in a "core" group of supporters of world organization headed by Americans United but including some pacifists; and pacifist/left groups (including the WILPF) who set up shop in San Francisco and maintained contact, despite their criticisms, with the consultants and with the Administration. The consultants tended to steer a middle course between support for the new organization, criticisms of the veto and trusteeship, and proposals for change influenced by their own constituencies and other sectors of the movement.

The consultant system became the primary means for altering the Dumbarton Oaks proposals to accord with movement prerogatives at San Francisco. Consultant groups again opposed the major power veto as well as the lack of strong language favoring self-determination of colonies. They also argued for stronger powers of debate in the General Assembly. If the Great Powers could veto decisions in favor of action, groups contended, they should not be able to restrict "democratic" discussion and de-

---

[44] The Friends' Peace Committee expected to be included as a consultant. Robins, *Experiment in Democracy*, Appendix XVII and XVIII, pp. 199–201; Carrie A. Foster, *The Women and the Warriors: The U.S. Section of the Women's International League for Peace and Freedom, 1915–1946* (Syracuse: Syracuse University Press, 1995), pp. 317–21; Memo on Coordination of Private and Public Relief Activity in the International Field, May 12, 1942, RG59, Records of Leo Pasvolsky (1942). United Nations Conference on International Organization, Papers of Charles F. Darlington and Henry Reiff, Harry S. Truman Library.

bate in the organization at large. All of these positions represented moves toward egalitarianism in the new organization.

Consultant groups, finally, articulated explicit provisions for human rights as an area of UN competence. State Department planners had begun to track unofficial groups' efforts to secure human rights guarantees, spearheaded by the American Law Institute, in early 1942, though such guarantees did not figure in the Department's own initial assumptions regarding postwar order. But especially after Dubarton Oaks, the movement promoted measures ensuring self-determination and human rights. At San Francisco, this effort coalesced into a "tri-faith" statement of major Catholic, Protestant, and Jewish denominations. Movement groups urged delegates at San Francisco to approve the statement, which called for an international "bill of rights," the codification of international law, and arms limitation. The U.S. Delegation received thousands of letters from individuals and groups urging that these measures be included in the new organization.[45]

Peace group claims did not succeed in eliminating the veto or the trusteeship system at San Francisco, but their insistence on an explicitly humanitarian element to the new organization resulted in the inclusion of human rights provisions in the final Charter. The consultant system, according to observers, allowed "religious and moral forces" the opportunity to make "their influence powerfully felt." Resulting provisions in the Charter included the affirmation of "respect for human rights and for fundamental freedoms" in Chapter 1(3), as well as the requirement that the Economic and Social Council (ECOSOC) set up a Human Rights Commission.[46] Moreover, the work of consultants ensured the inclusion of a provision granting observer status to nongovernmental organizations formerly called "private voluntary organizations") in ECOSOC and the General Assembly. Finally, pacifists, churches, and the NAACP led the critique of mandates and trusteeship that helped to bring the issue of colonies back to the forefront of debate and encouraged attention to the "right" of self-determination and independence. All of these measures set up param-

[45] J. Jones to Leo Pasvolsky, February 24, 1942, Division of Special Research, Box 2, RG59, National Archives; San Francisco Conference, No. 2, April 25, 1945; No. 25, May 22, 1945; No. 27, May 24, 1945, OPOS, RG59.

[46] Robins, "Experiment in Democracy," chap. 7; OPOS, San Francisco Conference, No. 2, 25 April 1945; No. 25, 22 May 1945; No. 27, 24 May 1945; "Records of the U.S. Delegation," Box 196; "America," 26 May 1945, from OPOS, US Opin. 39, No. 29, 26 May 1945, RG 59, National Archives. Clark M. Eichelberger, "Organizing for Peace: A Personal History of the Founding of the United Nations," (New York: Harper & Row, 1977); pp. 266–72. President's Secretary's File, Conferences, 1945–July 1947, Box No. 162, Papers of Harry S. Truman.

eters for future nongovernmental organizations' attempts to influence the United Nation's multiple agendas and opened the way for continued debate on rights, independence, and economic distribution.

The final element necessary for "constructing" the United Nations consisted in selling it to the larger public. Ensuring its legitimacy was of special concern in the United States, given the Senate's prior rejection of the League. The U.S. administration, especially the State Department, therefore actively recruited unofficial groups to help it to publicize and gain acceptance of the UN organization beginning with the Dumbarton Oaks Conference. Peace groups, despite their claims that the new organization was not democratic enough and did not provide sufficient mechanisms to check great power interests, compromised with the administration and participated in the legitimization process.

Secretary of State Hull stated his anxiety in the planning committee over the "interest groups and opposing ideological influences that would inevitably bring their strength to bear against the constructive views on peace settlement and world improvement" developed by the committee. As a result, "it was necessary to consider . . . how to help public opinion to educate itself." Consequently, the administration organized a massive legitimization campaign concurrent with and extending beyond San Francisco. State Department officials matched the eagerness of "organizations of interested citizens," including many peace groups, for mutual discussion of Administration proposals during the fall of 1944 by speaking at numerous public meetings throughout the country as well as to group leaders for off-the-record discussions. According to the Department, approximately one hundred organizations "took part in these efforts to facilitate and encourage wide public discussion of this basic postwar foreign policy." According to Secretary of State Stettinius, these groups included "Not only organizations specialized in the study of international relations, but business, labor, and farm groups, service clubs and associations of ex-servicemen, women's organizations and religious societies, professional associations and groups of educators."[47] Most of these groups, with the exception of veterans and some business associations, were either peace groups themselves or affiliates of umbrella peace organizations.

Moreover, the State Department created the Office of Public Information in January 1944 at Roosevelt's request, to collect material on organizations' opinions and activities concerning foreign policy. The Office kept

---

[47] Notter, *Post-War Foreign Policy*, pp. 92, 93, 378–79; Edward Stettinius statement, December 1944 Department of State Bulletin, quoted in Robins, *Experiment in Democracy*, pp. 71–72.

tabs on women's, church, business, labor, and farm groups, concluding, for example, that "The Churches constitute the largest aggregation of groups in the United States expressing opinions on international relations issues." The Office also warned that although the Churches opposed isolationism and provided some of the strongest support for the UN Charter they were not completely satisfied with it and did not approve of international cooperation founded on "physical power."[48]

Thus in the words of one columnist, the State Department's interaction with groups promoting global international organization compelled it to engage in "establishing diplomatic relations with the American people." According to the State Department, "the views of the public received through these channels, and in letters from individual citizens and from organized groups, were the subject of regular study and report to all superior officers of the Department of State concerned with the improvement of the Proposals and the final steps in the negotiation of the Charter."[49] The fundamental purpose of these discussions and speeches was not to provide a conduit for public input into the process but rather to obtain public approval of U.S. participation in world organization along the lines of administration proposals. But the process of dialogue and debate, and the claims put forward by peace groups and their affiliates, resulted in a relationship of mutual influence.

Perhaps more significant, because "competence to interpret and to inform public opinion and to enlist public cooperation in the guidance of postwar policy had become a major need," the administration turned increasingly to a wide variety of groups, including peace groups who were already working on the issue, to help it "sell" the new organization to the public. Their legitimizing power was fully recognized by the State Department, which approvingly cited the results in 1948: "Public opinion polls show that the mass of the American people have discarded isolationism. One of the significant factors which has sustained this popular abandonment of isolationism has been the work of the international relations organizations. They wield an influence much greater than is suggested by their numbers (100,000–200,000 adults) since they include, or reach,

[48] This office eventually was renamed the Office of Public Opinion Studies. Schuyler Foster files, 1943–65, RG59, National Archives; "Public Attitudes on Foreign Policy, Special Report," no. 69, 18 August 1945, Schuyler Foster Files, RG59, National Archives.

[49] Anne O'Hare McCormick, *New York Times,* 3 March 1945. McCormick was also a member of the postwar planning commitee. "Dumbarton Oaks Reports," no. 14, 6 March 1945, Box 23, RG59; These views were analyzed by the Office of Public Affairs and the Division of International Organization. Notter *Post War Foreign Policy.*

citizens who translate their interest in foreign policy into significant action."[50]

In Britain it had also become clear that a universal membership organization would provide the basis of the new international order. "The slow-moving processes of traditional diplomacy" were finally outmoded and "diplomacy by conference" had become "a daily necessity, not only for idealistic reasons but on grounds of practical self-interest and convenience." The Foreign Office, which earlier had avoided unsolicited advice, began to enlist the LNU in the cause. After Dumbarton Oaks, Anthony Eden expressed his appreciation "that the League of Nations is going on with its task of shewing the people of this country how much they are concerned in the construction of a World Organization for the maintenance of international peace and security and the achievement of international cooperation in the solution of international economic, social and other humanitarian problems." Similarly, in 1945 the Foreign Office communicated its desire to have the group "carry on a vigorous campaign in favour of the San Francisco Charter." For British peace groups who had met to study and debate their own and official proposals throughout the war, the Charter once again provided the foundation for peace and economic fairness in the postwar order.[51]

It could be argued that the use of social groups' legitimizing power during the construction of the United Nation was an aberration due primarily to U.S. leadership and in particular the personality of Franklin Roosevelt. Roosevelt was known for his keen political sense and his ability to decide on the programs he needed to advance his political agenda, and to push through only those programs he knew he could "sell." This is a common argument, for example, regarding Roosevelt's public relations campaign in favor of the New Deal. But this type of analysis assumes as a corollary that Roosevelt was able to control the process of legitimization by ensuring that public input was used merely to popularize his own programs and not to permit additional claims to be heard. Yet, however much it was Roosevelt's intention to control the process of postwar planning for international organization, he in fact could not wield complete control over the United Nation's universalist form or normative content. Even

---

[50] "A Report on Thirty National Private Organizations Which Are Primarily Concerned with U.S. Foreign Policy," 5 February, 1948, Schuyler Foster Files, OPOS 1943–1965, RG59;

[51] Geoffrey L. Goodwin, *Britain and the United Nations,* prepared for the Royal Institute of International Affairs and the Carnegie Endowment for International Peace (London: Oxford University Press, 1957), p. 46; Eden to Cecil, 2 December 1944; Cecil to Cranbourne, 4 August 1945, Cecil Papers, British Library.

though it offers insightful twists on evolutionist and creationist themes, this narrative still overlooks the role of social contestation and debate in legitimizing norms underpinning the agenda of global international organization.

Thus, neither the evolutionist nor the creationist schools of thought adequately explains the continuation of global international organization and the creation of the United Nations. League officials themselves did not believe in automatic evolution and had always recognized the importance of societal legitimization in promoting and continuing their work. But by the beginning of World War II, neither governments nor many peace groups resorted to the League. Governments had always maintained a stance that was ambivalent at best. Peace groups continued to support global international organization, but as they had done many times earlier, resorted to extra-League mechanisms to address immediate problems. With the advent of full-scale war, they then turned their attention to reconstituting a new global organization in the postwar world.

The ability of peace groups to articulate and promote the reasons why a universal membership organization was necessary affected the postwar planning process instigated by the major powers, in particular the United States. Movement groups entered the process of constructing a new international organization from the start of the European war in 1939. They debated and promoted significant components of the form and content of the United Nations through the war and intensified their efforts from 1943 to 1945. Moscow defined the structure of the new organization, while debate over its contours continued at Dumbarton Oaks and San Francisco. After Moscow, peace groups focused on opposing proposals for a Great Power veto and regionalism (both of which negated equality of status) put forth at Dumbarton Oaks and on ensuring human rights provisions. Dumbarton Oaks, for them, represented both an explicit move toward institutionalizing a global international organization and a qualification of this move through the veto and regional alliances. Movement groups at San Francisco sought to weaken Great Power management, the resort to alliances, and colonialism, insisted on freedom of debate in the General Assembly, and brought a new dimension to global international organization by articulating rights pledges. Most peace groups were dissatisfied with the resulting UN Charter, especially the provisions for the Great Power veto in the Security Council and the restatement of states' sovereign rights in Article 2(7). Nevertheless, as they had done with the League, peace groups regarded the organization as a tool, one that provided a less-than-perfect alternative to security based on realpolitik, but an alternative nonetheless. They also regarded the new Economic and Social

Council as an important forum in which to develop their incipient humanitarian, human rights, and economic development agendas.

Peace groups' hopes for the United Nations in the postwar era diminished during the Cold War, when the superpower conflict overshadowed their demand that the United Nations be understood and used as an alternative to individualistic state security policies. With the onset of the Cold War, the role of the United Nations was called into question, as the organization became increasingly sidelined in addressing international tensions.

Moreover, while the Cold War made resort to multilateral decision-making a mere appendage of U.S.–Soviet management of world conflict, its ramifications on the domestic level forced many peace movement groups into a struggle for their existence. The consequences of the McCarthy era in the United States were extremely serious for social forces who wished to debate ethical choices in terms different from those promoting American values, and to have a voice in decision making on issues of peace and security. McCarthyism also had ramifications in Britain. In both countries the "movement for international organization" split again into a liberal internationalist wing who became increasingly supportive of U.S. leadership in the United Nations and U.S. military intervention abroad, and a smaller left/socialist/pacifist wing, made up of groups who soon began to channel their demands into a "nuclear pacifist" stance.[52]

Cold War politics temporarily displaced both the normative influence of social forces and the material influence of the United Nations. But if we return to the meaning of global international organization for social forces and the question of the role of social movements in world politics, the issue of how these movements legitimized the United Nations remains significant. The concluding chapter explores these questions.

---

[52] Lawrence Wittner, *Rebels against War: The American Peace Movement, 1933–1983* (Philadelphia: Temple University Press, 1984); Milton S. Katz, *Ban the Bomb: A history of SANE, the Committee for a Sane Nuclear Policy, 1957–1985* (Westport, CT: Greenwood, 1986); Maurice Isserman, *If I Had a Hammer: The Death of the Old Left and the Birth of the New Left* (New York: Basic Books, 1987).

Social Movements, Narratives, and Critical Analysis

Postmodern scholarship invites us to "make strange" that which is familiar, in order to call into question the underlying bases of knowledge that have become "foundational." The interwar period, however, already appears more strange, confusing, and apparently irrational to international relations than other historical periods. The discipline strives hard to make it understandable, and the resulting categories—realism/idealism; isolationism/internationalism—have become entrenched and fraught with ethical and intellectual implications. Postmodern scholars themselves, ironically, at times shirk from "making strange" traditional interpretations of the interwar period. Not only is the realist/idealist (or utopian) dichotomy entrenched in our thought, so is the modernist/postmodernist temporal bifurcation. Both dichotomies contain an implicit (and sometimes explicit) critique of "modern" or "utopian" notions of "progress."

But what was at stake for interwar peace movement activists was only partly "progress." Progress would have been welcomed, but more important for peace activists was the necessity of coming to grips with the implications of then-contemporary state security practices. The apparent necessity of finding alternatives thus entailed the redefinition of traditional notions of security, diplomatic practice, and participation on the part of both states and peoples. Security for peace movements was an integral part of the quotidian and could not be placed above or apart from decisions regarding social or economic aspects of life. Moreover the intertwining of security with economic and social concerns was not necessarily susceptible to liberal notions of "harmony." State and international security practice needed to be altered to prevent doom as much, if not more than, to ensure progress.

Traditional security practices and policies rely heavily on their separation from other aspects of international life. The strength of interwar peace movements' normative challenge to traditional security practices thus provoked a strong reaction in the form of an academic/policy alliance in favor of something called "realism." E. H. Carr, inspired by Karl Mannheim, was the first to create the presumably even-handed "realist/ utopian" dichotomization of beliefs and practices in foreign affairs. John Herz, soon placed "utopianism" under the more inclusive rubric of "idealism," at the same time being careful to separate the terms *realism* and *idealism* in international politics from their philosophical antecedents.[1] This allegedly conferred theoretical cachet on both realism and idealism, each designating competing but coequal understandings of the realities and possibilities of international politics. But although realism was used to denote the recognition of "power" and "interest" in international politics and the impossibility of transcending them (i.e., what "is"), the terms *utopianism* and *idealism* (i.e., what "ought to be") have always represented an imposed category in international politics (on those perceived to be unrealistic).

The realist/idealist dichotomy quickly gained strength in the aftermath of World War II. Pundits and theorists created realism to propound the idea that if certain prescriptions for state behavior were followed (and the unrealistic assumptions and behavior of social movements comfortably ignored), disasters such as World War II could be avoided in the future. In the postwar United States, especially, "realism" married "internationalism" in a new alliance that promoted U.S. intervention abroad to shore up U.S. "interests." In an odd twist that best exemplifies Carr's use of the harmony of interests notion, the new internationalist agenda was believed to retain some of its cosmopolitan, disinterested character while being carried out explicitly through military means for particularistic purposes. For example, Manfred Jonas, in his influential 1966 book *Isolationism in America 1935–1941,* argues that isolationism in the 1930s was "an expression of unilateralism" that did not and could not survive World War II. Reflecting on the thesis in 1990, Jonas asserts that American actions "involving

---

[1] E. H. Carr, *The Twenty Years' Crisis, 1919–1939: An Introduction to the Study of International Relations,* 2d ed. (New York: Harper & Row, 1964); Karl Mannheim, *Ideology and Utopia, An Introduction to the Sociology of Knowledge* (New York: Harcourt Brace Jovanovich, 1936); Herz, *Political Realism and Political Idealism* (Chicago: University of Chicago Press, 1951), p. 17.

Korea, Cambodia, Afghanistan, Angola, Israel, Nicaragua, Grenada, Libya, and Iran, among others" demonstrate that "not even a trace of isolationism survives in an American foreign policy which assumes that events anywhere in the world affect American interests and may require American intervention in some form."[2] Yet these were all essentially unilateralist, rather than internationalist, interventions. Thus realism, boldly and without a trace of irony, became internationalism redefined as U.S. military unilateralism.

The move toward equating realism and internationalism with the explicitly interventionist postwar U.S. military stance was made possible by subjugating alternative normative stances that were labeled idealistic, utopian, isolationist— or a combination of these. The power of the realist superiority complex derived in large part from fostering the sense that challengers were simply irrational. William T. R. Fox, in reflecting on interwar international relations scholarship in the 1950s, criticized the "emotional drive" in the field that "often leads to unclear thinking." Fox asserts, "From the invasion of Manchuria to the signing of the Molotov–Ribbentrop agreement, students of international relations too often found themselves emotionally and intellectually unprepared for the event."[3] But while the pro-League academic specialist came under fire for Fox, Carr, and others, interwar peace movements became even easier recipients of the emotional, irrational, and utopian labels.

This trend toward equating emotionalism with utopianism had an interesting parallel in social movement theory during the early Cold War. Studying mass behavior, social movement scholars of the late 1950s viewed movements as irrational responses to breakdown.[4] Their successors have been trying to recover from the stigma ever since.

Perhaps the main irony inherent in the dominance of realism is that it derived its strength and persistence from narratives of ethical rationales for going to war in 1939–1945. That peace groups' (especially pacifists) membership and reputation suffered after World War II was due to the

[2] Manfred Jonas, *Isolationism in America, 1935–1941,* new ed. (Chicago: Imprint Publications, 1990), pp. viii, xi.

[3] He continues, "If they are to be taken seriously in the 1950s, they must show that they now know what went wrong, that they now know what sorts of data and analysis would have given them in the 1930s the answers that were then denied them." William T. R. Fox, "Interwar International Relations Research: The American Experience," *World Politics* (October 1949): 67–68.

[4] Neil Smelser, *The Theory of Collective Behavior* (New York: Free Press, 1962); W. Kornhauser, *The Politics of Mass Society* (New York: Free Press, 1959); see also Jean L. Cohen, "Strategy or Identity: New Theoretical Paradigms and Contemporary Social Movements," *Social Research* 52 (Winter 1985): 663–716.

very anguished and sometimes public self-questioning that groups and individuals themselves undertook from the late 1930s onwards. Activists such as Laura Puffer Morgan, writers such as Storm Jameson, and those who gave up conscientious objector status to fight in the war believed their change of position necessary, but found it disconcerting.[5] Peace groups and individual activists' ethical dilemmas, present in debates over economic appeasement, League sanctions, and neutrality, were thus laid bare during the events leading to war. The ethical choice in favor of war paradoxically shored up realism's ability to subjugate ethics (or any ethics apart from the promotion of "American values") to "interests" in the postwar era.

The interwar period, as this book demonstrates, was rife with examples of the difficulties involved in carrying out purely self-interested policies. Realist policy prescriptions are predicated on knowledge of either clear and understandable interests or clear and attainable goals. In interwar Britain, the dominant realist narrative defined security interests as maintaining the Empire, policing trade routes, and balancing France and Germany in Europe. Even without taking internal social needs into account, it is highly questionable whether all of these goals could have been met simultaneously. In the United States, similar problems obtained. It is unclear that the United States could have attained simultaneously the goals either of staying out of European conflicts while promoting U.S. trade around the world or of controlling events both in Europe and Latin America.

Even a more "classical," or prudential, realist understanding of interests and security runs into problems because when goals are multiple or unclear, it is difficult to figure out what type of policy is most prudent. This is why it was at times relatively easy to redefine "interests" to accord with peace movement positions, although the rationales of peace movements or governments for adopting similar positions differed. It also becomes easier to understand how and why peace movement criticisms of *un*realistic government security goals were so potent and why alternative policies of disarmament, arbitration, and collective security appeared viable and necessary.

The interwar period, therefore, poses the realist dilemma starkly. But the dilemma has not disappeared. The Cold War was not immune to instances of conflicting or unattainable U.S. and British goals and interests, as witnessed in Suez and Vietnam. In the present post–Cold War era,

---

[5] Phyllis Lassner, *British Women Writers of World War II: Battlegrounds of Their Own* (New York: St. Martin's Press, 1998); "The Anti-War Movement since 1914," Imperial War Museum, London.

therefore, theoretical attempts to rescussitate realism in new guises should be viewed with skepticism.

Yosef Lapid has called the "'idealism versus realism' schism" the first of three far-reaching debates that have marked and transformed intellectual discourse on international relations. Yet the practice of international relations has been for new debates to be superimposed on to the old. Consequently, the first debate remains an obdurate pentimento, continually betraying its contours despite the overlay of subsequent theoretical developments. Thus, R. B. J. Walker argues, it "has provided the context within which other disputes about appropriate method or the priority of state-centered accounts of world politics could occur at all."[6]

Neoliberal institutionalists, for example, take pains to distinguish their belief in the possibilities of "cooperation" from the hopes pinned on the League of Nations by interwar advocates of international organization. The neoliberal institutional framework thus "barricades itself from idealism."[7] Conversely, those who advocate the incorporation of historical contextuality, agent–structure relationships, and critical perspectives into theories of global politics also validate the term *realism,* either by appropriating it in new forms or by elevating its "classical" articulation above its "neorealist" successor. But such validation runs the risk of recreating the same hedges that, according to Jack Donnelly, diluted early realism's "distinctive character" and marked it with inconsistencies.[8] Thus if the term *"realism"* was used inappropriately to discipline efforts by interwar social

---

[6] Yosef Lapid, "The Third Debate: On the Prospects of International Theory in a Post-Postivist Era," *International Relations Quarterly* 33 (September 1989): 236. The second and third debates concern, respectively, the "history versus science" controversy of the 1950s and 1960s and the positivist versus post-positivist debates current since the 1980s; R. B. J. Walker, "History and Structure in the Theory of International Relations," repr. in James Der Derian, ed., *International Theory, Critical Investigations* (New York: New York University Press, 1995), p. 314.

[7] Robert O. Keohane and Lisa L. Martin, "The Promise of Institutionalist Theory," *International Security* 20 (Summer 1995): 39; Christine Sylvester, *Feminist Theory and International Relations in a Postmodern Era* (Cambridge: Cambridge University Press, 1994), p. 7.

[8] Barry Buzan, Charles Jones, and Richard Little, *The Logic of Anarchy, Neorealism, and Structural Realism* (New York: Columbia University Press, 1993); Robert Cox, "Social Forces, State, and World Order: Beyond International Relations Theory," *Millennium: Journal of International Studies* 10, (1981), esp. pp. 127–131, and "Multilateralism and World Order," *Review of International Studies,* 18 (1992); Richard Ashley is more circumspect. See "The Poverty of Neorealism," *International Organization,* 38 2 (Spring 1984), esp. 263–76. A major exception is David Campbell, *Writing Security: United States Foreign Policy and the Politics of Identity* (Minneapolis: University of Minnesota Press, 1992); Jack Donnelly, "Twentieth-Century Realism," in Terry Nardin and David Mapel, eds., *Traditions of International Ethics* (Cambridge: Cambridge University Press, 1992), p. 97.

movements to act as powerful agents in world politics, contemporary theorists should reassess the underlying utility of the term and the antithesis it was intended to oppose.

This returns us to the question of how we interpret the role of social movements in world politics. Social movements can rarely be cited as unitary "causes" of "state" behavior in the traditional sense, yet they were critical in contesting and delegitimizing traditional diplomatic norms and conventional notions of interest. They were also critical agents in legitimizing norms underpinning the United Nations. Yet their significance is only partially due to an ability to reconstruct state "interests" or influence policy, although moves in these directions sometimes occurred. Rather, their primary significance lies in their ability to contest, to loosen the boundaries of conventional notions of interest by exposing their contradictions (as in the Coolidge Conference and Kellogg–Briand Pact debates), and to use discursive compromises to open the way toward further contestation (as in their success in incorporating principles of universal membership and human rights into the UN Charter).

Interwar peace movements advanced claims and analyses that promoted particular meanings and interpretations of state and international practices. Their demands incorporated a normative agenda that posed significant challenges to traditional norms of state behavior. The result was debate and struggle for legitimacy of conflicting ethical and pragmatic norms. Neither the peace movements nor governments achieved many of their goals during the interwar period. Yet the peace movements did wield power and had significant political effects, contesting traditional security norms and legitimizing norms based on universal participation. Laying bare the normative positions of interwar movements forces us to look at the reasons why peace groups acted as they did; that is, it forces us to compare the logic of their behavior against that of the "lessons" taught by the dominant narratives and to ask anew whether the former should of necessity be seen as naive and the latter as prudent.

When we look at the construction and reconstruction of Anglo-American peace movements over the course of the nineteenth and early twentieth centuries, for example, we see that they did not represent a monolithic form of "idealism." Rather, they reproduced certain elements of contemporary political practice, but, depending on their interpretations of historical events, at times reformulated the normative underpinnings of practice. Thus free trade was debated, legitimized, questioned, and finally evaluated according to whether or not it aided or hindered imperialism. Similarly, the more peace movements became politically involved in articulating their own versions of security, the greater the role that economic redistribution and humanitarian concerns played in their claims and demands.

Interwar peace movements articulated a conception of international order they believed would promote peace and security that also included attention to economic justice and humanitarian goals. This conception was based on norms of equality of status and universal participation of states and peoples. As seen in Chapters 3 through 6, these norms often conflicted with, rather than abetted, British and U.S. perceptions of their interests. Neither the British nor the U.S. governments were enthusiastic about the World Disarmament Conference of 1932, held under League auspices, precisely because they did not wish to be held to standards of parity or equality in armaments, and it took the British peace movement ten years to convince a (Labour) government to sign the Optional Clause, which committed Britain to "obligatory arbitration" in the event of conflict. Norms such as universal participation and equality of status, although they were only partially institutionalized in twentieth-century global international organizations, do more than mask the interests of the powerful in maintaining the status quo; they also provide a mechanism for furthering and legitimizing change in world politics, often (though not always) in opposition to Great Power interests (as in the era of decolonization).

Thus peace movements saw the promotion of universal rights and responsibilities in 1945 as the best and perhaps only means of negating an Anglo-American "harmony of interests" in favor of an anti-imperial, "just" world order. Social struggle and debate over the meaning of human rights and security and the role of economic redistribution in attaining peace continued though in a muted fashion during the Cold War.

This reinterpretation demonstrates that a critical analysis of the interwar period and the role of peace movements in it not only disturbs entrenched categories and ways of theorizing, but also tells us something useful about the role of social forces in international life. Peace movements helped to foster and to legitimize norms underpinning global international organization. But what is important about global international organization is not so much whether or not it represents a decline in state sovereignty or whether it fulfills state goals. What is important is that it has represented an important site of social struggle over the normative meaning and legitimacy of state practice and an alternative to the state for social groups to enable new practices to take form. The state and international organization are both permeable as well as powerful entities, and both have functions that can and are constantly reevaluated, reinterpreted, and recreated, in large part because of the claims and demands advanced by social movements.

Thus for peace groups, both the League and the United Nations represented a site in which they could advance their claims that individual states could not provide security, peace, or a better quality of life through balance-of-power politics or self-help military policies. Global international organization also represented a site for participation in universal mechanisms for resolving conflict that placed constraints on state power and enabled the creation of new international practices to address humanitarian and economic needs. Although peace movements never obtained all that they wanted from either the League or the United Nations, both represented important fora for struggle and debate over the boundaries and limits of the state and the possibilities of international cooperation. Thus attention to social agency is critical if we are to understand the rearticulation and reformulation of legitimate political practice over time.

During the Cold War, the superpower conflict and nuclear stand-off overshadowed debates over the meaning of security, human rights, and economic redistribution. Yet social movements continued to contest dominant narratives and normative implications. For example, during the debate in the 1950s and 1960s over nuclear weapons, Nigel Young argues, "the moral opprobrium of nuclear first-use was greater in 1962 than four years earlier, because of CND (the Campaign for Nuclear Disarmament) and, in the USA, SANE (the Committee for a Sane Nuclear Policy.)" Richard Taylor argues that CND "was part of the process that broke the post-war consensus," through a "whole ethos of involvement and concern" that focused on "ordinary people's RIGHT to be heard on centrally important issues." For others, such as Milton Katz, SANE's strategy "enlarged the area of accepted political action." Finally, in the last years of the Cold War, Thomas Rochon points out that the 1980s European peace movement was able to "deepen the critique" of nuclear weapons "past the point at which it might be answered by a shift of nuclear strategy." For society as a whole, the movement initiated "the authoritative discussion" of eliminating intermediate nuclear forces from Europe and to a large degree controlled the terms of that discussion. In the process it transformed what had been a military problem into a political issue that challenged state prerogatives to set security strategy. Moreover, "the biggest impact of the movement" concerned "the spread of interest in alternative approaches to defense in Europe" or what then became known as "defensive defense."[9]

[9] Nigel Young, in John Minnion and Philip Bolsover, eds., *The CND Story* (London: Allison & Busby, 1983), p. 62; Richard Taylor, *Against the Bomb, The British Peace Movement, 1958–1965* (London: Clarendon, 1988), p. 340. Milton S. Katz, *Ban the Bomb, A History of SANE, the Committee for a Sane Nuclear Policy, 1957–1985* (Greenwood, 1986), p. xii; Thomas R. Rochon, *Mobilizing for Peace: The Antinuclear Movements in Western Europe* (Princeton: Prince-

Debate over ethical norms and the inherent worth of "universalist" rights and responsibilities, however, has resurfaced with particular force in the post–Cold War era. This book does not assert that peace movements, during the interwar period or after, possessed the means to resolve this ongoing debate. Rather, it argues that the way in which social movements confront and attempt to influence history has profound implications for which political practices are considered acceptable and legitimate and which are not. This is true of both "progressive" social movements and "reactionary" ones.

Moreover, the way in which we interpret the role of social movements has implications for our ability to understand the bases and outcomes of normative contestation in international politics. Narratives of social movement activity, once constructed, have ethical and normative implications. Examples are easy to find—in the extreme case, witness the conflict between reified narratives in the Middle East or the reconstructions of history that have justified slaughter in the former Yugoslavia and Rwanda. Not only should we be wary of the narratives constructed by participants in these cases, but we should also be critical of the narratives we construct to analyze them. These can lead, for example, to an oversimplified view of religion and culture as causing a "clash of civilizations" or to the story that because democracies are "good," nondemocracies should be subject to intervention under international law.[10]

Thus we must be more aware of social movement activity as a constant in international politics. In so doing, we should take both agency and intentionality seriously. The interwar case demonstrates, moreover, that attempts to paint particular kinds of social activity as inappropriate to international life closes down inquiry into the significant ways in which movements can engender change on the international level. More generally, the unquestioning adherence to dominant narratives regarding the role and impact of social movements inhibits our understanding of movements deemed either naive or dangerous at first glance. Thus we must subject our interpretive lenses and resulting narrative constructions to constant critical analysis.

---

ton University Press, 1988), esp. chaps. 1, 2, and 9; Rochon, "Political Movements and State Authority in Liberal Democracies," *World Politics* 42 (January 1990): 299–313.

[10] Samuel Huntington, "The Clash of Civilizations?" *Foreign Affairs,* 72 (Summer 1993); Fernando R. Tesón, "The Kantian Theory of International Law," *Columbia Law Review* 92 (January 1992), pp. 81, 92–93.

Archives and Private Papers

Great Britain

Viscount Robert Cecil, Papers, British Library, Kew
Austen Chamberlain, Papers, Public Record Office, Kew
Sir John Simon, Papers, Public Record Office, Kew
Anthony Eden, Papers, Public Record Office, Kew
Cabinet Correspondence, Public Record Office, Kew
Foreign Office Correspondence, Public Record Office, Kew
Foreign Office, Documents, British Foreign Policy, 1919–1939
Imperial War Museum, Department of Sound Records, "The Anti-War Movement since 1914"
League of Nations Union (LNU), Papers, British Library of Economics and Political Science (BLPES), London School of Economics (LSE), London
National Peace Council, Records, BLPES, LSE, London
Women's International League for Peace and Freedom, Records, British Section, BLPES, LSE, London
No More War Movement, Records, Peace Pledge Union and Library of the Society of Friends TEMP MSS 579, London
Peace Pledge Union, Records, PPU, London

United States

National Archives, Department of State Records, Record Group 59, including:
 Diplomatic and Consular Correspondence
 Peace and War in Foreign Policy, 1931–1941
 Records, Office of European Affairs (Matthews-Hickerson Files), 1935–1947
 Military Intelligence Report-Surveillance of Radicals in the United States, 1917–1941

Post-War Foreign Policy Preparations, 1939–1945, prepared by Harley A. Notter,
 Publication 3580, General Foreign Policy Series 15 (February 1950)
OPOS (Office of Public Opinion Surveys), Schuyler Foster Files
Norman Davis Papers, U.S., Library of Congress, Manuscripts Division
Fellowship of Reconciliation (FOR), papers, Harvester microfilms
Manley O. Hudson Papers, The Harvard Law School Library
League of Nations Association, Papers, Swarthmore College Peace Collection
 (SCPC)
National Council for the Prevention of War, Records, SCPC
Women's International League for Peace and Freedom, Records, U.S. Section,
 SCPC
James Shotwell, Papers, Columbia University, New York
Harry S. Truman Library, Independence, MO, including:
  The United States Conference on International Organization, Records
  President's Secretary's Files
  Papers of Charles F. Darlington
  Papers of Henry Reiff

Geneva, Switzerland

League of Nations Archives
  Adrian Pelt Papers
  Archives of the International Association of Journalists Accredited to the League
   of Nations (1921–1939)
  Archives of the International Union of League of Nations Associations, 1921–
   1939
  Conference for the Reduction and Limitation of Armaments, Records, 1932–
   1934
  Information Section Papers
  Preparatory Commission for the Disarmament Conference, Papers, 1925–1931
  Eric Drummond Papers, 1920–1933
  Laura Puffer Morgan Papers
Women's International League for Peace and Freedom, Records, International
  Section, Geneva

Index

AAUW. *See* American Association of University Women
Abolitionist movement, 45, 46, 47
Abyssinia invasion (1935), 97, 114–18
  and imperialism, 97
  and Kellogg–Briand Pact, 90, 114
  and League of Nations, 93, 114, 117–18, 190
  and peace movement complexity, 36
  and peace movement divisions, 27, 33, 36, 111, 117–18
  traditional realist narrative, 93, 95
  and U.S. neutrality, 163–64
  and weapons of mass destruction, 107
Adamthwaite, Anthony, 121
Addams, Jane, 33, 52, 145
Advisory Committee on Problems of Foreign Relations (United States), 194–98
AFSC. *See* American Friends Service Committee
Agent-structure debate, 15
Aghnides, Thanassis, 183
Allen, William, 43
America First Committee, 169
American Associaton of University Women (AAUW), 33, 168
American Farm Bureau Federation, 134
American Foundation, 144, 145
American Friends Service Committee (AFSC) (United States), 34, 159, 197, 202

American Interorganizational Council, 185
American Law Institute, 203
American Legion, 37, 140, 146
American Peace Society, 43, 49
Americans United for World Organization, 200, 201, 202
Anti-Corn Law League, 46–47
Antifascism, 36
Appeasement, 26–27, 66
  and collective security, 111, 112–14
  and Hoare-Laval Pact, 116–17
  and imperialism, 121–22
  and peace movement divisions, 110–12
  traditional realist narrative, 3, 93–96, 109–10, 111, 120, 121
  and U.S. peace movements (1920s), 128
  See also Munich Agreement
Arato, Andrew, 21–22
Arbitration, 42, 64, 130
  "Arbitration Petition" drive (1925), 75, 99
  and Geneva Protocol, 71–72, 75
  intramovement cooperation, 34
  and Kellogg–Briand Pact, 85, 89
  and League of Nations, 66, 69
  Progressive era, 50, 52, 57–58
  and Ruhr invasion, 68, 69
  and United Nations formation, 195
  and U.S. neutrality, 158
  and World War I, 56
  See also International law; World Court